REFORMATION WRITINGS OF MARTIN LUTHER

AETHERNA IPSE SVAE MENTIS SIMVLACHRA LVTHERVS
EXPRIMIT AT VVLTVS CERA LVCAE OCCIDVOS

· M · D · X · X ·

From a copperplate engraving by Lucas Cranach

THE EARLIEST KNOWN LIKENESS OF LUTHER, PROBABLY
AS HE APPEARED AT WORMS IN 1521, THOUGH SKETCHED
A FEW MONTHS BEFORE

REFORMATION WRITINGS
OF
MARTIN LUTHER

Translated with Introduction and Notes
from the Definitive Weimar Edition

by

BERTRAM LEE WOOLF

VOL. II
THE SPIRIT OF THE
PROTESTANT REFORMATION

LUTTERWORTH PRESS
LONDON

Printed in Great Britain by
The Camelot Press Ltd., London and Southampton

PREFACE

Luther lived in the climate of the Bible, not as if in the sunlit archipelago of a few chosen books; rather he was at home in the whole continent of Holy Writ, and was the first Biblical cosmopolitan for over a millennium. This fact is amply testified by even a small group of Luther's writings, and not least by those put forward, on the average of one per fortnight, during 1519-21; and is the more striking if we allow for the shift of geographical centre, the change of race, the lapse of centuries, and the growth and thrust of the alien ecclesiastical tradition of Rome and the papacy. Biblical study to-day, based on the scientific principles of historical and literary criticism, makes this fact clear enough, yet it partly obscures an important feature of Luther's Biblicism. Modern methods of study tend to the fragmentation of the Biblical message, and to wide differences in the value assigned to the various documents. Luther was capable of trenchant criticism of relative merits, including those of the very Gospels, yet he finds the word of God preached on every page. He calls Romans quintessential gospel, and Matthew, by comparison, a book that can be left on one side,[1] yet, in fact, he quotes and alludes to Matthew equally often, and regards its message as equally authoritative. These are striking observations, but not exceptional instances. In fact, Luther's thought is determined, and his idiom shaped, by every document from Genesis to Revelation; every page comes alive under his eye, and remains vivid in his mind. Only rarely is the same verse or passage quoted twice even when much the same subject is again under discussion; for it is now illuminated and enforced by other passages from the inexhaustible treasury; no page is left unscanned, no leaf unturned; any passage, however unfamiliar to most of us, may at any moment be laid under tribute. To read a score or so of Luther's writings and pay close attention to Scriptural detail and allusion[2] is to acquire a liberal education in the message and meaning of the Bible; a liberal education—because here is nothing of the slavish literalism which blights many devout minds, as it did that of Luther's immediate successors. Rather we have the first clear signs of the kind of study in which each passage is interpreted in the light of the whole of Sacred Writ, and in which,

---

[1] Cf. *infra*, p. 283 　　　　[2] Cf. the wealth of our Scriptural indexes

with increasing definiteness, the writer's original meaning and purpose are sought and made normative. He also impresses us with the vitality of every book, every chapter, and every sentence. We are made to feel how much we have missed for all our study, and that what we have missed is as much alive as anything we ourselves have come to treasure. He seems always to be a few steps ahead of us, to have dug a foot or two deeper, and to have found some gems in the gravel which had passed through our own mental sieves.

With the exception of one or two short pieces, everything in the present volume dates from the period between the autumn of 1519 (after the public debate with John Eck at Leipzig) and the high summer of 1521 (when Luther completed his New Testament in German). This is the period during which the issue between Luther and the Romanists reached its climax; when he had become the most talked-of public figure in western Europe; when he finally and publicly broke with Rome, and his position became unmistakeable to both friend, waverer, and foe; and when the mass movement in favour of the Lutheran reform began to flow and gather the impetus of a tidal wave.

Yet here we find an anomaly: Luther never sought to bring about a popular movement, but only to be the guide and mentor of those around him, near and far, who were looking for help in the ferment of the times. When reform came to affect more than half of Germany and disturb much of western Europe, he did not seek the role of formal leadership; still less, even in the rough appeal of some of his polemical writings, that of a demagogue. Amid the widespread turmoil, he was the man who, in all the world, remained most like his former self; amid all the excitement he retained the completest serenity, and, despite all the public occasions, he was the man who loved best his own quiet corner. He never surrendered to popular acclamation nor ever allowed himself to assume the tone of arrogant defiance of constituted authority. When he burned the bull and the books outside the Elster gate, it was by his own decision, and because he felt this was the only firm response to the bull excommunicating him, and to the campaign against his own writings. When he had performed this crucial, symbolical act, he immediately returned to his study and resumed the calm routine of the day.

Nevertheless, he knew that, unless he were first sent to the stake, the Romanists would sooner or later bring the issue before the emperor's court; and the growing tension was a sign that the time would be short. But Luther's daily life remained the same.

His lectures and sermons were entirely devoted to the subject in hand. This fact is well seen in his exposition of the Magnificat, which was interrupted by his journey to Worms, and completed afterwards, in precisely the same tone, during his stay in Wartburg castle.

Contrary to the received and universally accepted popular opinion, his attitude in the presence of the emperor was not defiant or arrogant; he was very quiet, humble, and submissive. His almost incredible firmness was not obstinate in tone, but respectfully insistent and courageous. The respectfulness was due to a profound regard for the emperor, the council, and for public order; and he was firm because his conscience was firmly bound by the word which the Bible had preached to his heart. By comparison, his own views, like his own fate, were unimportant. This unimportance is the secret at once of his genuinely humble spirit and of his unexampled courage and strength in maintaining the position with which he had become identified.

Paradoxically, this position was one which alone offered him ultimate peace, and yet it was that into which the Romanists forced him. In this sense, too, Luther was in chains, but chains in which, like Paul at Philippi, he could sing at midnight. He was a slave who had found perfect freedom. That paradox is at the heart of the Protestant reformation, and is indispensable to understanding every document in the present volumes.

The section on Luther at Worms reproduces, we believe for the first time in English, the earliest contemporary documentation of this epoch-making drama. No single account contains a record of all that took place; Luther's own version, in his letter to Charles V, is the least factual, but otherwise perhaps the most important. Great difficulty has been met, not only in attempting to reproduce briefly everything of substantial, historical importance, but also in deciding the actual form in which the material should be set out. It can scarcely be hoped that all the difficulties have been surmounted, and nothing left obscure; but perhaps this section will supply the English-speaking student with his essential needs in coming to close terms with the thought and the facts of the most momentous occasion since the sack of Rome in A.D. 410.

The period now covered extends by only about six or eight months that of our first volume, and it has therefore not been thought feasible to add an Appendix giving a chronological table of Luther's writings and contemporary events. Such a table may better be reserved for our third volume, already well advanced, and in which we hope to include the polemic against Latomus, of 1521; the Smaller Catechism, of 1529; the essay on Translating of 1530; and perhaps the Simple Method of Prayer of 1535; etc.

I wish once again to record my best thanks to the publishers of the Weimar edition, now Messrs. Hermann Böhlaus Nachfolger in Weimar, for their kind permission to make free use of their monumental *Historisch-kritische Gesamtausgabe von Luthers Werken*; and my gratitude to many friends who have allowed me to draw on their time and knowledge; in particular to Miss Doris Bushnell, M.A., LL.B., Messrs. S. D. Charles, M.A., Harry Cowlishaw, Dr. Maria Hammerschmidt, Dr. Paul Meyer, Dr. Gordon Rupp, Principal Philip Watson, the staff of the Lutterworth Press, especially Miss Hilda M. Wilson, the Assistant Editorial Secretary; and last, but not least, to my wife for many hours of collaboration in times of stress and fatigue in the last ten years.

BERTRAM LEE WOOLF

Christmas, 1955
CHRISTCHURCH

CONTENTS

ABBREVIATIONS

in references to the Weimar Edition of Luther's Works

W.   The main section of the *Werke*, or general works, now nearly complete in about seventy volumes.

Br.   The *Briefwechsel*, or correspondence, in eleven volumes so far published.

Bi.   Luther's *German Bible*, in seven volumes.

T.R. The *Tischreden*, or Table Talk, in six volumes.

also

R.A. Deutsche Reichtagsakten unter Kaiser Karl V., ed. Wrede and Bernay, Gotha, 1896.

1

FOURTEEN COMFORTS FOR THE WEARY AND HEAVY LADEN

Shortly after the election of Charles V on June 28, 1519, at Frankfort-am-Main to the throne of the Holy Roman Empire, Frederick the Wise returned to Torgau and was taken so seriously ill that it was feared that he could not survive. Luther had received many favours and gifts from him as his patron, and it was therefore with a willing heart that he responded to a request from George Spalatin, the court chaplain, to write something that would encourage and sustain the Elector. When he sat down to write, he began simply with the Greek word *Tesseradecas*, Fourteen, as his title, because he wished that what he wrote should take the place of the fourteen helps in distress usually resorted to in such circumstances. These helps were fourteen saints who, according to a popular tradition, had been seen by a shepherd in central Germany when he was vouchsafed a vision of them surrounding Christ as a child. The legend dates from 1446, and the Church of the Fourteen Saints at Staffelstein still marks the spot. There is no point in listing the names or the special virtues of these medieval comforters, but only in saying that, in their place, Luther gave the weary and heavy laden two series of seven symbolic representations of the negative and the positive aids to fortitude and faith in times of stress. Taking his stand on Scripture, he first showed how the seven types of serious evil are of a minor character when seen in the light of the word of God; and, indeed, bear no comparison with the passion and death of the Saviour. He then went on to depict the riches of God's grace and mercy as seen in His sevenfold benefits, which are crowned by the highest blessing, Jesus Christ, risen from the dead, the Lord of lords and Conqueror of death, who had brought life and immortality to light.

Luther must have begun writing sometime during August, 1519, for by the 29th of that month he was occupied with the sixth reflexion of the first series, in the course of which he spoke of John the Baptist's day as "to-day". Apparently, he still found it easier to write a book of this character in Latin rather than in German, for on the twenty-second of the next month, he sent the completed MS. to Spalatin with the request that he would translate it "freely" into German before handing it to the Elector. It would seem that the immediate urgency had passed, for Spalatin took as much time to make the translation as Luther had required for the original. The work was only ready for the Elector at the end of November. Early in December, Luther asked for the return of the Latin copy, "in order to gain comfort from it himself". This request of Luther's speaks not only of the anxieties through which he was passing, but also of the deep convictions and the entire sincerity with which he had written. Like all great preachers, he had been writing for his own instruction and admonition.

Up to this point of time, he had had no thought of publishing the little work, at least in its Latin form; but Spalatin, who had doubtless sent him the German translation along with the Latin original, persuaded him to print both versions. On December 18, Luther sent his friend the news that the *Tesseradecas* was being printed in Wittenberg in both languages. The Latin version appeared on February 5, and the German on February 11, 1520, a year which was to see the publication of so many of Luther's most important works.

Although definitely intended from the first for the Elector, Luther did not write a dedication, but left it to Spalatin whether to provide one or not. Such a dedication prefaces the first edition of the German version, but not of the Latin. The latter concludes, however, with a paragraph addressed to the "illustrious prince", a paragraph which only becomes clear in the light of the prefatory dedication. Luther himself explained this situation when he wrote to Spalatin on February 5, 1520: "The introductory letter has been omitted, leaving the booklet, to my distress, quite out of shape." He would appear to have written the Preface in December 1519, but had been away from Wittenberg when the first quires left the press, the Preface having been omitted by a printer's error. Several editions appeared in the same form, until 1535, when Luther revised the text, removed interpolations in many places, and restored the original preface. This was in a sense a new edition. Nevertheless, he purposely left untouched views which he no longer held, and which he had outgrown, saying that this would make it plain to all the world how far he had progressed in his inner self. He added, with characteristic irony, that it would also provide his enemies with "material on which to exercise their malice", and contemporary know-alls with something to think about, because it was pervaded with the atmosphere of Christ's presence.

Luther is said not to have held the work in high esteem; but it was gratefully accepted by Frederick the Wise, and also by John, the bishop of Meissen, even after Luther had entered the lists against him. In 1523, Erasmus commended it to Christopher, bishop of Basle, and said, "I am sending you a pamphlet of Luther's containing fourteen reflexions which many praise highly, including some persons who contest his opinions in every form."

The present translation is made from the text printed in the Weimar Edition of Luther's Works, Vol. VI, pp. 104-34. The translation published by Henry Cole in *Select Works of Martin Luther*, Vol. II, pp. 127-74, seems to be based on one of the interpolated texts which Luther finally set aside in 1535.

FOURTEEN COMFORTS FOR THE WEARY AND HEAVY LADEN

BY M. LUTHER, AUGUSTINIAN, OF WITTENBERG
Martin Luther

THIS book is one I wrote at an early stage,[1] and I addressed it to that excellent prince, duke Frederick of Saxony, at a time when he was seriously ill; but in accordance with a widespread desire, it was printed for circulation. After having been reissued several times, however, it has become so distorted and mutilated that many passages are lacking, and even I myself am not able to guess their original phraseology. As far as possible, I have restored the meaning, and this, I believe, in accordance with my original intention. Even had I been able, I had no desire to introduce at this stage any changes or embellishments. In this book I wish to make it plain what progress I have made, and to throw a few crumbs to the carping critics[2] that they might have something to vent their spite on. As for myself, I shall be content if I do the good pleasure of Christ, my Lord, and of His saints. I render thanks to God with heartfelt joy if I am hateful to the devil complete with his scales.[3]

To the most Illustrious Prince and Lord, the Lord Frederick, Duke of Saxony, Arch-Marshal and Elector of the Holy Roman Empire, Landgrave of Thüringia, Margrave of Meissen, His most gracious Lordship

Jesus, our Lord and Saviour, left a commandment which applies equally to all Christians, that we should perform kindnesses, or rather (as Scripture calls them) works of mercy, to those who are afflicted and in distress; that we should visit the sick, endeavour to set prisoners free, and do other things of this sort for the benefit of our neighbour, in order that, in this way, his present ills may be to some extent

---

[1] This preliminary paragraph was specially written by Luther in 1535, for the Latin text in its final form

[2] *Antilogistis*, i.e. people like John Faber who, in 1530, published *Antilogiarum Mart. Lutheri Babylonia*; their delight was to search Luther's writings for changes, contradictions, and inconsistencies

[3] It was common at the time, as is seen in many of the illustrations to Luther's Bible, to represent the devil as a dragon with a scaly tail

relieved. And, indeed, our Lord Jesus Christ Himself gave us the most signal example of this commandment when, on account of His immeasurable love towards mankind, He came down from the bosom of the Father, and entered into our woes, indeed our prison, the prison, I mean, of our flesh and of our life with all its misfortunes. He took the penalties of our sins upon Himself that we might be saved. This accords with what Isaiah says in chapter 43, Thou hast made me labour among thy sins and burdened me with thy iniquities, etc.[1]

If this signal example does not move a man, and if, in addition, the authority of the divine commandments does not impel him to perform these works of love, surely that person will deservedly hear at the last judgment the voice of an irate judge: Depart, accursed, into everlasting fire. For I was sick, and you did not visit me; but, in deep ingratitude for the great benefits which I conferred on you and the whole world, you have not rendered the slightest assistance to your brethren, nay, to Me, Christ, thy God and Saviour, in thy brethren.[2]

When, therefore, most illustrious prince, I see your Lordship suffering from a severe disease, and Christ at the same time suffering in you, I considered it my duty to send your Lordship something in writing to act as a sick visitor. For I cannot pretend not to hear Christ's voice crying to me from within your Lordship's body and flesh, and saying, Lo, I am here, sick. For it is not we Christians, but Christ Himself, our Lord and Saviour, in whom we live, who suffers these diseases or other evils. Such is Christ's plain testimony in the gospel: Whatever you have done for the least among my (brethren), you have done for me. And while we owe a certain duty of visiting and encouraging all who are afflicted with illness, yet we have a special duty to those of the household of faith. For even Paul clearly distinguishes between strangers and those of our household or those who are bound to us by any claims of necessity. Galatians 6.[3]

But I have other reasons supporting this duty of mine. I feel that, as one of your Lordship's subjects together with

[1] Cf. Isa. 43:24   [2] Cf. Matt. 25:31ff.   [3] Gal. 6:10

the rest of your numerous subjects, I cannot but share in your Lordship's sickness, and endure illness, as it were, just as a member does with the head. All our fortune, all our safety and felicity depend on you. We recognize your Lordship to be another Naaman through whom God is giving well-being to-day to Germany, just as formerly he gave well-being to Syria through that good man. This is the reason why the whole of the Roman empire turns its eyes to your Lordship alone, venerates you, and regards you as the father of the country, the signal ornament and guardian of the whole empire, and especially of the German people.

Nor is it our only duty to your Lordship to give you what comfort we can, and bear your present prostration as if it were our own, but much more, to intercede with God for your health and well-being; and I hope this is what is being done in all earnestness and with all diligence by your Lordship's subjects. As for myself, since your Lordship's numerous and outstanding favours and benefits have put me in your debt more than others, I recognize that it is required of me to show my gratitude by some unusual service. Because both mentally and materially my resources are poor, and I cannot offer anything of great value, Dr. George Spalatin, who is one of your Lordship's chaplains, made me the welcome suggestion that I should write something that would afford spiritual comfort, and said, if I sent it to your Lordship, this action would be most acceptable to your Lordship. Being eager to follow this friendly advice, I have composed these fourteen chapters arranged like an altar tablet. I have given them the title of *Tesseradecas* with the idea that they would replace the fourteen canonized persons whom current superstition has conjured up and called defenders against all evils. This is not a tablet of silver but of the spirit', designed not to ornament the walls of temples, but to uplift and strengthen a devout soul. I hope that it will be indeed helpful to your Lordship just now. It is divided into two parts, the first of which contains aspects of the seven evils and is meant to mitigate your present troubles when you think them over. The second part contains aspects of the seven good things brought together for the same purpose.

Would your Lordship therefore accept this little work of mine, and find such pleasure in it that the constant reading and consideration of these aspects may give you a little comfort?

I pay your Lordship my humble respects as your subject.

MARTIN LUTHER, *doctor*.

PREFACE

When in Romans 15 the apostle Paul went on to outline the things which help the Christians, he said, Brethren, everything that has been written has been written for our instruction, that we may derive hope from the messages of endurance and courage contained in the Scriptures.[1] In this passage, he plainly teaches us to seek encouragement in the holy Scriptures. Now the holy Scriptures give encouragement in a twofold manner, placing before us two presentations of things intermingled in a most suitable way, those good and those evil, as the wise Ecclesiasticus says: in bad times remember the good, in good times remember the bad.[2] The Holy Spirit knows that every experience through which a man passes has value only in accordance with the meaning which he assigns to it; for what he regards as base and of no value will have little influence; it will give him but little pleasure if it comes, or regret if it departs. Therefore the Holy Spirit makes every endeavour to draw us away from material thoughts and feelings. When He has done so, all material things are alike to us. It is the Word which is most powerful in so drawing us away. It turns our thought from the thing which influences us now to the thing which is either absent or, if present, does not move us. We shall enjoy this encouragement at its best through holy Scripture which, in the day of evil, calls us away to contemplate the good, whether present or future; and in the day of good calls us away to contemplate what is evil. But in order better to grasp these two series of types or similitudes, let us divide each of them into seven parts.

[1] Rom. 15:4   [2] Cf. Ecclus. 11:25

Part I

Discussion of aspects of evil, namely, i. those within; ii. those in front; iii. those behind; iv. those near us on the left; v. those on the right; vi. those below; vii. those above.

CHAPTER I

The first aspect: the evil within

Whether one believes it or not, this fact is settled and certain, that no evil from which a man can suffer can be as severe as those that exist within him. What is more, the evils within him are far more numerous and of greater import than any from which he suffers pain. If he were to feel the pains of those that are within, he would experience hell; for he has hell within his own self. You say How? The prophet declares, All men are liars[1] and, again, No living man is aught but a vain show. But to be a liar and a vain show is to be destitute of truth and reality. And to be destitute of truth and reality is to be without God and to be nobody; in other words, to be in hell and damned. Hence, God, in His mercy, reveals to us and lays upon us only the more bearable evils when He chastises us. He knows that if a man were to be brought truly to understand his wickedness he would perish at once. Even so, He has given this experience to some, for we read, He bringeth down to the grave, and bringeth up.[2] It is therefore right to call our bodily pains as it were monitors of inward evils. And the apostle, in Hebrews 12, speaks of the fatherly disciplines of God, and says, He scourges every son He receives.[3] He does this in order, by the scourgings and small evils, to expel the great evils that we may never undergo them; so in Proverbs 22, Folly clings to the mind of a child; the rod of discipline drives it away.[4] Do not godly parents grieve more for their sons if they become thieves and

[1] Ps. 116:11   [2] 1 Sam. 2:6   [3] Heb. 12:6   [4] Prov. 22:15

wicked men than if they receive wounds? Nay, they themselves chastise them, perhaps till they bleed, to prevent their
becoming evil-doers?

What then prevents this true evil from being felt? Surely
it is, as I have said, that God has arranged it thus lest a
man be overcome by the sight of his profound evil. He has
hidden it, and decreed that it should be discerned by faith
alone, when He discloses it by the evil of which we are aware.
Hence, In the day of evil, remember the good.[1] How good a
thing it is not to know all our depravity. Keep this blessing
before your mind, and you will suffer less from the pain you
feel. Similarly, in the day of good things, keep in mind the
evil. In other words, when you are not suffering from your
true evils, be grateful for the respite, and remember the
true evils; then you will find that you feel the sensible evils
the less. It is evident, therefore, that, in this life, a man's
freedom from pain is always greater than his pain, and this,
not because the whole evil is not present, but because its
influence and effect are not felt since, by His goodness, God
keeps it hidden.

Hence, when their true depravity has been made known to
them, how violently these men react. Whatever else they
must endure throughout their whole life, they count as
nothing, if only it will prevent them from feeling the hell
within. That is what everybody else would do if he but felt
or truly believed in his own inward evil. Of his own initiative,
he would summon external evils, toy with them and never
be more downcast than when he had no evils to bear, as we
know to have been the case with many of the saints, e.g.
David in Psalm 6.

The first aspect, therefore, in which we find our comfort is
when we say to ourselves, As yet, sir, you do not feel your
depravity. Rejoice and be thankful that you are not compelled to feel it. By making this comparison, the smaller
evil lightens the greater evil. This is what some mean when
they say, I deserve far worse than this, indeed hell; which is
easy to say but dreadful to bear.

Moreover, however deeply this ill may be concealed, it

[1] Ecclus. 11:26

still brings forth fruits that can be perceived plainly enough, namely, the fear and uncertainty produced by anxiety of conscience; and thus faith is assailed. Meanwhile, the man does not know, or at least is in doubt, whether he is in God's grace and favour, and these fruits are the more bitter as his faith is the less robust. This infirmity alone, when properly weighed, and because it is of a spiritual nature, is far more important than any bodily thing, which, by due comparison, seems a very slight matter.

Stretching beyond these inward ills is that whole tragedy described by Ecclesiastes when he declares, All is vanity and vexation of spirit.[1] How many of our plans miscarry? How many of our desires mock us! How many things do we see, how many hear, to which we are averse! Nay, the very things which we wish run contrary to our wishes. In fact nothing is complete and perfect. Moreover, all these things are the larger, the higher one's rank or station; for one who is highly exalted must of necessity be tossed about by tides and billows and storms far more than others labouring under the same burdens. Rightly does Psalm 103 say, In the sea of this world there are countless swarms of animals and reptiles great and small.[2] For this reason, Job 7 calls man's life a testing time.[3]

And, indeed, these ills do not become less alive because they are less felt, but because, by the charity of God, they become of little account through use and custom, and their effect and influence are blunted thereby. Therefore rare occurrences disturb us more when we have not learned by familiarity to treat them with contempt. Hence the truth that we feel scarcely the thousandth part of our ills; and the further truth that we assess them, and either feel or do not feel them, not on account of their real nature, but by their influence and effect.

[1] Eccles. 1:2, 14   [2] Cf. Ps. 104:25   [3] *Tentationem*; Job 7:17ff.

CHAPTER II

The second aspect: future evil, or the evil before us

It will lighten present ills considerably if you turn your attention to those that are to come. These are so many, of such a nature, and so great, that from this one cause arises that sense of fear which is one of our principal emotions. Some people have defined fear as the apprehension of future ill, and so the apostle says in Romans 11, You have no reason for pride, rather for fear.[1] Future evil is the greater the more it is uncertain in what form, or with what force, it may come. Hence the familiar saying, At no age are we proof against scurvy (which by the by is a childish and even infantile malady). In fact, no man is safe from the ills to which mankind is heir, and what one man undergoes to-day his neighbour may suffer to-morrow. Here is the sting of all history, and of the tragedy of every age; here the woes of the whole world. Here is the relevance of the point that someone has made that there are more than three hundred named diseases from which the human body can be afflicted. If there are so many diseases, how many other misfortunes, do you think, may not befall our outward circumstances, our friends, and especially our very soul which is the chief objective of all evils, and the chief resort of sorrow and all ills?

The greater and worthier one's status, the greater the intensity of the force and feeling associated with one's ill-fortune. In an exalted station, poverty, ignominy, and all kinds of indignity, may happen at any moment; and, since all things hang by a slender thread, not unlike the sword which Dionysius[2] the despot hung over the head of his guest, one must be constantly alert to danger.

Should one of these things not befall us, we must count it our good fortune, and no little consolation for any evil that has come. Indeed we are compelled to say with Jeremiah, It is by God's mercy that we have not been brought to an end.[3]

[1] Rom. 11:20, Knox [2] sic; in error for Damocles [3] Cf. Lam. 3:22f.

Nay, if one of those evils does not befall us, it is because the right hand of the Most High has been our protection, a rampart on every side of such strength that, as proved in Job, Satan and his wiles are inadequate, and are warded off. This shows how dearly we ought to love the Lord, no matter what evil befalls us, for in any one evil, our Father, in His great love, calls upon us to consider how many evils press around us and would fall upon us if He Himself did not hinder them. It is as if He said to us, Satan and the hosts of evil[1] desire to have you and to sift you as wheat.[2] But I have laid down the confines of the sea, and have said, So far shalt thou come and thy proud waves be stayed.[3]

Granted that, if God so will, none of these things has come about, yet the most dreadful of all known evils, namely death, is very certain to come, though its hour is most uncertain. This is indeed so great an evil that we know there are many who would rather live in the midst of all the evils we have spoken of, than have them brought to an end, and meet death once. The Bible despises the other evils, but recognizes this; it says, Keep your last day in mind; then you will never sin.[4] Look round and see how many meditations, how many books, how many regulations, have been accumulated for the purpose of deterring men from sin by fixing their minds on this one evil. They have sought to make the world disdainful, to lighten sufferings and hardships, to comfort the afflicted, by drawing a contrast with this horrible, and great, yet necessary evil. There is no one who would not prefer to suffer any other hardship if only it would enable him to escape the evil of death. It is something the very saints have feared, that Christ underwent with trepidation and bloody sweat. All this has meant that the divine mercy has nowhere done more to encourage us in our faint-heartedness than in respect of this evil, as we shall see later on.[5]

All the above evils are common to the whole of mankind, just as the blessings of salvation are available to all who are in the midst of those very evils. But for Christians, there is

---

[1] Chaos   [2] Cf. Luke 22:31   [3] Job 38:10f.   [4] Ecclus. 7:36
[5] Cf. *infra*, p. 50.

another reason for fearing future ills, a reason peculiar to them and which easily exceeds all that have been mentioned. It is that which the apostle depicts in 1 Corinthians 10 when he says, Let anyone who thinks he stands secure, take care lest he fall.[1] So slippery is the way, so powerful the foe who is, moreover, armed with our own forces (i.e. the flesh assisted by all its wicked passions), attended by the innumerable armies of the world, its delights and pleasures to our right, the bitter and perverse inclinations of man on our left, to say nothing of the thousand ways of hurting, seducing, and destroying, an art in which he is himself the past-master. The condition of our life is such that not for a moment are we certain of the good that awaits us. In his epistle, *de mortalitate*, Cyprian, in dealing with many things of this sort, teaches that death is to be preferred as a swift way of escaping these ills. And it is true that, wherever there have been high-minded men who calmly discussed hell and its infinite perils, we find that they were disdainful of both life and death (i.e. the aforesaid evils), and preferred to die[2] in order at the same time to be rid of the sinful evils in the midst of which they lived (as we discussed in the first chapter) and into which they might fall, which is our present topic. These are indeed two very weighty arguments not only for preferring death but also for disdaining every kind of ill, not to mention any that can be readily borne. If God grant a man to be persuaded by them, it is due to His gift that we are ever affected by them. What true Christian would not prefer to die, not to mention being sick, when he sees, and finds by experience, that, while in health, he is in the midst of sin, in constant danger of running into more sins, and daily does so; and meanwhile he is continually acting against the most loving will of the most loving Father? It was with this degree of fervent wrath with himself that Paul was moved in Romans 7 when, after complaining that he could not do the good that he willed, but only the evil that was against his will, he cried out, Unhappy man that I am, who will rescue me from a nature thus doomed to death? His answer is, The grace of God through Jesus Christ, etc.[3] A man has but little

---

[1] Cf. 1 Cor. 10:12   [2] Cf. Phil. 1:23   [3] Cf. Rom. 7:19, 24f., Vulgate

love for God who prefers this evil of sinning to the ill of dying. God has appointed death that the former evil might at some time reach an end, and that death might be the servant of life and of righteousness. I shall discuss these points in the sequel.

CHAPTER III

The third aspect: past evil, or the evil behind us[1]

Here more than anywhere else does the tender mercy of God shine out and encourage us, no matter what our distress. No one is more aware of the presence of the guiding hand of God than he who reviews his life through the years. St. Augustine says, If a man were given the choice of either death or reliving his past life, then, in view of the numerous perils and evils from which he has barely escaped and even that with difficulty, he would choose death. This remark will be found only too true if duly pondered. From this standpoint, a man may perceive how often, without planning it, without intending it, or even apart from and contrary to his wish, did he perform or undergo many an ill. So little thought did he give to them before they were taking place or while they were being performed that, when all was over, it was only then that he wondered with astonishment, however have these things happened to me when I never gave them a thought and indeed was thinking of something very different? This is what gives point to the proverb, Man proposes, but God disposes. In other words, He lays down and carries to effect something different from what man proposes. From this one consideration, it is impossible for us to deny that our lives and our actions have been governed, not by our own sagacity, but by God's marvellous power and wisdom and goodness. This makes plain how often God has been with us unfelt and unawares, and how truly Peter said, His concern is over us all.

If we never read a book or heard a sermon, but if we pondered our life as it traces its course through so many ills and perils, it would abundantly commend to our attention the goodness of God which is very near to us and very tender, and which, far beyond our own wisdom and understanding, bears us in its bosom. It is as Moses says in Deuteronomy 32,

[1] This and the following chapters depart from the sequence first proposed, *supra*, p. 21

The Lord kept him as the apple of His eye, leading him by another route, carrying him on his shoulders.[1]

This condition of affairs is what gave rise to the exhortations in the book of Psalms, I remember the days of old; I meditate on all Thy works; I muse on the work of Thy hands.[2] I will remember Thy wonders of old.[3] Again, I remembered Thy judgment of old and took courage.[4] These and similar exhortations are all intended to teach us that, if we see God to have been present with us at a time when we did not think or feel that He was near, we should not doubt that He is present even when He seems far from us. If He sustained us without our aid in many a needy time, surely He will not forsake us in our smaller need, although He may seem to be doing so. What is said in Isaiah is in point, For a moment and for a little I have forsaken thee, but with great acts of mercy will I show pity on thee.[5]

Here are further considerations: Who was it that cared for us many a night while we slept? How often, too, while we were at work or at play, or doing all those innumerable things when we had no thought for our own selves? Indeed, for how much of our time do we take care of ourselves? Even a miser, with all his concern to get wealth, must cease caring for his own self while he is getting and gaining. Thus it appears that, whether we will or not, the entire care of ourselves reverts to God alone, and hardly ever are we left to our own devices. And when the Lord does this, it is in order to teach us how to perceive His goodness, and, when we do, that we may see the great difference between His care and ours. That is why, at times, He allows us to be embarrassed by some slight disease or other ill while disguising His care for us (although He never ceases to care); but He does not allow all the evils that surround us to fall upon us at once. Thus, as if we were His dearly-beloved children, He tests whether we are willing to trust His care which has been known to us throughout our life, and to learn how vain and weak are our

---

[1] Cf. Deut. 32:10f. This is quite an inexact recollection of the Vulgate text. The term *circumduco*, used in its classical and etymological sense and only in general reproducing the original, is made very apposite to Luther's purpose

[2] Ps. 143:5   [3] Ps. 77:11   [4] Cf. Ps. 119:52   [5] Isa. 54:7

efforts to care for ourselves. What is it that we do, or can do for our own selves throughout our life, when we are unable at any moment to protect ourselves from some particular hurt to one of our limbs?[1]

Why then are we so distressed about any particular peril or ill, and do not leave it in His hands, since our whole life bears witness that we have been delivered and preserved by Him from innumerable evils without any help from us? To know these facts is to know the works of God, to meditate on His ways, and to draw encouragement from remembering them in times of adversity. Those who do not know, run up against the passage in Psalm 27, Because they understand not the works of God, nor the works of His hands, Thou wilt pull them down and not build them up.[2] Those who will not trust themselves to His care in any small matter show no gratitude for all God's care of them throughout their life.

[1] Perhaps a reference to the accident with his sword when setting out from Erfurt in the Easter vacation to visit his parents; cf. W. J. Kooiman, *By Faith Alone* (The Life of Luther), p. 20

[2] Ps. 28:5

CHAPTER IV

The fourth aspect: infernal evil, or the evil beneath us

So far, in all the evils under which we labour, we have
always found the goodness of God; and this goodness is so
great that, among the innumerable evils by which we are
surrounded and almost invested throughout life, very few
are allowed to assail us, and this only at intervals. This means
that, whatever may be the evil by which we are oppressed,
it is only a signal of some great benefit with which God is
favouring us, in that He does not permit us to be crushed by
the multitude of evils round about. How marvellous it would
be if a man, at whom unnumbered blows were aimed, was
touched at most by one! It is a mark of grace not to be
struck by all, a miracle to be struck by but a few.

The first of the evils beneath us is death, the second is
hell.

If we ponder death in its varied and terrible forms such as
we see other sinners suffer, it will be evident how great is our
gain when we suffer less than our deserts. How many men
are hanged, burned at the stake, drowned, or beheaded, who
perhaps committed sins less than ours by far! Their death
and affliction are brought vividly to our attention by Christ,
so that we may grasp how much we ourselves have merited.
When news was brought to Him about the Galileans whom
Pilate slaughtered while they were bringing their sacrifices,
Luke 13 says that He responded, Do you think because they
suffered in this way that they were worse sinners than the
rest of the Galileans? Not so, I tell you. But unless you
repent you will all perish as they did. And those eighteen
men who were killed when the tower of Siloam fell, do you
think that there was more against them than against all the
others that dwelt at Jerusalem? Not so, I tell you. But unless
you repent, you will all perish as they did.[1] It is impossible
to believe that we who have committed greater, or only

1 Luke 13:1ff.

similar, sins should have a lighter account against us. Neither the justice nor the truth of God, by which He will render to each man according to his deeds, will become unjust or false for our sakes, if we do not hasten and make satisfaction by at least bearing patiently our own little hardships.[1]

In hell and eternal damnation, how many thousands are there who have not committed one thousandth part of our sins? There, too, are hosts of virgins, youths, and those whom we call "innocents"; hosts of conventuals, priests, married couples, who seemed to serve God throughout life, and yet, perhaps by a single lapse, receive eternal punishment! Nor can we ignore the fact that the justice of God is one and the same towards any sin whatsoever. He hates and condemns sin in the same way no matter in whom it is found. Does it not show the infinite mercy of God through which He has not condemned us though we have often deserved it? And I ask, what can we undergo in our whole life that will compare with the eternal punishment which those deservedly suffer for a single dereliction? Yet we are still free and safe because God has not taken account of our many sins. Surely it is due to our ingratitude and the hardened state of our unbelief if we are indifferent to these divine blessings, or give them a cold glance.

We must also take account at this point of the unbelievers, the heathen, the Jews, the people under age: if they had been granted the blessings we enjoy, they would not now be in hell but in heaven, and would have sinned far less than we have done. Christ brings us face to face with this aspect when He says in Matthew, Woe to thee, Corozaim, Woe to thee, Bethsaida, because if the mighty works done in you had been done in Tyre and Sidon, they would already have done penance in sackcloth and ashes; and I say this to you, that it will go less hard with Tyre and Sidon in the day of judgment than with you. Woe to thee, Capernaum, who hast been lifted heaven high, thou shalt go down into hell, because, if the mighty works had been done in Sodom which have been done in thee, it might have stood to this day. And I say this,

---

[1] Luther soon abandoned this view of satisfaction

that it will go less hard with the district of Sodom in the day
of judgment than with thee.[1] This shows how greatly we
ought to praise and love our most blessed Lord no matter
what the ills from which we are suffering, which are but as a
drop in the bucket of our deserts, and these Job compares
with the ocean and the sands of the sea.[2]

[1] Matt. 11:21-24   [2] Job 6:3

CHAPTER V

The fifth aspect: sinister evil or evil on the left hand

We must now direct our gaze to the many men who are hostile to us and of wicked intent. The first thing to notice is the numerous evils which they desired to bring upon ourselves, our affairs, our good name, our very souls, but were unsuccessful because, by the providence of God, they could not. The higher one's station and the broader one's sway, the more one is exposed to such people with their many traps, machinations, innuendos, and attacks. Throughout, we may well perceive and experience that God's hand is very close, but would it be strange if occasionally one of them succeeds? Next, we must notice the evils which they themselves endure, not that we may have pleasure in them, but exercise compassion on them. They themselves are exposed to all the same evils to which we are exposed, as we can readily see in the previous chapters. But their state is more deplorable than ours in this respect that they are outside our fellowship[1] in both body and soul. Any misfortune that we suffer is as nothing compared with the fact that they live in sin, in unbelief, subject to the wrath of God, under the mastery of the devil, wretched slaves of impiety and sin, and this to such an extent that, if the whole world were to lay its curse upon them, it could not call down anything worse. If we give all these things due consideration, we shall see, when we are called upon to bear some slight bodily inconvenience, how much more richly we enjoy the grace of God in our faith, in the kingdom of Christ, in the service of God. Surrounded by such a wealth of the best things, we, who have humble Christian hearts, ought to feel so much sorrow for their unhappy lot, that our own troubles would seem pleasurable by contrast. Accordingly, Paul says in Philippians 2, Let each have regard for the interests of others and not merely his own. Let this conviction be yours as it was that of Christ

[1] The communion of saints

Jesus, who, though He was in the form of God, took the form of a servant, etc.[1] That is to say that, out of His very tender love, He assumed human form, acting in our hard lot as if it was His own. He was so unmindful of Himself and so stripped of His own advantages, that He was completely in human form. He considered nothing human foreign to Himself, and was entirely subject to human afflictions.

Since they are moved by this love and stirred by this example, saints are accustomed to pray for the wicked no less than for their enemies, and to follow in all respects the example of Christ. Forgetful alike of the injuries from which they suffer or the rights they might claim, they were anxious about the way in which they might free these people from the afflictions from which they suffered far more severely than from their physical ills. In 2 Peter 2, St. Peter speaks similarly of Lot, For when he resided among (the people of Sodom), day after day his righteous soul was tormented by their wicked ways.[2] You now see how profound are the evils that come to light, and how great is the reason for showing pity and compassion. At the same time, we ought to be forgetful of our own small hardships, if the love of God dwells in us, for what God lets us suffer is as nothing compared with what they suffer. The reason why these things move us so little is that our inward eye is not sufficiently clear for us to see the squalid and pitiable condition of the man who is enthralled by sin, and therefore separated from God and possessed by the devil. Who is so hardhearted as not to feel revulsion at and pity for those lying at the entrances of our churches, or in the squares, with disfigured faces, noses eaten away, eyes and other organs horrible with blood and putrefaction, until our minds recoil from the thought, and our senses are numbed by the sight? God's purpose with these deplorable creatures, who bear the likeness of our flesh and blood, is to open the eyes of our understanding to see how far more dreadful a sight the soul of a sinner exhibits, with its sores and rottenness, even although he himself be clothed in purple and gold and lives among lilies and roses, as if he were already the heir of heaven. And how many

[1] Phil. 2:4ff.　　[2] 2 Pet. 2:8

sinners are there in the world compared with one of those
with running sores!

When we think lightly of the evils which are unlimited in
degree and number among our neighbours, it will follow that
any single evil of our own, be it never so small, will seem to be
both singular and of great importance. Enough! there must
be people who are physically greater sufferers than we are.
But even if they were to obtain and gain possession of everything that they wished, what sweet and pure enjoyment
could they have if their conscience was not at rest? Is there
an evil more cruel than the unrest caused by a mordant
conscience? Isaiah 57 says, Wicked men are like the restless
sea, whose waters throw up mud and mire. There is no
peace for the wicked, saith God the Lord.[1] Similarly a
passage in Deuteronomy 28 applies to them, which says, The
Lord will give thee a trembling heart, eyes that fail with
longing, and a soul consumed with sorrow. Thy life shall be
lived in suspense. Thou shalt be fearful by day and by night,
without confidence in thy life. In the morning thou wilt say,
Would it were evening; and in the evening, Would it were
dawn, for the dread of thy heart which brings thee terror,
and because of the things which thou seest with thine eyes.[2]
In short, if one were rightly moved by all the evils suffered
by the wicked, whether friends or foes, not only would a man
forget his own evils and seem to suffer nothing himself, but
also, similarly to Moses[3] and the apostle Paul,[4] he would
yearn to die for them and be "accursed from Christ" as it
says in Romans 9, for them to be set free. This was the zeal
and fervour with which Christ burned when He both died and
descended into hell for our sakes, leaving us an example, so
that we should be likewise concerned for the hard lot of
others, wholly forgetful of our own, nay eager to bear it.

[1] Isa. 57:20f.   [2] Deut. 28:65-67   [3] Cf. Exod. 32:32   [4] Rom. 9:3

CHAPTER VI

The sixth aspect: dexter evil, or evil on the right hand

To the right are our friends. It mitigates our own afflictions when we contemplate theirs. Hence St. Peter teaches in 1 Peter 5, Resist the devil, firm in your faith, knowing that the same sufferings are required of your brethren who are in the world.[1] So, too, the petitions offered by the church pray that we may be stirred by the example of the saints to imitate their fortitude in suffering. She sings:

> What torments all the saints endured
> When they a martyrs' crown ensured.

From these words and from the hymns of the church, we learn that the saints' days, their memory, temples, altars, names, and images are to be honoured and added to in order that we should be inspired by their example to bear the same afflictions as they bore. Unless they are reverenced for this reason, every other form of their cultus must contain an element of superstition. Thus there are many who perform all these observances in order to avoid the afflictions which the saints teach us how to bear by their example and memory; and so they become different from the very ones whose feasts they celebrate in order to become like them.

By far the finest discussion of this kind of encouragement is given by the apostle in Hebrews 12, In repelling the attacks of sin, you have not yet resisted to the point of shedding your blood, and you have forgotten the words of comfort in which you are addressed as sons, namely, My son, do not regard lightly the discipline of the Lord, and do not lose heart when you are reproved by Him. For the Lord chastises one whom He loves, and scourges every son whom he receives. Be patient, then, while discipline lasts. God is dealing with you as His children. Was there ever a son whom his father did not correct? Correction is the common

[1] 1 Pet. 5:9

lot of us all; you must be bastards, not true sons, if you are
left without it. We have known what it is to accept correction from earthly fathers, and yet to reverence them; shall
we not submit far more willingly to our spiritual Father, and
draw life from Him? For the time being, all discipline is painful rather than pleasant, but afterwards it yields thereby a
harvest of good dispositions, to our great peace.[1] These are
Paul's words.[2] Who can fail to be fearful at these words of
Paul's? He plainly declares that those who are not disciplined
by God are not sons of His. What could confirm us more
strongly and encourage us more effectively than to hear that
the Lord loves those whom he disciplines; that they are His
sons, endowed with the fellowship of all the saints; that they
do not suffer alone? This urgent exhortation makes discipline desirable.

Nor does it lay the way open for the plea that some have
an easy lot, whereas others have a hard one. Temptation is so
moderated for each one that it shall not exceed his strength.
Accordingly it says in Psalm 79, Thou wilt feed us with tears
as our daily bread, and a measure of tears wilt thou give us
for our drink.[3] Paul too says the same thing. God can be
trusted. He will not allow you to be tempted beyond your
powers, providing a happy issue[4] with each temptation, so
that you will be able to endure it.[5] Hence the heavier the
affliction, the happier the issue and the greater the divine
aid. Thus the inequality in the distribution of the sufferings
is more apparent than real. This very day[6] we commemorate
St. John the Baptist and his beheading by Herod. We are all
disturbed and amazed by the fate of so great a man. There
was no greater born of woman,[7] the close friend of the
bridegroom, the forerunner of Christ, more than a prophet;[8]
yet he was put to death, not after a public trial, not even
after a false accusation as Christ was, nor to please the
people, but to please a dancing girl, daughter of an adulteress.
The ignominious death of this one saint, his life so vilely and
shamelessly betrayed into the hands of an adulteress full of

[1] *Fructum pacatissimum exercitatis per eam reddet justitiae*
[2] Cf. Heb. 12:4-11 and the brilliant translation by Ronald Knox
[3] Ps. 80:6   [4] *proventum*   [5] 1 Cor. 10:13   [6] August 29
[7] Matt. 11:11   [8] Matt. 11:9; John 3:29

the bitterest hatred, serves to make all our own affliction light. Where was God then, that He could look on such things? Where was Christ that He remained silent after receiving the news? He perished as if unknown to God, to man, or to the entire world. Compared with the death of this man, of what sufferings must not we be ashamed, not to say take pride in? What will our place be if we bear no suffering willingly, when such great men suffered so ignominious a death without cause, and, after death their body was handed over to the mockery of enemies? It says in Jeremiah, Lo, if those who had not been condemned to drink the cup, nevertheless did drink it, shalt thou be left blameless? Thou shalt not continue to be regarded as blameless; drink you must.[1]

A certain eremite, who used to fall sick year by year, was full of sorrow and lamentation when he had good health for one whole year, because he felt that God had forgotten him and denied him grace. The discipline of the Lord is very necessary and salutary for all Christian people.

It is obvious then that all our sufferings are as nothing when we consider the endless torments endured by the saints: nails, prisons, the sword, fire, wild beasts; or if we ponder over the trials of men now living, who undergo the severest of the devil's persecutions. And there are some who suffer in both body and spirit more sharply and seriously than we.

At this point, some may say, My difficulty is that my sufferings are not on the same basis as those of the saints; being a sinner, I am not worthy to be compared with them. While I suffer for my sins, they suffer for their innocence, and it is no marvel if they bear everything gladly. To say this is very stupid. If you suffer for your sins, you ought to rejoice; your sins are being purged; and have not the saints once been sinners? Need you fear to be like Herod and the thief crucified on Christ's left hand? Not so, if you exercise your patience. It was patience or impatience that distinguished the thief on the left from the thief on the right. Granted you are a sinner; the thief, too, was a sinner, but by

[1] Jer. 49:12

his patient endurance he earned the glory of justification and holiness. You must do likewise. You can only suffer for the sake either of sin or of justification. In either case, if you prize it, suffering sanctifies and blesses. Hence no plea holds good. In fact, the sooner you confess that you are rightly suffering for your sins, the sooner you will become righteous and godly like the thief on the right. We are justified and sanctified by confessing sin because it is true to fact; and so, from the moment of making this confession, you suffer, not for sin, but for your innocence. You have been made righteous by confessing both that your sufferings were deserved and that you were a sinner. It is therefore right and proper to compare your sufferings with those of the saints, just as it is to compare your confession of sin with the confession made by the saints. In each case, the truth, the confession, and the suffering of affliction, are all one, besides being the true communion of the saints in all and through all.

CHAPTER VII

Supernal evil, or the evil above us

Lastly, let us lift up our hearts and ascend with the bride into the mountain of myrrh.[1] Here, crucified, is Jesus Christ, head of all saints, prince of all sufferers of whom, fittingly, many have written much, and all have written all.[2] His memory is commended to the bride when it says, Set me as a token on your heart and as the sign of the cross on your arm.[3] The blood of this lamb, as a sign on the threshold, wards off the destroying angel.[4] The bride is commended by him, because the hair of her head is as glossy as the king's purple, meaning that when she meditates, she flushes at the memory of Christ's passion.[5] This is the tree that Moses was ordered to cast into the waters of Marah, meaning the bitterness of suffering, and they were made sweet.[6] There is nothing, not even death, that this suffering does not sweeten. The bride says, His lips are like lilies dripping prime myrrh. What is the relation between lips and lilies, since the former are red and the latter white? But she is speaking mystically, because the words of Christ are very white and very pure. There is no cruel bitterness or envy in them, but only sweetness and gentleness; yet into them he distills and coaxes prime and choice myrrh (meaning the bitterness of death). Death, like prime myrrh, removes at once the corruption of sin, and, by these purest and sweetest of lips, can itself be made sweet, fair, white, and desirable. How does all this take place? Surely when it comes to your ears that Jesus Christ the Son of God has, by His most holy touch, consecrated and sanctified all kinds of suffering, including death itself. He has turned the curse into a blessing, glorified shame, enriched poverty, until death has been made the gate of life, the curse a

---

[1] Song of Sol. 4:6
[2] All have written all: probably meaning that all the Biblical writers have written between them all that could be said
[3] Cf. Song of Sol. 8:6, Vulgate
[4] Exod. 12:7.13   [5] Song of Sol. 7:5   [6] Exod. 15:23-25

fount of blessing, and shame the mother of glory. Such being
the case, how can you be so hard and ungrateful as not to
choose and love all manner of sufferings, imbued as they are
with the most pure and holy body and blood of Christ, and
rendered to you holy, harmless, good for your salvation,
blessed?

If He sanctified any water used at baptism by the fact that
water had touched His wholly innocent flesh, how much more
will it be the case that, by its contact with His wholly
innocent flesh and blood, He has sanctified every form of
death, all kinds of sufferings, wrongs, curses, and humilia-
tions, and made them convey a baptism of the spirit or of
the blood.[1] He speaks of this baptism of suffering in Luke
12, I have a baptism to be baptized with, and how I am
constrained until it is accomplished![2] Lo! how greatly He was
constrained, how He yearned, how He thirsted to hallow
suffering and death and make them lovely, because He saw
that we were fearful of suffering, and that we trembled and
shrank from death. Like an entirely dutiful pastor and quite
trustworthy physician, He hastened to set a limit to our
sense of affliction, and hurried to His death in order to
commend to us what He himself had tasted. The consequence
is that death is to be regarded by a Christian after the manner
of the brazen serpent of Moses, which retained all the
appearance of a serpent, but was quite without life, without
movement, without venom, without sting.[3] In stupid men's
eyes, the righteous seem to die, but they are at peace.[4] We
ourselves resemble men who die, and to all appearance our
death is like theirs, yet the facts are different. To us death is
dead. Similarly, everything else that we suffer is like the
sufferings of other men. That is how it appears, but, in fact,
our sufferings introduce our freedom from suffering, just as
death is the beginning of life. This is what John means:
Anyone who is true to my word shall never see death.[5]
How shall he not see it? Because, when he is dying, he is

---

[1] Dr. Steinhaeuser rightly sees here a reference to the medieval conception
of a threefold baptism, namely, (i) the sacrament of baptism by water; (ii)
the baptism of the spirit, or repentance; (iii) the baptism of blood, or martyrdom. Cf. Holman, I, p. 138n.
   [2] Luke 12:50   [3] Num. 21:8f.   [4] Wisd. 3:2f.   [5] John 8:51

beginning to live, and so he cannot see death because of the life which he beholds. Now, the night is shining like the day,[1] since the light of dawning life is brighter than that of departing death. All this is valid for those who believe in Christ, but not for unbelievers.

If, therefore, you kiss, love, and fondle, the robe of Christ, the vases, waterpots, and whatever else He may have touched and used, as the most desirable of relics consecrated by contact with Him,[2] much rather should you love, fondle and kiss the pains and penalties inflicted by the world, nay, its shame and death, which are not only consecrated by His touch, but also tinged and blessed by His blood in all its purity. They were willingly accepted by Him and embraced with the highest of constraining love. And you should do this more especially as there are greater merits, rewards, and blessings for you in these afflictions than in those relics. In the former, you are offered victory over death and hell and over all sins; in the latter, nothing at all. O would that we could see the heart of Christ, constrained, when He was hanging on the cross, to render death dead and contemptible. How ardently and with what grace did He embrace death and its pains for those who are fearful and shrink from death and its pains! How willingly He first drank this cup for us who are sick, that we ourselves should not be afraid to drink! We discern that, by His resurrection, no evil touched Him, but only good. If we could but see all this, then undoubtedly that prime myrrh, instilled and commended by the lips and words of Christ, would become most delightful and sweet, like the fragrance and beauty of lilies. Compare what Peter says in 1 Peter 4, Christ's mortal nature has been crucified, and you must arm yourselves with the same intention;[3] and Paul in Hebrews 12, Take your standard from Him, from the great enmity the wicked bore Him, and you will not grow faint, you will not lose heart.[4]

[1] Ps. 139:12
[2] A reference to the medieval practice in the worship of relics, the possession of which was consequently a source of revenue and power to the church or owner that had collected them. Frederick himself had a large collection in the Castle church in Wittenberg, so that Luther's remarks here have a very topical reference; cf. Kooiman, pp. 53, 59
[3] 1 Pet. 4:1   [4] Cf. Heb. 12:3

If, from the foregoing chapters on the evils beneath and around us, we have learned to bear afflictions patiently, surely in this last chapter, when we are lifted up above and beyond ourselves, caught up into Christ, made superior to every affliction, they will appear not merely something to be borne, but to be loved, chosen, sought. The more remote a man is from this state of mind, the less to him is the value of Christ's passion. He will be like those who use the signs and symbols of Christ to guard against misfortunes and death, lest they be either afflicted or die, the very opposite of zeal for the cross and death of Christ. Hence, from this seventh aspect, whatever ills we shall have to bear, must be seized with avidity. Far from grieving us, they must give us joy. Then this aspect of affliction will penetrate to our heart and take its place among the deeper feelings of our soul.

End of the first series. A second follows.

Part II

The seven aspects which we are now to discuss are the antitheses of those in the first series, and are, i. the good within; ii. future good; iii. past good; iv. good beneath; v. good on the left hand; vi. good on the right hand; vii. supernal good.

CHAPTER I

The first aspect: the good within

Can anyone enumerate just those good things which everyone possesses within his own self? i. How great are our physical endowments: beauty, strength, health, liveliness of mind, qualified in the male by a high nobility due to his sex, fitting him to do many things in both public and private life, and for outstanding deeds unsuited for women. If, by the grace of God, you enjoy the pleasure afforded by these gifts for ten, twenty, or thirty years, is it a serious matter to endure hardship for a short while at times? A popular proverb says, It's only a passing squall; and another, A little good luck is worth a little bad.[1] What is to be made of us, if, after we have enjoyed long periods of happiness, we cannot bear a bit of hardship? That shows how great are the blessings that God showers upon us, whereas, in the majority of cases, we are scarcely touched even by a few evils.

The good God, not contented with giving these blessings, adds riches, a wealth of goods of all kinds, and these, if not to everyone, certainly to many, and especially those too weak to bear hardships. Moreover, as I have said above,[2] where He gives fewer possessions or physical advantages, He gives more of the mental kind. Thus all is made fair and He disposes all things justly. Great wealth does not give greater

---

[1] *Es ist umb ein bose stund zuthun;* and *Ein gutt stund ist eyner posen werdt*
[2] Cf. *supra,* pp. 37ff.

comfort than a cheerful disposition. In addition, to some He grants children, and it is said that offspring are the highest pleasure, influence, rank, honour, fame, glory, favour, etc. If He grants the enjoyment of these for a long time, or even only temporarily, we are readily persuaded by them how to act in some little distress.

But the good things of the mind are more excellent than any of these: intelligence, knowledge, judgment, erudition, discretion. As before, so also here, He tempers His rule with equality in such a way that though He gives more to some men, He does not prefer them to those to whom He has given instead greater peace or cheerfulness of mind. In all these things we ought to pay grateful attention to the bountiful hand of God, and find comfort in our time of weakness. Then, surrounded by many blessings of great value, we shall not marvel if a little bitterness is intermingled. To epicures, roast meat is unsavoury when unsalted; and scarcely any food is to our taste without a certain bitter flavour either natural or added. A continuous and unalloyed sweetness is so distasteful that it is said that "Pleasure long continued brings on loathing" and "Sooner or later, pleasure becomes hard to bear". In other words, in this life we are not fitted to enjoy good things not tempered by ills, because the good things are too excessive. Hence the proverb, "You need to be strong to bear good fortune".[1] When turning over this proverb, I have often marvelled how wonderfully true was its sentiment: namely that human wishes are at odds with themselves. Men seek only to be happy, yet they are less able to bear happiness than hardship.

What God commends to us by these things is that the Cross of Christ is something miraculous even to its foes, and that by virtue of its relics[2] all things must needs be tempered and sanctified and thus preserved, just as meat is salted down lest it breed worms. Why then should we not gladly receive this tempering sent by God? If He did not send it, we should call for it on our own initiative, because life would be

---

[1] *Oportere ossa esse robusta, quae ferant dies bonos*

[2] *Sic*; with a prime reference to the prevailing reverence for relics of the Cross. Yet the dominating thought is, surely, that a modicum of Christian suffering tempers and sanctifies

intolerable with naught but pleasure and felicity.[1] This is the
truth in what the Wise Man says of God, Wisdom exercises
a mighty sway to the limits of the world and disposes all
things propitiously.[2] These blessings, on examination, will
make plain how true is that which Moses said, Deuteronomy
32, He carried him on his shoulders, cared for him, and kept
him as the apple of his eye.[3] With these quotations we can
silence those ungrateful babblers who say that life contains
more evil than good, since there is no lack of good things or
of infinite favours for our delight. The lack is of those who
share the insight of him who said, The earth is full of the
mercy of the Lord,[4] and, The earth is full of His praise,[5] and
Psalm 103, The earth is full of Thy riches;[6] Thou hast made
me rejoice in Thy creation.[7] This is the reason why we sing
daily at mass, Heaven and earth are full of Thy glory. Why is
this done? Because of the many good things for which He
should be praised, although it is done only by those who
perceive how many they are. When discussing the first type of
evils,[8] we said that the afflictions a man is called on to bear
are only as great as he thinks or feels them to be. Similarly,
although our blessings approach and pour in upon us from
all sides, yet they are only as great as the value we set upon
them. Everything that God does is exceedingly good,[9]
though not acknowledged as such by men like all those
mentioned in Psalm 77, They despised the pleasant land.[10]

Of the type we are discussing, Job offers the most beautiful
and instructive example. When he had been deprived of all,
he said, If we accept good from God's hand, why not evil
too?[11] That is a saying worth its weight in gold, and is a great
help when we are being tried. Job not only endured sufferings
in himself, but also his wife tried his patience when she said
to him, Are you still keeping inoffensive? Curse God and die.[12]
It is as if she said, Plainly He is not God if He abandons you

---

[1] *Nisi ille mitteret, impotens nostra voluptatum et bonorum vita sponte
accerseret*

[2] Cf. Wisd. 8:1   [3] Cf. Deut. 32:10f.   [4] Ps. 33:5   [5] Hab. 3:3

[6] Ps. 104:24   [7] Cf. Ps. 92:5   [8] Cf. *supra*, p. 23   [9] Gen. 1:31

[10] The quotation is from Psalm 106:24, which may be regarded as a
summary of Ps. 78

[11] Job 2:10   [12] Job 2:9

in this way. Why trust in Him, instead, rather, of renouncing
and cursing Him, and showing yourself mortal, a man for
whom there is nothing left after this present life? This and
the like are suggested to each one of us by one's wife (i.e.
one's feelings[1]) in times of trial because our perceptions[2] do
not grasp the ways of God.

All that we have discussed so far are physical blessings,
common to all. A Christian enjoys other, and far superior
blessings within, namely, faith in Christ. This is described by
Psalm 44, The king's daughter is all glorious within: her
clothing is of wrought gold.[3] We said of evils of the first type[4]
that no evil in a man can be so great that it is the worst of
those within him.[5] Similarly, the Christian is not able to
see the best of the blessings that are within him; should he
feel them, he would be already in heaven, for (as Christ said)
the kingdom of heaven is within us.[6] To possess faith is to
possess the truth of God and the word of God, and to possess
the word of God is to possess God the creator of all things.
If these blessings were to be revealed to us in all their fulness,
in the twinkling of an eye our soul would be set free from our
body by immeasurable happiness. It follows that the other
blessings which we mentioned are rightly to be regarded as
reminders of those inward blessings which God commends
to us by them. Our life could not bear them to be revealed,
and they are therefore mercifully hidden by God, until they
reach their perfect time. Similarly, parents may sometimes
lovingly give their children small and trifling gifts, leading
their childish minds to look for something nobler.

Nevertheless, these blessings show themselves sometimes.
They break out when we consciously rejoice in our faith in
God, speak of Him freely, hear His word gladly; when we are
quick and happy to serve Him, to do good, or to suffer wrong,
etc. All these things are clues to the infinite and incomparable

---

[1] *Sensualitas*   [2] *Sensus*

[3] So Ps. 45:14, A.V.; Luther's text reads, *omnis gloria eius regis ab intus
in fimbriis aureis circumdata varietate*

[4] Cf. *supra*, p. 21

[5] As it stands, the sentence is self-contradictory; the meaning is: no
inward evil *of which we are conscious* is the worst, etc.

[6] Luke 17:21

blessing within, which drips these little drops to form a tiny rill without. Sometimes, to the contemplatives, a fuller revelation is granted until, in ecstasy, they know not where they are. St. Augustine and his mother, and many others, acknowledge this to be their case.[1]

[1] Cf. Aug., *Confessions*, IX, 10

CHAPTER II

The second aspect: future good, or the good that lies in front

Not much comfort can be given by speaking of future blessings to those who are not Christian, when they endure present afflictions. In cases like these, there will be a great deal of talk about the renowned virtue of hope, for it is only human to encourage each other to look for better things. Too frequently, we are led to plan splendid things for the uncertain future, yet always in vain. In the gospel according to Luke, 12, Christ tells of a man who said to his soul, I will pull down my barns and build greater ones; and I will say to my soul, Soul of mine, take thy rest now, eat, drink, make merry; thou hast goods in plenty laid up for many years to come. But God said, Thou fool, this night thou must render up thy soul; and who will be master of all thou hast laid by? Thus it is with the man who lays up treasure for himself, and has no credit with God.[1]

Nevertheless, God has not so far abandoned humankind as not to comfort them with the feeling that their afflictions will pass, and good things come. Granted that they are still uncertain of the future, yet they have assurance when they hope, and this, meantime, buoys them up, lest, unable to bear their present afflictions, they fall into the evil of despair, and make things worse. It follows, that hope of this kind is given by God, although it is not such that He wishes them to rely on. But it should suggest to them that substantial hope which is found in Himself alone. God exercises forbearance in order that He might lead them to repentance,[2] as it says in Romans 2, nor does He allow them all to be at once deceived by this false hope, if they may still find heart again and a true hope.

Beyond the twofold blessings of this kind, Christians are assured of very great future blessings, yet only through death and suffering. While it is true that they, too, rejoice in the

[1] Luke 12:18, 21ff.　　[2] Rom. 2:4

universal hope of the end of present evil and the increase of the corresponding good, they only entertain that hope in order that their proper blessings may increase, namely, the truth as it is in Christ. They seek to grow in this respect from day to day, and for this they both live and hope. Beyond these things, as I have said, two blessings of the greatest kind lie before them in death, i. that death closes the universal tragedy of the ills of this life. Hence it is written, Precious in the sight of the Lord is the death of His saints;[1] and again, I will both lay me down in peace, and sleep;[2] again, Although the righteous man be overtaken suddenly by death, he will be at rest.[3] On the contrary, death is the beginning of afflictions for the wicked, as it is written: The death of the wicked is a very evil thing[4] and, Evils shall seize the wicked man in his destruction.[5] Similarly, Lazarus, who endured a hard lot in life, will be solaced, whereas the man who feasted will be tormented because he enjoyed his advantages here.[6] Thus, whether in life or in death, the Christian enjoys the better part; so blessed a thing is it to be a Christian and to believe in Christ. On this basis, Paul says, To me to live is Christ, and death is gain;[7] and Romans 13, He who lives, lives to the Lord; He who dies, dies to the Lord. Whether therefore we live or die we are the Lord's.[8] Christ has gained this assurance for us because He died and rose again, to become the Lord of the quick and the dead, able to keep us safe in both life and death, as it says in Psalm 22, Should I walk in the midst of the shadow of death, I shall not fear evil, because Thou art with me.[9] If we are scarcely moved by this advantage which death offers, it is because our faith in Christ is feeble, and does not sufficiently prize the reward and advantage of a happy death, or does not yet believe that death is a good thing, being prevented, perhaps, by the old self, which is still alive, and by worldly wisdom. We must therefore endeavour to attain to the knowledge and love of this privilege of death. It is important that death, which is the greatest of evils to others, should be our greatest prize. If Christ did not perform this for us, what has He done at

---

[1] Ps. 115:16   [2] Ps. 4:8   [3] Wisd. 4:7   [4] Cf. Ps. 34:22
[5] Cf. Ps. 140:11   [6] Luke 16:25   [7] Phil. 1:21   [8] Rom. 14:8   [9] Ps. 23:4

the great cost of His own self? The work He wrought
was entirely divine, and there is therefore no room for
wonder if He made the evil of death into something very
good.

Hence, to believers, death is already dead, and retains no
terror beyond its appearance and the mask it wears. It is like
a dead serpent whose appearance is as frightening as before;
but, in fact, only the appearance remains and the harmful-
ness is dead and cannot hurt. In Numbers 21, Moses ordered
a brazen serpent to be set up, at the sight of which living
serpents perished;[1] similarly, our death dies if we steadily
contemplate the death of Christ, and retains nothing but the
shape of death. By these lovely similes, God in His mercy
reveals beforehand to us in our infirmity, that, although
death cannot be taken away, He has drained its power until
it remains only in appearance. Wherefore, the Scriptures call
it sleep rather than death.

The other benefit of death is that it not only puts an end
to the pains and penalties of this life, but, what is more
important, ends its vices and sins. This fact, as I have already
said,[2] makes death far more preferable to believing minds
than the blessing now discussed. Evils in the soul, namely
sins, are far worse than bodily afflictions, and, if we were wise,
would of themselves make death most desirable to us. If this
is not their effect, it is a sign that we do not sufficiently
feel and hate the sins of our soul. Since our present life
is a very perilous thing, with insidious sin lying in wait for us
on every hand, and we cannot live without committing sin,
death, in its excellence, delivers us from these perils, and cuts
sin off from us altogether. The praise of the righteous man in
Wisdom 4 ends with the words, He pleased God and was made
His beloved; and after living among sinners, he was translated to heaven. He was speedily removed lest wickedness
should spoil his understanding and falsity beguile his soul.
The fascination of frivolity beclouds things that are good,
and the changing forms of evil desires subvert an innocent
mind (O how certain and insistent are they). Though he
reached his end soon, he did enough to fill a long life. His soul

[1] Cf. Num. 21:8f.   [2] Cf. *supra*, pp. 41ff.

pleased God, who therefore hasted to take him away from the midst of iniquity.[1]

In this way, through the mercy of God, death, which is punishment for the sinner, becomes, for the Christian, the end of sin and the beginning of life and righteousness. Anyone, therefore, who loves life and righteousness does not dread, but must of necessity love, death, their servant and subordinate. Otherwise, he never attains life and righteousness. Let him for whom this is impossible, pray God to make it possible. We are taught to say, Thy will be done,[2] for we are unable to do it of our own selves, because we fear death more, and love death and sin more, than we delight in life and righteousness. That God ordained death to put an end to sin may be deduced from the fact that He imposed death on Adam immediately after his sin and to make amends for sin.[3] He did this before He drove him out of paradise in order to show us that death does us no harm but brings every blessing, since it was imposed in paradise as penance and satisfaction. It is true that death entered the world through the envy of the devil,[4] but, by the surpassing goodness of God, when it had entered, it was not allowed to do us much harm; it was taken in hand from the start and made to be the punishment and death of sin.

This is what He meant when He gave a commandment which foretold the death of Adam. Nor was He silent afterwards, for He imposed death anew, and tempered the rigour of His commandment. He did not so much as mention death, but said only, Dust thou art, and unto dust shalt thou return; and, Until thou return to the ground out of which thou wast taken.[5] It was as if He so hated death that He did not deign to name it, according to the passage, Wrath is in His indignation, but life in His purpose.[6] He seems to have said, If death had not been necessary for abolishing sin, He would not have known nor named, much less imposed it. Thus God in His hostility armed death against sin, though it was the very thing which sin had brought about. This exemplifies what the poet says:

[1] Cf. Wisd. 4:10-14   [2] Matt. 6:10; Lk. 11:2   [3] Cf. Gen. 2:17
[4] Wisd. 2:24   [5] Gen. 3:19   [6] Ps. 30:6, Vulgate

> Knowest thou not,
> That by the same device his art has framed
> The artist falls?[1]

Similarly, sin is destroyed by its own fruit, and slain by the death which it brought forth, like a viper by its own progeny. It is a splendid sight to see how sin is destroyed by its own act and not that of another, beheaded by its own sword like Goliath by his.[2] Goliath was a figure for sin, a terrible giant to all except David a stripling, namely Christ, who laid him low single-handed, cut off his head with his own sword, and afterwards said that there was no better sword than that of Goliath.[3]

If, then, we meditate on these joys, which issue from the power of Christ, and on these blessings of His grace, why should a minor evil cause us distress when, in a great evil that lies in the future, we can see such great blessings?

---

[1] Ovid *Ars amat.* I, 656   [2] I Sam. 17:51   [3] I Sam. 21:9

CHAPTER III

The third aspect: past blessing, or the blessing behind us

It is easy to discuss this blessing in view of its contrary type, namely, past evil.[1] Nevertheless, let us help any who are giving it attention. On this subject, St. Augustine, in his *Confessions*, shows himself an outstanding master when, in beautiful language, he rehearses God's blessings to him from his very birth.[2] The fine Psalm 138 makes the same point, Lord, Thou hast searched me, where the Psalmist, marvelling among other things at the providence of God, declares, Thou hast understood my thoughts from afar, my path and my portion hast Thou scrutinized. It is as much as if he said, Whatever I have thought, whatever I have done, and whatever I shall achieve and possess, I now see are not the result of my own diligence, but have been ordained long ago by Thy care, for Thou hast foreseen all my ways. There is not a word in my tongue. Where then? In Thy power.[3]

This we learn from our own experience. If we call to mind our past lives, is it not astonishing that we thought, or willed, or did, or said things such as we could not envisage in advance? How very differently we should have acted if we had been left freely to our own devices. That of which we now first grasp the significance, we discern to have been, as it were, His instant care or His constant concern for us. Unless He had granted it, we should have been unable either to speak or to will or to think. It therefore says in Wisdom 7, For in His hands, are both we and our words;[4] Paul says, It is He that worketh all things in us.[5] In the hardness of our unfeeling hearts, ought we not to hang our heads in shame, when, taught by our own experience, we see how God has cared for us to the present moment, and given us all our blessings? Yet we are unable to transfer to Him our cares when in some small affliction; we act as if He had abandoned us, or could do so in some way! Not so Psalm 39, which says,

[1] Cf. *supra*, pp. 28ff.   [2] *Confessions*, I, 6   [3] Cf. Ps. 139:1ff.
[4] Wisd. 7:16   [5] I Cor. 12:6

I am poor and needy, yet the Lord thinketh upon me;[1] on which verse St. Augustine comments, Let Him who made thee care for thee. Will not He, who cared for thee before thou hadst being, care for thee now that thou art become that which He wished thee to be? We propose a kingdom divided with God. We scarcely grant, even tepidly, that He made us; we arrogate to ourselves responsibility for ourselves, as if He had made us and immediately departed, leaving it to us to control our own affairs.

If our wisdom and foresight prevent us from seeing God's care over us, because many things have perhaps turned out according to our own plans, let us go back and probe ourselves with Psalm 138, My bones were not hidden from Thee when Thou madest me in secret (meaning, Thou didst see and form my bones in my mother's womb, before I had being, before my mother knew what was taking place in herself) and my substance in the lower parts of the earth[2] (meaning, the form or shape of my body was not hidden from Thee even in the secret recesses of my mother, because Thou wast giving it shape). The Psalmist intended with these words to give us a striking illustration of God's unceasing care for us without our participation. Who can boast that he co-operated when he was formed in his mother's womb? Who gave our mother the care through which she suckled, fondled, and loved us, and performed all her maternal offices before we were conscious of our life? We should know and remember none of these things, unless we saw their like done to others and believed they must have been done to us also. These things are done to us exactly as if we were asleep, or even dead, or rather not yet born, as far as our own knowledge of them goes.

Thus we learn that, without our aid, God's mercies and comforts bear us up. And yet we doubt and even despair of His care for us up to the present. If anyone is not taught and moved by this experience, I know not what will teach or move him. This is what we see plainly before our eyes in every little child we meet. So many examples are placed there before us in our ignorance and hardness of heart that

---

[1] Ps. 40:17   [2] Cf. Ps. 139:15

they ought to fill us with deep shame when we doubt that the slightest good or evil cannot touch us apart from God's special providence for us. Thus St. Peter says, 1 Peter 5, Casting all your care upon Him, for He careth for you;[1] and Psalm 36, Cast thy care on the Lord and He will provide for thee.[2] In his *Confessions*, St. Augustine addresses his own soul and says, Why dost thou stand over thyself and yet thou dost not stand? Cast thyself upon Him, He will not withdraw His hand and let thee fall;[3] and again 1 Peter 4, Why then, let those who suffer according to the will of God commend their souls with their good deeds to their faithful creator.[4]

O, anyone who confesses God in this way, how tranquilly, how peacefully, how happily will he live! He would truly possess God, and know for certain that all things, whatever they were, that have happened or are happening to himself are in accordance with His most gracious will. Peter's word holds good: He careth for you. What can we hear that is sweeter than this word? He says, Therefore cast all your care on Him.[5] If we fail, and are solicitous for our own selves, this only means that in all we do we are seeking to impede God's care; and at the same time we make our life sad, and laborious, anxious on account of many fears, cares, and much restlessness. Moreover, all is in vain, for we bestir ourselves to no good purpose. Rather, it is as Ecclesiastes says, This is vanity of vanities, and affliction of spirit.[6] The whole of that book discusses this experience, as if written by one who had tried many things for himself, yet had found in them all nothing but weariness, vanity, and affliction of spirit. He therefore concludes that it is God's gift when a man eats and drinks and lives joyfully with his wife; in other words, when he commends his cares to God and lives without anxiety.[7] For this reason, we ought to have no other anxiety for ourselves than this, namely, not to be anxious about ourselves and negate God's care for us.

As for the rest, anyone can work it out for himself from the contrary type (as I have said)[8] and from his memory of all his past life.

---

[1] 1 Pet. 5:7 [2] Ps. 37:5, 55:22 [3] Aug., *Confessions*, VIII, 9
[4] 1 Pet. 4:19 [5] 1 Pet. 5:7 [6] Eccles. 1:2.14 [7] Cf. Eccles. 5,18; 9:7.9
[8] Cf. *supra*, pp. 28ff., Past Evils

CHAPTER IV

The fourth aspect: the good below or beneath us

Thus far we have been considering those blessings which are personal to and within us. Let us now consider those which are in others and outside ourselves. The first of these is found in those who are beneath us, namely, the dead and the damned. Why marvel if any blessing is to be found among the dead and the damned? The power of the goodness of God is everywhere so great that it makes it possible to see blessings in the greatest afflictions. If we first compare those creatures with ourselves, we shall find that our advantages are incomputable, as we can easily see by a consideration of the evils of the contrary type.[1] The greatness of the afflictions of death and hell to be seen in them are undoubtedly proportionate to our advantages, which are the greater as their afflictions are greater. None of these things are to be despised light-heartedly, for they urge upon us the splendour of God's mercy. If we think these things but slight, there is the danger of ourselves being found ungrateful, and of being condemned together with them, and even more cruelly tormented; because the more we see they suffer and bemoan their lot, the more we ought to rejoice in the goodness that God has shown towards us. This is what Isaiah 65 says: Behold, my servants shall eat, but ye shall be hungry; behold, my servants shall drink, but ye shall be thirsty; behold my servants shall rejoice, but ye shall be ashamed; behold my servants shall sing for joy of heart, but ye shall cry for sorrow of heart, and shall howl for vexation of spirit; and ye shall leave my name for a curse unto my chosen, etc.[2] In other words, as I have said,[3] the example of those whose death is dreadful and of the damned (as discussed by St. Gregory in his Dialogues)[4] should serve to admonish and

---

[1] Cf. *supra*, pp. 31ff. [2] Isa. 65:13-15 [3] Cf. *supra*, p. 31
[4] Cf. Greg. *Dialogorum*, Book IV, which contains a number of examples of the terrible end of the wicked; so A. E. T. Steinhaeuser, Holman, Vol. I, p. 157, n.

instruct us well. Our advantage in this respect, being quite familiar, scarcely affects us, although it should be reckoned as of the highest importance; and people who have delicate sensibility set much store by it. There are many passages of Scripture that bear upon it, namely, those that teach of God's wrath and judgments and threats. The highly salutary quality of these teachings is what is rightly made a positive thing for us by the example of these very unhappy creatures.

Examples like this only come home to us when we enter into the feelings of those who endure such things and, as it were, put ourselves in their place and person. Then they will indeed move and rouse us to praise the goodness of the God who has preserved us from these things.

Let us compare these people with God Himself in order that we may see the divine righteousness in them, a difficult task, but one that we must attempt. Since God is a just judge, His righteousness ought to be loved and praised. Similarly, we ought to rejoice in God even when He utterly destroys the wicked in both body and soul, because the height and ineffability of His righteousness shine forth here also. It follows that hell, no less than heaven, is full of God and of supreme goodness; and therefore not only His mercy, but also His righteousness and His judgments are to be loved, praised, and preached to the utmost. This was David's meaning when he said, At the sight of such vengeance, the good shall exult, and wash his hands in bad men's blood.[1] This is the reason why the Lord forbade Samuel, 1 Kings 16, to mourn any longer for Saul, when He said, How long wilt thou mourn for Saul, seeing I have rejected him from reigning over Israel?[2] It is as if He had said, Does My will displease you so much that you prefer a human will to mine? In short, this is the strain of praise and joy that runs through the whole book of Psalms. It says that God is the judge of the widow and the father of orphans; that He will maintain the cause of the poor and the rights of the needy; that His enemies will be confounded, the wicked perish; and there are many similar utterances. If any should be inclined by their foolish pity and for the sake of the company of

[1] Ps. 58:11, Moffatt   [2] 1 Sam. 16:1

wicked men[1] to condole with this species of men of blood,
who killed righteous men, including the very Son of God, he
will soon be found sharing in the joys of their iniquity and
approving their actions. He will deserve to perish in the same
manner as those whose sins he would have unpunished, and
to hear what is said in 2 Kings 19, Thou lovest thine enemies
and hatest thy friends.[2] That is how Joab spoke to David
when he grieved too sadly over his son Absalom, a wicked
man and a murderer. From our present standpoint, therefore,
we ought to rejoice in the piety of all the saints and in the
righteousness of God, on account of which He has most rightly
punished the persecutors of religion in order that He might
set His elect free from them. In this way, too, it can be seen
that not small, but very great blessings shine forth in the
dead and the damned; and, in particular, punishment for all
the injuries done to the saints, and for your own if you are
righteous as they were. If so, would it be astonishing if God
were using your present affliction in order to punish your
bodily sin? Certainly, you ought to rejoice at the service
done by God in His supreme righteousness which, in this
way, without your asking, kills and destroys your worst
enemy, namely, sin in your heart. If you feel sorry for your
body, you will turn out to be the friend of sin and an enemy
of the righteousness which is at work within you. Be very
careful on this point or it will be said to you also, You love
them that hate you, and hate them that love you.[3] You
ought to rejoice greatly at the righteousness which is wrath
with your sin; and, similarly, rejoice when it is wrath with
sinners, who are enemies of all mankind and of God. Such
considerations show that it is possible to see the highest
good in the greatest evils, and to rejoice in the worst afflictions, not because they are evil, but on account of the
supreme righteousness of our Avenger.

[1] *Impiorum cumulo*   [2] 2 Sam. 19:6   [3] 2 Sam. 19:6

CHAPTER V

The fifth aspect: the good to the left, or on the left hand

We are now to deal with those foes who are still alive,
just as in the preceding chapter we dealt with the damned
and those assimilated to the devils. We must look at them
from a different angle, and we shall see that the blessings they
enjoy are of two kinds. In the first place, they have an
abundance of temporal blessings; so much so that even the
prophets were well-nigh moved to envy their prosperity.
Psalm 72 says, I almost slipped, I nearly lost my footing,
because I was jealous of the wicked when I saw the serenity
of the sinners; and later, Lo, these are the sinners. They
abound in the worldly wealth which they have obtained.[1]
Jeremiah 12 says, Thou art righteous, O Lord, when I complain to Thee; yet let me talk with Thee of Thy judgments.
Why do bad men prosper? Good fortune is on the side of all
who play false and do wrong.[2]

Why does He spontaneously pour out and waste so many
good things on them, unless it be to comfort us, and to show
how blessed are they whose heart is righteous,[3] as it says in
that very Psalm 72? If such is His goodness to the wicked,
how much greater must be His goodness to the good? This
is not to say that He does not vex the wicked with any
afflictions, but that He tests the good with many afflictions
in order that they may know that their blessings lie, not so
much in present benefits, as in those that are hidden and in
the future. Then they will repeat the verse in the same psalm,
It is bliss for me to hold fast to God, and to place my hope in
the Lord,[4] which is as much as to say, I will retain my trust,
even if I suffer from what I see they are free of, because God's
blessings are far greater to me than they are to them. In this
way, the good things which the wicked enjoy are an incite-
ment to us to hope for invisible blessings and to despise the
evils we suffer. This accords with what Christ said in

[1] Ps. 73:3.12   [2] Jer. 12:1   [3] Ps. 73:1   [4] Ps. 73, 28

Matthew 6, when He commanded us to consider the birds of
the air and the lilies of the field, and said, If God so clothes the
grass which is growing to-day, but to-morrow is cast into
the oven, how much more in your case, you of modest faith.[1]
Thus, by comparing the good things with which the wicked
abound, and the evils from which we suffer, our faith is exercised, and we find in God the only comfort that is holy. Then, of
necessity, all things will work together for good to the godly.

The second blessing, and it is much the more marvellous,
is that things which are afflictions to them are benefits to us.
Even if those sins are a stumbling block to the weaker sort,
they offer to the stronger sort an exercise of their virtue, an
opportunity for battle, and one of greater merit. Blessed is
the man who endures under trials. When he has proved his
worth, he will win the crown of life.[2] What greater temptation
can there be than a host of bad examples of that kind? For
this reason, the world is spoken of as one of the enemies of
saints of God because, with its enticements and wicked ways,
it provokes us, allures, and attracts us from God's way into
its own. Thus Genesis 6, The sons of God saw that the
daughters of men were beautiful and formed of flesh;[3]
and Numbers 25, The sons of Israel slept with the daughters
of the Moabites.[4] It is therefore salutary that we should be
always under the pressure of some disadvantage, lest, in our
weakness, we are caught in the snares of the world, fall down,
and sin. Peter commends Lot in this way, 2 Peter 2, when he
had suffered much from the evil practices of the people of
Sodom, and yet, through them made progress in his own
righteousness.[5] Offences of this kind come of necessity, and
move us to struggle through to victory; but woe unto the world,
because of offences.[6] If, then, God works so much good in us
through the sins of others, how much more firmly ought we to
believe with all our heart that He will work good in us through
our troubles, even if our mind and body judge otherwise?

Nor is that good less which is conferred on us by the world
by its other sort of evils, namely, its adversities. When it is
unable to swallow us up by its enticements, and incorporate

---

[1] Cf. Matt. 6:25ff.   [2] Jas. 1:12   [3] Cf. Gen. 6:1
[4] Num. 25:1ff.   [5] 2 Pet. 2:7   [6] Matt. 18:7

us with itself by its snares, it endeavours to cast us out by sufferings, and drive us off by sharp pains; it is always making traps for us in the example of sinners, or loosing its fury on us in the anguish of its punishments. The world is a monster, a chimera, with a maiden's head, seductive; the body of a lion, cruel; and the tail of a serpent, deadly; because the end of the world, with its voluptuousness and its tyranny, is poison and eternal death. But, despite our being in the midst of the sins of the world, God enables us to find blessings for ourselves; and, similarly, He has ordained that the persecutions we suffer from it should be neither useless nor otiose, but should increase our blessings. The very things by which we are harmed are compelled to help us on. St. Augustine, discussing the case of the innocents whom Herod slew, says he would never have been able to do so much good by his favour as he did by his hatred. St. Agatha, the blessed martyr,[1] went to prison as if to a banquet; and this is what she said: If you do not make the executioners treat my body badly, my soul will be unable to enter paradise with the victor's palm; for a grain of wheat is not stored in the barn until it has been stripped of its husk and well beaten on the threshing floor.[2]

But why discuss such questions, however briefly? The whole of Scripture, the writings and sayings of all the fathers, the lives and acts of all the saints obviously bear it out that those who do most injury to believers do them most benefit. Peter says in 1 Peter 3, Who will do you wrong, if you are eager for what is good?[3] Psalm 88, His enemy shall get no further with him, and no miscreant shall succeed in hurting him.[4] If he often kills, how is it that he will do no harm? Because by harming, he does us the greatest good. Thus, from every standpoint, if we use our sagacity, we find we dwell in the midst of blessings in spite of being in the midst of evils. All things are kept within their limits by the overruling of divine providence.

[1] *gloriabunda*
[2] St. Agatha is the patron saint of Catania, Sicily. She died in prison on February 5, 251, after having been cruelly tortured and sent to the stake, from which, however she was delivered by the people when an earthquake occurred which they felt to be a divine sign
[3] Cf. 1 Pet. 3:13   [4] Cf. Ps. 89:23

CHAPTER VI

The sixth aspect: the good on the right, or on our right hand

Our subject is now the church of the saints, those created anew by God, brethren and friends of ours in whom nothing but blessing is to be seen, indeed, nothing but encouragement; although, granted, not always visible to ordinary sight (where they might seem to belong to the contrary type of the afflicted) but to spiritual vision. Still, we must not disregard their visible blessings, but learn from them how God can comfort us. Even Psalm 72 does not go so far as to condemn all who have gained worldly wealth; it says, If I had been speaking in this way, I should have been offending against those who were Thy people.[1] The meaning is, If I had intended to call wicked all men who were wealthy, healthy, and esteemed, I should have been condemning many among them who were saints of Thine. Even the apostle instructs Timothy to teach those who have worldly wealth not to think highly of themselves, but he does not forbid their wealth.[2] The Scriptures record that Abraham, Isaac, and Jacob were rich men.[3] So, too, Daniel and his companions were raised to high honour in Babylon itself.[4] Further, many of the kings of Judah were saintly men. It is with these people in mind that the Psalm says: If I had been speaking in this way, I should have been offending against those who were Thy people.[5] I assert that God does give to His own people a wealth of blessings of this kind for their own enjoyment and that of others; although it must be granted that such things are not their true blessings, but the shadows and signs of those that are truly good, namely, faith, hope, love, and other gifts and graces, all of which alike come through love.

This is the fellowship of the saints, and we glory in it. He who believes that this is the truth, may vaunt himself about

[1] Ps. 73:15 [2] 1 Tim. 6:17 [3] Cf. Gen. 13:2, 26:12f., 32:13ff.
[4] Dan. 2:48f. [5] Ps. 73:15

it even in the midst of afflictions, and say, in effect, that the good things the saints enjoy are his, and his afflictions are theirs. In writing to the Galatians, the apostle put it graphically, Bear one another's burdens, and so fulfil the law of Christ.[1] Is it not good for us to be in the place where, as it says in 1 Corinthians 6, If one member suffers, all members suffer with him; if one is exalted all the members rejoice with him? Hence, when I suffer, I do not suffer alone; Christ and all Christians suffer with me, as it is written, He that toucheth you, toucheth the apple of his own eye.[2] In this way, others bear my burden, and the strength of others is my own. The faith of the church succours me in my trepidation, the purity of others helps me when I am lustful, the fasts of others are my merits, another's prayer is my consolation; in short, the members encourage one another, so that those who have been more enriched, protect, serve, and enrich those who are needy, in the way beautifully described in 1 Corinthians 6.[3] Then, of a truth, I can take pride in the blessings of others as if they were my own; and in fact they are my own when I rejoice and take pleasure in them. While I myself may be only base and vile, yet those whom I love and applaud are fair and beautiful. By my love, I make my own, not only their good things, but also their very selves. In this way, my ignominy is enriched by their splendour, and my need is supplied from their abundance, their merits cure my sins. What man, then, could fall into despair if he fell into sin? What man would not rejoice in his sufferings if he had not to bear his own sins and sufferings, or at least, not alone? He is aided by the host of the saints of God, nay, by Christ Himself. This shows how great a thing is the communion of saints and similarly the church of Christ.

If any one does not believe that these things are so, or that this is how they happen, that man is an unbeliever, and he denies Christ and the church. Even if he is unaware of it, yet this is the way of things; but who is unaware? Why are you not overcome by despair, why not give way to impatience? What is the reason? Your own strength? Not by

[1] Gal. 6:2   [2] Zech. 2:8   [3] 1 Cor. 12:22ff.

EML

any means, but the communion of saints. Otherwise, you would not be able to bear up after only a venial sin, nor endure it when any man spoke against you. So near is Christ, and also the church. This is what we are saying when we repeat, I believe in the Holy Spirit, the Holy Catholic Church. To believe in Holy Church is nothing else than to believe in the communion of saints. In what does the communion of saints consist? In both good and evil. All things belong to all. This is symbolized in the sacrament of the altar by the bread and wine, when the apostle says that we are one body, one bread, one cup.[1] Who can hurt any part of the body without giving pain to the whole body? Anything felt in the tip of the toe is felt by the whole body, and any good done to our feet makes the whole body happy. Similarly, we are one body. I feel and bear whatever anyone else suffers; and whatever is good for him is good for me. Thus Christ says that what is done to the least of those who belong to Him, is done to Himself.[2] If a man partakes of the smallest fragment of the bread of the altar, we say he partakes of the bread. Would not anyone who despised a crumb of it be said to have despised the bread?

Hence if we sorrow, or suffer, or die, here is our weak spot.[3] Let us believe firmly and be assured that in affliction we are not alone, but Christ and the church sorrows, suffers, and dies with us. It is not Christ's wish for us that we should tread that path of death alone, which all men fear. Rather, we enter upon the way of suffering and death in the company of the whole church, and the church bears it with greater fortitude than we in ourselves alone. It would be appropriate to quote what Elisha said when his servant was afraid, 4 Kings 6, Fear not, for they that be with us are more than they that be with them. And when Elisha prayed he said, Lord, open this lad's eyes, that he may see. The Lord opened his eyes and he saw, and lo! the mountain was full of horses and chariots of fire round about Elisha.[4] The one thing that remains for us to do is to pray that our eyes may be opened to see the church round about us; I mean the eyes of faith.

---

[1] Cf. 1 Cor. 10:17 [2] Matt. 25:40
[3] *Huc feratur intutus* [4] 2 Kings 6:16f.

Then there will be nothing which we shall fear; so, too, Psalm 124, The mountains are round about it, and the Lord is round about his people both now and for ever.[1] Amen.

[1] Ps. 125:2

CHAPTER VII

The seventh aspect: supernal good, or the good above us

I am going to say nothing of the good things which are eternal and celestial, and which the blessed enjoy when they see God face to face; or rather I speak of them only in faith and insofar as they can be comprehended by us. Hence the seventh type is Jesus Christ, the king of glory, risen from the dead, just as the seventh type of evil was His passion, death, and burial.[1] Here we can see the highest joy of our hearts and the surest of blessings. There remains no evil of any kind, because, having risen from the dead, Christ dieth no more; death hath no more dominion over Him.[2] Here is the furnace and the fire of God in Zion.[3] And Isaiah says, Christ is born unto us; and not only so, but He is given unto us.[4] For this reason, His resurrection and all that He wrought by it are mine; and, as the apostle exclaims in an exuberance of joy, Romans 8, Shall He not with Him give us all things?[5] What did He effect by rising from the dead? Listen! He destroyed sin, aroused righteousness, abolished death, restored life, conquered hell, and procured everlasting glory. These benefits are beyond compute, and the human mind scarcely dares to believe that they have been given to us. It is like Jacob's case in Genesis 45: when he heard that his son Joseph was a ruler in Egypt, he was like a man waking out of a deep sleep. He did not believe them until they repeated the whole story, and also showed him the wagons sent by Joseph.[6] It would have been equally difficult for us to believe the great blessings procured for us poor creatures by Christ, unless He had manifested Himself to His disciples in many conversations and many epiphanies. So also He has taught us a similar faith by the "wagons" of use and experience. A wagon it was of a most delightful kind when He was made by God to be our righteousness, sanctification,

---

[1] Cf. *supra*, pp. 41ff. [2] Rom. 6:9 [3] Cf. Isa. 31:9
[4] Cf. Isa. 9:6 [5] Rom. 8:32 [6] Gen. 45:26ff.

redemption, and wisdom, just as the apostle says in 1
Corinthians 1.[1] I am a sinner, but I ride in the righteousness
which He has given me. I am unclean, but His holiness, in
which I ride at ease, is my sanctification. I am foolish, but
His wisdom carries me. I am guilty, but His liberty sets me
free, and is a wagon of the safest kind. So that, if a Christian
only believes it, he can boast of the merits of Christ and all
His blessings just as if they were his own doing. So fully are
they his, that he may now safely dare to look forward even
to the divine judgment which, however, is something that
cannot be borne. That is the measure of faith; that is the
extent of the good things which it imparts to us; with such a
high degree of glory does it establish us as the sons of God.
We cannot be sons unless we inherit the Father's blessings.
Let the Christian say with confidence, O death where is thy
victory? O death where is thy sting, namely, sin? The sting of
death is sin, and the law is the strength of sin. But thanks be
to God who has given us the victory through Jesus Christ,
our Lord![2] That is to say, the law makes us sinners, and sin
condemns us to death. What conquered these two? Our
righteousness? our life? No! rather Jesus Christ risen from
the dead, condemning sin and death, imparting to us His
own righteousness, giving to us His own merits, placing His
hands upon us. Now all is well with us: we fulfil the law and
conquer sin and death, for which be honour, praise, and
thanksgiving to God for ever and ever. Amen.

This then is the highest type of all; in it we are raised, not
only above our own evils, but even above our own blessings.
We who before had our lot cast among evils heaped up by
another's sin[3] and increased by our own, live now surrounded
by another's good things produced by another's labour. We
live, I say, in that righteousness of Christ by which He
Himself is righteous, because we ourselves cling to that
through which He pleases God, intercedes as our mediator,
and makes Himself in every way our high priest and protector.
Just as it is impossible for Christ, with His righteousness, not

---

[1] 1 Cor. 1:30   [2] Cf. 1 Cor. 15:55ff.

[3] *Alieno peccato*, which may mean either the sin of some other man, or of
Adam

to please God, so it is impossible for us, with the faith by which we cling to His righteousness, not to please God. By these means, a Christian may become omnipotent, a universal lord, owning everything, doing anything, wholly free from sin.[1] Even if he still be in sin, yet it must needs be that the sins do no harm, for they are forgiven for the sake of the unconquerable righteousness of Christ which brings all sins to an end, and to which our own faith is conjoined when we firmly believe that Christ is such as we have just described. He who does not believe it, hears the tale with deaf ears. He does not know Christ, neither does he understand for what He is helpful, nor who may enjoy Him.

It follows that, even if there were no others, this type alone, when considered properly and with all one's heart, can imbue us with so much encouragement that, far from grieving over our afflictions, we should glory in tribulations, scarcely feeling them on account of the joy that we have in Christ. May Christ Himself, our Lord and God, instruct us in this glory, blessed as He is for evermore. Amen.

The end.

With these few remarks of mine, most illustrious prince, which testify to whatever service is within my poor resources, I commend myself to your most illustrious Lordship. I shall be most ready to offer things of greater value, if ever the power of my spirit equals my desires. I shall always remain a debtor to any neighbour of mine, but especially to your most illustrious Lordship, whom may our Lord Jesus Christ, in His good clemency, long preserve to us in safety, and at length, by a happy end, take to Himself. Amen.

For your most illustrious Lordship,
professor[2]
brother Martin Luther
Augustinian of Wittenberg.

---

[1] Cf. *R. W.*, Vol. I, pp. 357 *passim*, esp. e.g. §15   [2] Latin: *Orator*

2

WHY THE BOOKS OF THE POPE AND HIS FOLLOWERS WERE BURNED BY DOCTOR MARTIN LUTHER

ALSO LET ALL WHO WILL TAKE NOTE WHY THE ROMANISTS BURNED DOCTOR LUTHER'S BOOKS

Introduction

WHEN the bull against Luther was finally published, no great stir was felt in Germany, the region primarily affected. The secular princes left the initiative to the church authorities, but the archbishops and bishops dallied; the universities refused their co-operation on the alleged grounds of faulty drafting; and the populace was hostile. For a while nothing happened of a decisive character. The bull would have failed of any effect, had it not been for the special envoy from Rome. The man chosen by the curia was Jerome Aleander, a good linguist, who was the head of the Vatican Library, and who, according to Erasmus, was born for the work. With Marino Caracciolo, he was sent as nuncio to Germany. In accordance with his instructions, he made his way at once to the emperor's court in the Netherlands to get the authority of Charles for carrying out his plans. He thought that the best means of making the bull known, and producing the desired effect on the people at large, would be to burn Luther's writings publicly. By what he afterwards boasted of as his "great energy and craftiness", he was able to secure that, "as early as the third day after his arrival in Flanders, the necessary imperial mandate was given, and before the emperor and his counsellors had fully grasped what was afoot, Luther's writings and other condemned books had gone up in flames".

The first occasion was at Louvain before the middle of October, 1520.[1] There was a similar bonfire at Cologne on November 12, with Hochstraten taking a leading part; and yet another at Mainz on November 29, after a first failure.[2] Meanwhile, by John Eck's tireless energy, the University of Ingoldstadt obeyed the bull's instructions in the same way on October 29.[3]

Luther was not astonished. He had received no definite intimation that his doctrines had been condemned when he heard of the mandate against his books; but he had no hesitation about the nature of his reply. "If they condemn and burn my books, my response, unless fire fails me, will be to condemn and destroy in

[1] Erasmus was in residence at Louvain from 1517 to 1521, and must have quaked with fear at the proceedings. Perhaps this fear was largely responsible for his gradually parting company with the movement for reform as led by Luther, since the divergence dates from about this time

[2] Crotus Rubianus wrote a long and lively letter to Luther with "all the news" on December 5, 1520, but without mentioning Mainz. He was surprised that Luther was not alarmed; urged him to be cautious, and not to go to the length of martyrdom. cf. *Br.*, Vol. II, No. 358

[3] Cf. Aleander's report, P. Balan, *Monumenta reformationis Lutheranae*, pp. 4ff. Erasmus's views: *Eras. opp.* ed. Cleric. III, col. 592. qd. *W.*, Vol. VII, p. 152, and cf. notes there

public the whole papal law, that quagmire of heresy, and end the submissiveness and the useless respect which I have shown till now, for I am unwilling to increase still further the puffed-up pride of the enemies of the gospel."[1] He felt that there was so much error and dangerous doctrine in the papal law that it ought to be flung on "a blazing pyre".

Before the end of November he received word of what had happened in Louvain and Cologne, but was not disquieted. "There is so little need for me to quake, that I have nought but pity for their blindness and wretchedness, and especially for their childish folly." It was only when things began to happen nearer Wittenberg that he felt drawn to take some action. It was rumoured that his books had been burned at Merseburg, and that the same would soon be done at Leipzig. On December 3, Spalatin wrote to the elector Frederick to say that "Doctor Martin has arranged for the bull and the decretals to be burned one and all at the same time as soon as he receives trustworthy news that they have had the presumption to burn his books at Leipzig", and he expected that Luther would make a public pronouncement in the pulpit. It is not known whether there was a holocaust in Leipzig, but only that Luther carried out his own intentions.

Melanchthon posted up a notice on the door of the parish church at Wittenberg[2] inviting the youth of the university, and whoever loved the evangelical teaching, to assemble at 9.0 a.m. on December 10 near the chapel of the Holy Cross outside the town; for there, "in accordance with ancient and apostolic custom", the ungodly volumes of the papal law and of scholastic theology would be burned. Crowds streamed out into the open space beyond the Elster gate. A master of arts built the pyre and lit it at the appointed time. Luther himself placed the papal law books and other writings on top. And then, as he flung into the leaping flames the bull of Leo X which had condemned his teachings, he cried: "Because thou hast betrayed the Holy One of the Lord, so may eternal fire destroy thee."[3] Then the *Te Deum* was sung and, accompanied by many doctors, masters, and others, Luther returned to the town, taking no further part in the events of the day (some of which were excessively boisterous).[4] It would seem that, on returning to his rooms, he immediately wrote Spalatin, giving details of the writings he had burned.[5]

Luther was fully conscious of the significance of what he had done: he had broken with the Roman Church and the papacy, and had pitted strength against strength. Next day, before beginning

---

[1] *Br.*, Vol. II, No. 310
[2] Given as Appendix I to the present document: in *W.*, Vol. VII, p. 183
[3] More or less echoing John 7: 25, Mark 1:24, and Acts 2:27
[4] *Vide* Appendix II in *W.*, Vol. VII, pp. 184-86
[5] *Br.*, Vol. II, No. 361

his lecture on the Psalms, he spoke about it with great earnestness to his audience. But some public explanation was required, and Luther gave it in German in the present document. The first edition was printed in Wittenberg and published before December 27, but several other editions appeared in various parts of the country before the end of the year, one of which was printed by Hans von Erfurt in Worms where the delegates were assembling for the imperial council. A Latin version appeared in two recensions, the earlier being printed in Worms by the same press before the end of 1520. Although the translation was made anonymously, it would seem to have been done by the humanist, Hermann von dem Busche, and was intended for the benefit of the emperor (who spoke nothing but French, and had difficulty in understanding Latin) and the many foreign delegates attending the imperial council, who spoke little or no German. All were deeply stirred by the unheard-of act of burning the books of the canon law, to say nothing of the bull. The prolonged discussions between Frederick the Wise on the one hand and Aleander and important delegates on the other showed how complex, delicate, and dangerous was the situation.[1]

The writing was not meant merely as an apology for a daring act. It was intended to inform the German people at large of the profound issues that were at stake, and was therefore essentially a piece of instruction. It is a terse discussion of the vital differences between two different conceptions of religion, and of the foundations on which evangelical Christianity must be built. It gives ample documentation on the one hand in the canon law and the like (shewing, incidentally, the extent and precision of Luther's scholarship in this field), and, on the other hand, in the Bible—a juxtaposition which is an additional argument in itself. It must therefore be regarded as one of the fundamental works which Luther contributed to the Protestant Reformation—hence its place in our selection.

The following translation is made from the original German text, often illuminated by the contemporary Latin version, as given in the Weimar Edition of Luther's Works, Vol. VII, 152-60, 161-82.

[1] Cf. P. Kalkoff, *Der Grosser Wormser Reichstag*, pp. 50ff.

WHY THE BOOKS OF THE POPE AND HIS FOLLOWERS WERE BURNED BY DOCTOR MARTIN LUTHER

ALSO LET ALL WHO WILL TAKE NOTE WHY THE ROMANISTS BURNED DOCTOR LUTHER'S BOOKS

Text and Notes

𝔍𝔢𝔰𝔲𝔰

I, MARTIN LUTHER, possessing the title of Doctor of Holy Scripture, an Augustinian monk of Wittenberg,[1] make it known to one and all that by my wish, advice, and co-operation, on Monday after St. Nicholas' day[2] in the year 1520 the books of the pope of Rome were burned together with those of his followers. Since many will be surprised and, as I foresee, ask for what reason and by what authority I did this, I ask them to accept the following answer.

Firstly, it is an ancient custom to burn poisonous and evil books. We read in Acts 19 that, as a result of St. Paul's teaching, they were burned to the value of 5000 pence.[3]

Secondly, though unworthy, I am a baptized Christian. In addition I have taken the oath as doctor of Holy Scripture. Moreover, I am a regular preacher and, as such, obliged by name, status, oath, and office to destroy false, seductive, and unchristian doctrines, or at least rebut them. Although there are many others who have the same duty, but who do not wish, or are not able, to do what I have done, perhaps through lack of judgment or because weakened by fear; nevertheless, were my own conscience sufficiently clear, and my own spirit sufficiently awakened by God's grace, I should be without excuse if I were to let myself be stayed by another's example.

[1] Luther opens with this solemn, official kind of phraseology, as employed in the decrees issued by the governing authorities, in order to give formal and weighty character to the pamphlet
[2] December 6, 1520, fell on a Thursday   [3] Acts 19:19

Thirdly, I would not have ventured such an act unless I had learned to see by experience that the pope and the papal deceivers had erred and deceived. Indeed, although I myself had frequently, but vainly, explained my teaching to them, they were so stubborn and obstinate in their unchristian errors and their corruption of soul that, not only would they refuse to be shown or taught, but they even closed their eyes and stopped their ears, blindly condemned the evangelical teaching, and consigned it to the flames, as if thus to confirm and preserve their own teaching, which is antichristian and devilish.[1]

Fourthly, I do not believe that the Romanists had received the relevant orders from pope Leo X himself with his personal knowledge, my information being to the contrary. I hope, too, that the books I burned were not to his taste even if they were written by his predecessors; but whether he liked them or not was not an issue with me. On the basis of trustworthy information, I know that the people of Cologne and Louvain, who boast they had permission and orders from his imperial Majesty to burn my pamphlets, do not speak the truth, for they purchased permission to do what they did by making a present of several thousand guilders to certain officials.

Fifthly, by burning those books of mine, they may have done great harm to the truth, and given a false idea to simple, ordinary people, to the hurt of many. Therefore, by the leading of the Holy Spirit (as I hope), and in order to strengthen and support these people, I burned the books of my enemies because it was hopeless to teach them better.

Therefore, no one should let himself be perturbed by high-sounding titles, the name and fame of the pope's rank, the canon law, or the long-standing use of the books now burned. Rather, first of all, hear and see what the pope teaches in these books, and what sort of poisonous and abominable teachings stand in the holy, canon law, and what it is that

[1] This is not the first time that Luther had raised the question of the antichristian character of the papacy: cf. letter to W. Linck on December 18, 1518, *Br.*, Vol. I, No. 121; further, *Br.*, Vol. I, No. 161, p. 359, II, No. 257, p. 49, etc.

we have hitherto venerated instead of the truth.[1] Then let him judge freely whether I have rightly or wrongly burned these books.

ARTICLES AND ERRORS IN THE BOOKS OF CANON LAW AND IN THOSE OF THE POPE, WITH REASONS WHY THE BOOKS WERE RIGHTLY BURNED AND ARE TO BE AVOIDED

The First

It is not required of the pope and his adherents that they be subject to God's commandments and obey them.

He clearly writes this abominable teaching in the chapter '*Solitae*', *de majoritate et obedientia*[2] where he expounds St. Peter's words: You ought to be subject to every authority,[3] by declaring that St. Peter did not mean himself nor his own successors, but their subjects.

The Second

St. Peter is not giving a commandment, but advice, when he teaches that all Christians ought to be subject to their own kings. *ibidem*.[4]

The Third

Among Christians, the sun is the emblem of papal authority while the moon is that of secular authority. *ibidem*.[5]

The Fourth

There is no obligation for the pope and his see to submit to Christian councils and regulations.[6]

---

[1] Very similar phraseology was used by Luther in a letter to Spalatin eighteen months earlier, March 13, 1519. cf. *Br.*, Vol. I, No. 16

[2] A quotation from the *corpus juris canonici*, like most of the quotations in the following articles. Here the reference is to *Solitae, 6, de majoritate et obedientia, tit. 33. lib. 1*

[3] 1 Pet. 2:13   [4] In the gloss to the reference given above

[5] Cf. note to The First

[6] Cap. *Significasti, 4, de electione, tit. 6. lib. 1*

The Fifth

The pope, in his own breast, has full authority over all laws.
In prolo. Sexti.[1]

The Sixth

Hence it follows that **the pope has power to set aside all councils and to break all regulations,** and does so daily; as a result neither power nor value is left to the councils or the Christian regulations.

The Seventh

The pope has the right to require oath and fealty from the bishops for their robes of office. Cap. *'Significasti'.*[2] Against this compare: Freely ye have received, freely give [3]

The Eighth

Even if the pope is so wicked as to send innumerable people in great troops to the devil, nevertheless no man is permitted to punish him for it. *Dist.* 40. *'Si Papa'.*[4]
This article, even if it stood alone, would be sufficient cause for burning all papal books. What devilish and unchristian things could they not set in motion by unashamedly holding and teaching such abominable things? Yet, O Christian, that is what canon law teaches you.

The Ninth

Next to God, the salvation of the whole of Christendom depends on the pope. *Ibidem.*[5] Against this is: I believe in one, holy church, etc.[6] By this article, all Christians would go to perdition as often as there were a wicked pope.

[1] *Sexti Decret. lib. 1, tit. 2, de constitutionibus, Cap. 1;* so Borcherdt and Merz
[2] *Vide* the note to The Fourth   [3] Matt. 10:8
[4] *Si Papa,* 6, dist. 40   [5] As in note to The Eighth   [6] As in the Creed

The Tenth

No man on earth is permitted to judge the pope nor may anyone question his verdict. Rather he shall judge all men on earth. 9.q.3.c. *'Cuncta'*.[1]

This article is the principal article. In order to press it well home, it is cited ever and again in many chapters, and throughout almost the whole of canon law. This fact shows that canon law was composed solely in order that the pope might be at liberty to do, or to leave undone, what he would, make an opening for sin or afford a hindrance to the good. If this article holds good, Christ and His word lie prostrate; but if it does not hold good, it is the canon law together with the pope and his see, that lies prostrate.

But it does not hold good, for St. Peter commands, 1 Peter 6: You ought to be humble towards each other.[2] St. Paul, Romans 12: Let each one hold the other higher than himself.[3] And Christ often says: Let him that would be greatest, be the least.[4] In the same way, St. Paul reproaches St. Peter, Galatians 2, because he does not walk rightly according to the gospel;[5] and, Acts 8, St. Peter was sent forth (with St. John) by the other apostles as if he were under their authority.[6] Therefore it is not true, nor can it be true, that the pope is subject to no one and is to be judged by no one. He should be subject to everyone and be judged by everyone, since he claims to be the chief of all; and the canon law, because this is its basis and very nature, is against the gospel in every particular.

Of course it is true that the secular power should not owe obedience to its own lower orders; but Christ reverses and changes that relationship and says: You must not be like the secular lords.[7] His will is that each one of us should be subject to the leaders of the people and accept their authority, as He says, Luke 22: The princes of the Gentiles exercise authority over them, but it shall not be so with you; but he who would be the leader among you must be the humblest.[8]

---

[1] *Cuncta per mundum*, 17. IX. qu. 3   [2] 1 Pet. 5:5   [3] Rom. 12:10
[4] Matt. 20:26ff.; 23:11, etc.   [5] Gal. 2:11f.   [6] Acts 8:14
[7] Luke 22:25f.   [8] Luke 22:25f.

But how can the pope be a subject if he will not permit any-one to judge him?

If we were to try to force the words of Christ (as some do) and understand them to mean that, in his heart, the pope should respect the lowest, but not show it outwardly, then we must also say that, in his heart, he must be loyal to the authorities without showing it outwardly; for both must be spiritual and in the heart, or else both must be outwardly shown, if Christ's words are to hold good.

This is the article which has given rise to all the wrong to be found anywhere in the world. Therefore the canon law must be regarded as a poisonous thing, which should be destroyed or evaded with good reason. All this leads to an inference which is immediately obvious, and which has in fact been drawn, that we can neither repel evil nor promote the good, and we are compelled to be spectators watching the gospel and the faith go under.

The Eleventh

The Roman see is the source of the authority and power of all laws, but is itself subject to none of them. xxv.qu.i.[1] That is as much as to say that its will is law, but it is not bound to keep one of these laws. It is like that which Christ says in Matthew 23 of the Jewish Pharisees: They lay heavy burdens upon the backs of men, but are unwilling to touch them with a finger.[2] St. Paul speaks against this practice and says, Galatians 6: Stand in your liberty, and be not subject to human laws.[3]

The Twelfth

The rock on which Christ, Matthew 16, builds His church is called the see of Rome. *Dist. xix* and its context.[4] Nevertheless Christ alone is that same rock: 1 Cor. 10.[5]

[1] *Confidimus*, 1. xxv. qu. 1. and *Ideo permittente*, 16. xxv. qu. 1
[2] Matt. 23:4   [3] Gal. 5:1
[4] Cf. *Ita Dominus*, 7, dist. 19. *In novo testamento*, 2, dist. 21. *Quamvis universae*, 3, dist. 21. *Sacrosancta Romana*, 2, dist. 22
[5] 1 Cor. 10:4

F ML

The Thirteenth

That the keys are given to Peter alone.[1] Nevertheless, in Matthew 18, Christ gave them to the whole church.[2]

The Fourteenth

That Christ's priesthood was transferred by Him to St. Peter, *de constit. c. translato.*[3] Against this, David in Psalm 109, and Paul in Hebrews, say that Christ is the only eternal priest, and that this priesthood will never again be transferred to another.[4]

The Fifteenth

That the pope has authority to make laws for the Christian church. xxv.q.1 *'ideo permittente'.*[5] St. Paul says, to the contrary, in Galatians 5: You are called unto liberty by God.[6]

The Sixteenth

That the pope explains the passage, Whatsoever thou shalt bind, etc.,[7] **in the sense that he has authority to lay his mischievous laws on all Christendom**[8] whereas Christ's whole intention in these words was to bring sinners to punishment and repentance, and by no means to pile laws on others who are innocent. The words are clear on this point.

The Seventeenth

That under threat of excommunication, and by declaring it to be sinful, the pope forbids the eating of meat, eggs, butter, and so forth,[9] in spite of the fact that he has no such authority, and should only give friendly exhortation, leaving each person free to do as he pleases, without constraint.

---

[1] Cf. *Sacrosancta Romana*, 2, dist. 22   [2] Matt. 18:18
[3] *Translato*, 3, *de constitutionibus, tit. 2. lib.* 1
[4] Ps. 110:4; Heb. 5:6, 6:20, 7:21ff.
[5] *Ideo permittente*, 16. xxv. qu. 1. cf. *Sunt quidam*, 6. xxv. qu. 1
[6] Gal. 5:13.   [7] Matt. 16:19
[8] *Decret. pars. II, causa XXV,* qu. 1. Cap. 16. So Borcherdt and Merz
[9] Cf. *Denique Sacerdotes*, 6, dist. 4

The Eighteenth

That he has forbidden marriage to the whole priesthood[1] whereby, without due cause, he greatly multiplies sin and shame, and acts against God's commandment and Christian liberty.

The Nineteenth

That pope Nicholas, either the III or IV, in his antichristian decretal states, among many other wicked things, that Christ gave the keys to St. Peter and his successors with authority over the heavenly and the earthly spheres[2] whereas everyone knows well enough that Christ repudiated an earthly kingdom (John 6:15), and that all priests have the keys, and not a single emperor rules a heavenly and an earthly kingdom.

The XX[3]

That the pope regards as true, and lends his support to the great, unchristian falsehood that the emperor Constantine had given him Rome, his country, and his authority on earth.[4] Christ, on the contrary, says, Matthew 6: You should not gather together treasures upon earth,[5] and again, You cannot serve goods and God.[6]

The XXI

That the pope claims to be the heir of the Roman empire, *de sen. et re. iud.c. 'Pastoralis'.*[7]

The XXII

That the pope teaches it is right and proper that a Christian should defend himself with force against force, against and in spite of what Christ says in Matthew 5: He who takes away your coat, let him have your cloak also.[8]

[1] Cf. *Presbyteris*, 8, dist. 27. *Diacon. quicunque*, 8, dist. 28. *Presbyter, si uxorem* 9, dist. 28
[2] *Omnes, sive Patriarchii*, 1, dist. 22. (of Nicholas II). Cf. *De Elect. Fundamenta*, lib. 6. (of Nicholas III)
[3] From this point, Roman numerals are used to distinguish the articles
[4] *Constantinus*, 13 and 14, dist. 96   [5] Matt. 6:19   [6] Matt. 6:24
[7] *Pastoralis*, 2, *de sententia et re iudicata, tit.* 11, in *Clem. lib.* 2
[8] Matt. 5:40

The XXIII

That subjects can be disobedient to their own princes, and that the pope can depose kings, in the same way as he has appointed them in many places, and often done so against and in spite of God's will.

The XXIV

That he also claims that he has the power to abrogate all oaths, covenants, and obligations between the higher and the lower orders of society[1] against and in spite of God when He says, Each should keep faith with another.[2]

The XXV

The pope is said to have power to set aside or change vows made to God, *de vot. et voti redempt.*[3] which again is contrary to and in spite of God's will.

The XXVI

He who delays fulfilling his vow owing to the pope's commands is not guilty of breaking the vow, *ibidem*,[4] which is as much as to say that the pope is above God.

The XXVII

No married person can serve God, and this in spite of the fact that Abraham and many of the saints were married, and that God Himself undoubtedly instituted marriage. Thus once more the Antichrist mounts to a place above God.

The XXVIII

That the pope makes his vain laws equal to the gospels and Holy Scripture, a fact of which there are many instances in the decretals.[5]

---

[1] Cf. *W.*, VI, 453, and our Vol. I, p. 276f.   [2] Zech. 8:16
[3] *De peregrinationis voto*, 1, *de voto et voti redemptione, tit.* 34, *lib.* 3
[4] *Non est voti*, 5, *de voto et voti redemptione, tit.* 34, *lib.* 3
[5] Cf. *Sic omnes*, 2, dist. 19. *Sicut sancti*, 2, dist. 15. *In canonicis*, 6, dist. 19

The XXIX

That the pope has the power to expound and apply Holy Scripture in his own way, and to allow no one else to expound it in a sense contrary to his will. Thereby he sets himself above God's word, which he overthrows and abolishes; whereas St. Paul, 1 Corinthians 14, says: The higher should yield to a revelation given to the lower.[1]

The XXX

That trustworthy rank, power, and honour were not given to the pope by Scripture, but to Scripture by the pope. This is one of the principal articles showing why he, as a genuine Antichrist, deserves that Christ should come from heaven and destroy him and his rulership as Paul predicted.[2]

These and similar articles, of which there are more than can be numbered, all tend in the same direction, and make out that the pope is above God and men; that he alone is subject to none, but that all, even God and the angels, are subject to him. The result is that his disciples say that the pope is a miraculous being; he is not God, nor is he man (perhaps the devil himself). This means that the words of St. Paul are fulfilled where he says: A man of sin will come forth, and a son of perdition, who will oppose everything and exalt himself above all that is worshipped as God and called God, by the operation of the evil spirit, etc.[3] Inasmuch as Paul calls him a man of sin and a son of perdition, he does not mean only him personally, but that his very rule is purely and simply sin and perdition; and that the only effect of his rule will be to lead the whole world to sin and hell. From the foregoing articles it is as clear and open as the day that the pope has brought nothing but sin and perdition into the world, and brings more every day.

Those who support the canon law themselves know, although kept secret, that it reeks of sheer avarice and arrogance. That also is true, and any man who refuses to lie must acknowledge that it is so. If you would know in

[1] 1 Cor. 14:30   [2] 2 Thess. 1:7ff.   [3] 2 Thess. 2:3ff.

brief what stands in the canon law, then listen. Here is the whole thing in a nutshell:

The pope is a god upon earth, set over all things, heavenly or earthly, spiritual and secular. Everything belongs to him, and no one has a right to ask him: What are you doing?

That is the abomination and foulness of which Christ speaks in Matthew 24: When you shall see the reeking abomination, which lays all things waste, standing in the holy city. . . .[1] It is that of which Daniel said, Let him who reads clearly understand, etc.[2] And St. Paul, He will sit in the temple of God (i.e. in Christendom) and give himself out to be a god.[3]

It is nothing to marvel at that very few, if any, have ever dared to tell the pope that such are his enormities, for the proclamation has been made that he will burn all who resist him, and in doing this will have the support of all kings and princes. If the Antichrist's corruption were so gross that everyone could remark it, or so small that kings and great leagues did not take an eminent part in it, it would have been pointless for the prophets and apostles to preach and to write so much and so earnestly.

When Christ walked on earth, many people who heard His words and saw His works, spoke against those who denied that He was the Christ, and said: When at length the Christ comes, how can He do more miracles than this man is doing?[4] In the same way, many people to-day are muttering, When at length the Antichrist comes, what more wickedness can he do than has been done and is done daily under the rule of the pope? It is truly incredible that, if his rulership were truly of God, he would allow so much depravity and sin to result from it. But we do not believe this to-day—nor perhaps until we are lost by recognizing the Antichrist too late.

From the beginning of creation, the greatest evils have always arisen from the best things. In the highest choir of angels, among whom God did His greatest works of all, Lucifer sinned and did great harm. In the garden of Eden, the greatest sin and shame happened to the first and best man. Afterwards, in Genesis 6, giants and tyrants sprang

[1] Matt. 24:15   [2] Dan. 9:27   [3] 2 Thess. 2:4   [4] John 7:31

from the very children of God.¹ And Christ the Son of God
was crucified in the holy city, Jerusalem itself, where He had
received the greatest honour, and had done many miracles;
crucified by none other than the princes and chief priests
and the most learned and most holy men. And it had to be
the case that Judas did harm, not to something of mean
standing, but to the apostolic status itself. In the same way,
God blessed no other city on earth with so many graces and
holy things as Rome, but did more for her than for any other
city. She, like Jerusalem, had to requite Him by doing the
greatest evil, and giving the world what is truly the most
pernicious Antichrist, who does more evil than formerly
Christ did good. That is the course things are certainly
taking, and that is what must happen to everything bearing
the name and likeness of Christ and God; but no one will
believe it, until He Himself comes and illumines that darkness with the light of His coming, as St. Paul says.²

These articles are enough for the moment. But if there is
anyone near the pope who wants to try to defend and fight
for these things, I will paint them in plainer colours and cite
many more examples. What I have said is only meant as a
prelude to something serious, for hitherto I have only made
fun of and joked with the question of the papacy. I have
begun my work in God's name, and I hope that, in due time,
and in God's name, it will itself effect its own conclusion
apart from me. In what I have written above, I meant to
include all the articles which have been condemned and
burned by the nuncio of the Antichrist in Rome in the
last bull,³ articles which, all the same, were Christian and
true; and to apply to the pope as many antichristian and
unchristian articles as mine which have been condemned. If
they dare to burn these articles of mine, in which (without
boasting, I can truly assert and prove) there is more of the
gospel, and a better foundation in Holy Scripture, than in all

¹ Gen. 6:4   ² 2 Thess. 2:8; 1 Cor. 4:5
³ The bull which John Eck obtained on June 16, 1520, in Rome against
Luther, and in which four principles contained in Luther's writings were
characterized as heretical. The bull was published by Eck and Aleander in
Germany at the end of September and, in particular, posted up in Mainz,
Merseburg, and Brandenburg. They came to Wittenberg at the beginning
of October, but the university decided not to publish it

the books of the pope, there would be much more reason on my side if I were to burn their unchristian law books, which contain nothing good. Even if they contained something good, as I must acknowledge in the case of the decree, everything is so distorted that it does evil and only strengthens the pope in his rule as Antichrist. Moreover, none of it is observed with very great seriousness, except whatever is wicked and harmful.

I myself would have everyone exercise his own judgment. What troubles me most is that the pope has never once logically refuted in writing anyone who has spoken, written, or acted against him. He always uses kings, princes, and other adherents to exercise force or to excommunicate his opponents. Or else he uses guile and false reports to hunt them down, burn, or strangle them. I am ready to prove all this to him in detail with chapter and verse. He has never yet allowed a court to judge, or listen to a judgment; but always pleaded that he was above all Scripture, every court of justice and other authority. Nevertheless, it is always true that truth and righteousness do not fear the courts, and indeed hold nothing dearer than to come to the light and to be judged accordingly; they gladly submit to test and proof. The apostles, Acts 4, let their enemies judge and said: Judge for yourselves whether it is reasonable to obey you rather than God[1]—so sure is the truth. But the pope tries to blind everyone's eyes, and lets no one judge; he alone is the judge of everyone, so uncertain and fearful is he about his case and his affairs. The effect of this gallimaufry of his in the dark, and of his fear of the light, is such that, even if the pope were an angel pure and simple, I could put no trust in him. Everyone is right in hating the works of darkness, and in loving the light. Amen.

In all I have said above, I beg to take my stand before the judgment of all.

Samson. Judges 15,

As they have done to me, so I have done to them.[2]

---

[1] Acts 4:19   [2] Judges 15:11

3

A WORD TO PENITENTS ABOUT THE FORBIDDEN BOOKS FOR THOSE WHO ARE GOING TO CONFESSION

Introduction

LUTHER had been excommunicated by a bull decreed on June 15, 1520, and published by Eck at the end of September in the bishoprics of Meissen, Merseburg, and Brandenburg, i.e. in Luther's immediate vicinity. Prelates and bishops were commanded to make a careful search for all books by Luther, and to burn them with due solemnity. The bull had been frankly opposed in many quarters, received in a few with scorn and contempt. Nevertheless, it made itself felt beneath the surface. The priests obeyed the instructions of their superiors and, in the confessional, made diligent inquiry about Luther's books; no one was given absolution, or allowed to communicate, before handing over any such books in his possession. It is easy to understand the qualms of conscience that would be felt by many of the adherents of Luther's teaching, for going to confession was still regarded as the duty of a Christian, and the Reformer himself still held confession to be the third sacrament.[1] About this period, Luther was almost overwhelmed by innumerable calls for advice, help, explanation, etc.[2] Three printing presses were entirely engaged in publishing his writings. These labours could not be avoided, nor would Luther have shirked them if they could. Spalatin seems to have suggested the present tract,[3] as he had done in many other cases also. This active encouragement must have been very grateful to Luther, and added to his inner resources.

The work of writing was finished on February 3, 1521, and published exactly a fortnight later. Copies were taken by Schott, the bookseller, to Worms before the end of the month. This piece of information is given by Luther when writing on February 27, 1521, to tell Spalatin that it was useless to send more copies to Merseburg or Meissen, because already there, "they have burned a waggon-load of my books".[4] Luther warned his enemies that it would not help them "to bend the bow too far". The present tract was a mild writing, and he gave it most careful thought. In other circumstances, he would have to write more plainly. He seems to have carried out this promise when, somewhat later in the year, he wrote about the pope's authority over the confessional.[5]

The following translation is made from the text as printed in the Weimar Edition of Luther's Works, Vol. VII, pp. 284-89, 290-98.

[1] Cf. *Pagan Servitude* Par. 3. Our Vol. I. pp. 279ff.
[2] Cf., e.g., his letter to Pellican, end of February, 1521, *Br.*, II, No. 379
[3] Melanchthon, writing to Spalatin on March 2, 1521, ascribes the suggestion to him. Cf. *W.*, Vol. VII, p. 284
[4] *Br.*, II, p. 270, No. 378   [5] Cf. *W.*, Vol. VIII, pp. 129/38-204

Jesus

To all those Christian Readers into whose hands this book comes, Martin Luther wishes Grace and Peace in Jesus Christ our Lord.

IT has come to my attention that certain Father Confessors have misled the people in publicly forbidding them to read my books. Indeed they have gone much further and exceeded their authority; they have threatened disobedience with God's displeasure, and have probed consciences about the matter in the confessional. The result is that the people have been denied the absolution which they sought. This being a matter of genuine Christian concern to me, I decided to say a word by way of clarification and instruction, and to do my best to leave no one in doubt about his soul's good. Let anyone, who thinks nought of my help, know that I am innocent of his blood in God's sight, according to God's commands. Amen.

1. I am fully convinced that my doctrine has come from God. Nevertheless, you should not forget that a large part of it has been condemned by the prelates of the church and by those we are accustomed to call scholars. Daniel 13 describes what happens to all prophets, apostles, and, indeed, to Christ Himself; "Evil comes from the rulers"[1] whoever they may be that rule the people. For this reason, I am not writing now for all and sundry. I have no wish to make everybody read my books, nor do I invite them to do so. I aim at those who feel in their consciences that my teachings are correct, but who, disturbed by the number and the eminence of those who deny me, feel driven to act against a good conscience because it is weak.

2. If the Father Confessor probes your tender spot when he inquires whether you possess my little books, or have read them, you should reply in a humble manner as follows:

[1] Cf. Susanna, v. 5

Please, Father, do not chase me into a corner, and put me in difficulty. I have come to confession for you to absolve me, not to cause me distress. As long as many learned and important people continue to discuss this subject from opposite sides without having yet reached any final conclusions, I feel that I, and you also, are in no position to pronounce a judgment out of hand.

3. If necessary, continue as follows: Please sir, you are a Father Confessor and not a taskmaster. It is my duty to confess what is on my conscience. It is not your duty to press me, nor to probe my private affairs; or you might be asking me how much money I have in my pocket. If I choose to say nothing about some thing I know about, that is my lookout, and does not concern you. Give me my absolution, as it is your part to do; and then argue the thing out with Luther, the pope, or whom you will. Do not make the holy sacrament of confession into a subject of argument or debate and danger for me. This sort of conduct has nothing to do with confession. I will give my reply when it is the right time to do so about these things.

4. In the same way, too, I beg the Father Confessors to restrain themselves, and not invade God's prerogative of judging, to whom alone the secrets of the heart belong; as it says in Psalm 7: "God trieth the heart and reins."[1] They ought to thank God that they are dispensed from the dangerous business of probing, and that their duty consists simply of hearing confessions and giving absolutions. There is no necessity to compel any man to reveal what is on his conscience. As is commonly said: No one ought to be driven to believe, but only drawn. If anyone is destined to come, God will call him and stir him (through you). But if God does not stir him, what is the use of your pressing? Hence St. Paul taught that, in such cases of tender consciences, one ought not to probe, lest we confuse and trouble them: I Corinthians 8 and Romans 13.[2]

5. Should the Father Confessor refuse to grant absolution, should he use the bull as a threat, the response to make is: Please, Father, many deeply religious people have no respect

[1] Ps. 7:10   [2] I Cor. 8:9ff.; Rom. 14:1ff.

for the bull. Moreover, you yourself know how the pope's decisions change; he plans one thing for to-day, and, to-morrow, abrogates it. So I refuse to be driven by you into such a quicksand of uncertainty that what I acknowledge to-day I deny to-morrow, as changeable as the wind. It is not my duty to follow you in such changes and uncertain actions. Grant me my absolution. That is an assured thing. And when the matters now under discussion have been clearly decided, urge them upon me then.

6. If he still withholds the absolution, I myself would prefer to let him keep it; I would rather depart from him as if he were similar to Lucifer in as far as he exceeds his place and his commission only to fall under God's judgment. This is what he does when he probes the secrets of the heart, which he has no right to do, and they are no concern of his. God will absolve where men refuse to do so. Similarly, if you desire baptism, or the sacrament of the altar, at the hands of a priest, and he refuses, by your faith and your desire, you nevertheless have fully partaken of them. It follows that, even though the Father Confessor refuses absolution, the penitent has no need for alarm; he may be quite assured he has received absolution just because he desired and sought to confess and to get absolution. In such cases, the Father Confessor is to be regarded as a thief and a robber, withholding and taking from us what is our right. We may claim, with glad hearts, that we have received absolution in God's sight, and, in addition, that we have undoubtedly received the sacraments.

7. But no word of mine is necessary to those men of bold and firm conscience, who understand what the truth is, and dare to confess it. Of their own selves, they will know what to do and what line they should follow. Nevertheless, I will be overzealous and state my view: If they have openly said, in their confession to the taskmaster or slave-driver, whether they have the books or not; and if he refuses absolution unless they promise never to own or read these books, then the thing to say is: Absolve me, and let the responsibility be mine. I refuse to leave the books alone, lest I sin against my conscience. You ought not to press me to act

against my conscience, as you yourself know, or should know, Romans 14.[1]

8. If he refuses and threatens the bull, confront him with St. Peter's word in Acts 4:[2] We should obey God rather than men. And, should the whole world side with the pope and the bull, we ought not to bow before it, because it is very clearly contrary to the gospel and the Christian faith. Indeed, the bull ought to be burned and destroyed. This would be to follow the example set by Christ. The whole world persecuted Him, but that did not mean that He was in the wrong. Similarly, Luther's teaching has not yet been defeated and found false. Up to now, it has only been met with violence.

9. If he will not grant absolution, say no more; let him answer on the Day of Judgment for neglecting his office and robbing you of the sacrament, which it was his duty to give you. The penitent concerned should not trouble further about Absolution, but on the basis of having made his confession in this way, and having sought absolution he should simply go and partake of the sacrament. Certain is it that, in God's sight, he has been absolved; and he must bear it in patience and be glad to suffer the loss of not having absolution pronounced upon him, just as he should bear the theft of material goods. The sacraments may be taken from us, denied and forbidden us; but the power and grace of the sacraments are unconditionally ours, and cannot be taken from us. God has not left our salvation or His own grace at the disposal of their authority or caprice; it is dependent on our faith, as He says: merely believe that you have received what you prayed for, and it is assuredly yours.[3]

10. Should the priest deny the sacrament of the altar to you on the ground that you have not first received absolution, you must ask humbly that he give it to you. When dealing with the devil and his works, we must proceed in all humility, while yet maintaining a courageous faith. If that is no use, let them all go: sacrament, altar, priest, and church; for God's word, which is under condemnation in the bull, is more important than anything else. Our souls cannot spare it, but they can spare the sacraments. For Christ, our true bishop,

---

[1] Rom. 14:1ff.   [2] Acts 5:29   [3] Cf. Mark 11:24

will nourish us with that same sacrament spiritually. Do not think it out of reason, even if you are a whole year without going to the sacrament. It is not your fault. You would gladly go, but are hindered; you are being robbed of your rights, and the commandments of the church will not touch you. They are striving with you contrary to God's word and your own conscience. No commandment can be made contrary to these; nor, if already made, can it be valid . . . and that is what they themselves teach.

11. So take care to let nothing on earth, nor even an angel in heaven, seem important enough to compel you, against your conscience, to depart from the teaching which you regard and revere as God-given. St. Paul says, Galatians 1,[1] "Though an angel from heaven were to preach otherwise than the gospel, let him be accursed." You are not the first, will not be alone, nor will you be the last to be persecuted for the sake of God's word. Christ says: Blessed are you when you are persecuted for righteousness' sake;[2] again, You shall be hated by all men for my sake;[3] again, The time will come when they that persecute you will think that they are serving God.[4] We must lay hold of such words, and draw strength from them; let us indeed thank and praise God, and pray that we may be worthy to suffer for His word's sake. Remember that it is prophesied that, in the days of the Antichrist, no one will dare to preach, and all will be as if under condemnation when they preach or listen to God's word. That is what is happening now, and has been the case for more than a century.

12. But if the epistles of certain prelates are insisted upon, epistles in which all sorts of blasphemous books and slanderous letters are forbidden, it will be our duty to be most obedient. No one who knows and believes God's word will ever find pleasure in blasphemous books and slanderous letters.[5] According to the law of the emperor, such evildoers may be beheaded, together with all those who read them, hear them, or possess them. Moreover, since the question

---

[1] Gal. 1:8   [2] Matt. 5:10   [3] Matt. 24:9   [4] John 16:2.
[5] Is there here a ref. to *Letters of Obscure Men*, to Erasmus's *Praise of Folly*, or his *Epistolae*, or what not else?

of conscience does not arise in this connection, I beg everyone
to defend himself from such books, and avoid them as if they
were deadly poison. But let no man include here, or prefer
to see included and numbered here, any books of mine. That
would be a slander and a terrible libel. Moreover, the law of
the empire says that where anyone is specially mentioned by
name, and his repute is libelled; . . . all this is against the
law, even though printed without the writer's name. He fears
the light, but he will nevertheless have done harm in the
darkness, biting in secret like a poisonous snake, as Solomon
says.[1]

Notice, however, that I have printed my name publicly in
all my books, and laboured in the daylight. I have offered
myself for correction, and continue to do so. Although I have
attacked the pope's régime, I have never touched his person;
nor that of any prelate or his subordinates. Nor have I
secretly slandered any person whatsoever, but always
spoken out in public, preaching as a preacher should and
as all prophets have done. If books of this kind are to be
called blasphemous, then, by contrast, vice among the
people cannot be punished; and again, the gospels and the
entire Bible must be called scandalous, containing as they do
so many and such severe penalties for vice. But it is unfortunately true that there are many scandalous books in
circulation without name or title. It would be reasonable to
forbid them, and they should in fact be forbidden; for they
are not only contrary to Christian love but also against
natural ethics.[2]

13. Finally, I beg all prelates and confessors in accordance
with the blessed gospel, to see their way not to storm at the
people in the name of authority, but to guide and instruct
them kindly and gently. Do not strain and torture the
consciences of penitents, for that would be an act of the devil.
In this way, they will be given no cause to ask, or, indeed, to
set inquiries afoot as to whence this authority derives, and
what is the origin of the secret confessional; for this might

[1] Prov. 23:32

[2] *Naturliche gesetze:* a reference to the customary distinction between
natural and revealed truth, moral principles, etc.

GML

give rise to turmoil, which would increase their difficulties. Although such confession is an extremely good thing, still we all know how matters go.[1] It is therefore necessary not to give grounds for such a salutary thing to be disturbed by wanton attacks on the part of the authorities. Take heed of the example of my case: how many things would have remained as they were, if the pope and his supporters had not wantonly stormed at me; how many things there are which they have lost but can never restore. I have warned each and all, and besought them to avoid compulsion by force.[2] Violence can serve no further purpose, so be careful and cautious. May God grant His grace to all of us. Amen.

[1] *Wye der peltz auf der ermelen stat.* This is a very frequent figure of speech in Luther, but has no terse English equivalent
[2] *und fur sturm gewalt gepethen haben will*

4

THREE SERMONS PREACHED AFTER THE SUMMONS TO WORMS

(i) A SERMON ON RECEIVING PROPERLY THE TRUE AND SACRED BODY OF CHRIST

Introduction

THIS sermon shows Luther at his best as a preacher speaking directly to his people. The simplicity of the style, the homely phraseology, the absence of technical language, the pure idiom, are all apparent in spite of the translation into another tongue. Nevertheless, it is difficult to reproduce adequately many passages the idiom of which, being that of the spoken language, is now lost. The best one can hope to do is to avoid serious blunders in these cases.

While reading this sermon, one is vividly conscious of the background of events, especially those personal to Luther during the preceding twelve months. This was a period during which Luther was at the peak of his literary activity, yet without a thought of being "literary". In spite of the very bull of excommunication, or perhaps rather, because of it, and because he had burned the bull, the books of the canon law—and his boats,[1] he now stood out as the recognized leader of the new movement. Yet it is not as a titular leader that he speaks in this sermon, but as one who is under divine constraint to preach and teach the truth as he sees it, or, in other words, as he is instructed by the word of God speaking in his heart.

Yet the broader background was of untold importance, because Luther had already received the mandate conveyed by Caspar Sturm from the emperor. All that he had stood for, prayed for, and laboured for since he first "saw the light"[2] and especially since he nailed the theses on the church door, were now rapidly mounting to a crisis, and putting Luther to the severest personal test. He was now on the point of setting out for Worms, where within three weeks he must face the emperor and the imperial council. With his unrivalled power for seeing things in the round, he must have been already well aware of the magnitude of the ordeal; yet, even with Sturm in his house and perhaps in his congregation, nothing in the sermon reveals any excitement nor any deviation from the task immediately in hand: his sermon was the word which God had given him for his people and for this occasion and on this subject. As a result, it comes alive when we read it to-day after more than four centuries, and in another tongue.

---

[1] Cf. *Why the books were burned, supra,* pp. 73ff.
[2] Cf. W. J. Kooiman, *By Faith Alone,* pp. 39ff.

It was preached on Maundy Thursday, March 28, 1521, in Wittenberg, and the congregation included the prince and archduke of Brandenburg. It was probably his last sermon before beginning his memorable journey. It was printed immediately by John Grunenberg in Wittenberg, 1521, and then in many other editions.

The present translation follows the text printed in *W.*, Vol. VII, pp. 792-94, 795-802. Another text, with much additional detail, as found in a surviving manuscript, is printed in *W.*, Vol. IX, pp. 640ff.

Text and Notes

Jesus

1. The sacrament should not be taken by open sinners or those given to some wickedness, such as hatred, or uncleanness and the like. They should not be permitted to partake, despite the command of the church, till they abandon these sins. For it is better to obey God's command rather than that of the church, and to omit the sacrament rather than to take it contrary to God's command, which denies the holy sacrament to these sinners.

2. Neither should the sacrament be taken by those whose attitude of mind is that they only come in obedience to the command of the church, or only by custom; i.e. in such a way that, if they were at liberty to follow their own wishes, they would not readily partake. For, as St. Augustine says, the holy sacrament demands that the soul should hunger, and thirst, and yearn, and long for it. Those who come by command or custom, lack the necessary yearning and desire; they are fearful and afraid, and they would prefer to be absent rather than present. A hungry heart does not wait for the command, and never thinks about the command or the custom; rather it is urged by its own need and desire, and the man's whole mind is drawn to the sacrament that he yearns for.

3. You may object that if that were true, it would soon be plain that few people anywhere would receive it, for scarcely anyone attends by his own choice, but only out of obedience

to the church. The answer is that that makes no difference. There needs must be hunger and thirst for this food and drink, or it cannot be taken without harm. Similarly in common experience: if the body is sated and replete, or else ill and averse to food, and yet a hearty meal is taken, the eater becomes sick and ill, and may die. If he is hungry and thirsty, however, he enjoys the food, and gets health and strength from it.

4. Hence the pope does too little, or rather, he does wrong, by giving orders that force the people to attend no matter who they are, and without previously and most diligently seeing to it that they bring this hunger and thirst when they come. In this way, he destroys their souls and drives them to sin; and he brings the fruit of the sacrament to nothing. It follows that his command should only apply to the hungry; otherwise it is a harmful and hurtful command. It should not be obeyed until you feel hungry, and until, apart from the command, you feel driven from within yourself. Then, of course, you never need the command. Neither the sacrament, nor God Himself, can give anything to a man who is unwilling. God's gifts, just because they are large, require great hunger and much desire on our part; they do not seek, and will not enter a heart that is constrained and unwilling to receive them.

5. Hunger and thirst for God's gifts will be produced in a man's heart independently of any commands if we can make him aware of his trespasses and sins. When he recognizes his woeful condition, he will conceive a desire to change it. The same will be the case if the man sees that he is weak in faith, cold in love, or faint in hope; or again when he discovers that he is given to hatred and impatience, to uncleanness, to envy, or whatever the wickedness may be. Nor is there any doubt that that is what you will find to be your own case, if you look at yourself properly; for that is what all the saints have found to be the case with themselves. Further, you may discover that you are inclined to some lurking transgression of this kind, and find pleasure in it; you should therefore look out for traces of it, and confess your sin. This alters your view, and works within till you feel you must get rid of

the iniquity and wickedness, and you long to be pure, chaste, gentle, sympathetic, humble, believing, loving, etc. That is the way this hunger and thirst begins.

6. According as this inward desire grows warm, you become fitted for this sacrament. That is also the reason why God has commanded us to confess our sin, why He punishes it severely; and why He threatens death, and hell, and many pains and punishments. He is seeking to constrain us to desire godliness and thus become fit for this sacrament. So constrained, a man worries no more about the command of the church; he is glad to go to the sacrament constrained by his own self, and by his sense of need, apart from any commands or compulsions. This is the doctrine that the pope and all the priests ought to impress on, and teach to, the laity; they ought to ignore their own commands, and leave each separate person free to choose. Anyone who in spite of all these aids does not conceive the desire, should be allowed to omit the sacrament. At present, only the commands of the church constrain them, and they come in troops; this does much harm to the Christian faith.

7. When the person has got to the point of feeling the hunger, and to that extent is ready for the sacrament, let him beware of relying on his own merit when he attends. Nor should he, as some do, merely offer the prayer in the verse: "Lord I am not worthy that you should come under my roof. Only say the word, and my soul shall be saved."[1] Not that I reject this petition, but maintain that we ought to lay hold of something more to the point, viz.: the words with which Jesus instituted the supper, and said: *"Take, eat, this is my body given to you. Take it and all ye drink it. This is the cup of the new and everlasting testament in my blood shed for you and for many for the forgiveness of sin."*[2]

This pronouncement, though spoken by the priest in a whisper (and please God that he would say it quite loud, so that all hear plainly, and in their own language) let each Christian at the Supper keep in the forefront of his mind, and pay heed to it alone and above all else. For the words, as we hear them spoken by the priest are just as if spoken by

[1] Matt. 8:8   [2] Matt. 26:26-28

Christ to all of us who stand around. We must each take them
to ourselves and build on them. Nor must we doubt that the
Lord has used these words to invite us to be His guests at this
rich banquet.

8. That is the meaning, indeed, when the priest elevates the
sacrament and the chalice, and the bell rings. This is merely a
reminder that we have heard Christ's word, much as if the
priest and servitor were to say to us all, "Listen, ye Christians, and look; take, eat and drink, etc. This is the body and
blood of Christ." Thus when the priest elevates the host, and
the bell rings, the laity are told in effect that they have
heard Christ's word plainly and clearly, although the priest
had read it in a whisper. So you must nourish your hungry
hearts on this word, and put your confidence in this divine
truth and promise; go to the sacrament, enter into God's
presence and say: Lord, although I am not worthy for Thee
to enter my house, yet I am longing for Thy help and yearning for Thy grace. I aver that I have come for no other
reason than that I may become a godly man. I have heard
this blessed word with which Thou hast invited me to Thy
table; Thou hast told me, unworthy though I am, that
I shall obtain forgiveness for all my sins, through Thy body
and blood. Therefore I eat and drink this sacrament. Amen.
Dear Lord, Thy word is true. I doubt it not, and at Thy word
I eat and drink with Thee; and may all be fulfilled according
to Thy word. Amen.

9. That is the way to go worthily to the sacrament. Our
fitness does not depend on our diligence, labour, work,
prayer, or fasting; but on the truth of the divine words. A
few people, in order to create the longing and desire for the
sacrament, have pretended to find several benefits in the
mass; some in one thing, some in another. Some write that
a communicant does not age while taking the sacrament,
and they tangle the skein to such an extent that they
represent the benefits of the sacrament as entirely physical
and temporal. For this they have no better ground than their
own imagination. They all pretend that if they take mass
they will be all the more certain of their daily bread, and of
good fortune. The mass thus understood, nothing remains

of the real sacrament, i.e. of the true meaning and proper use of the divine promise which is the essence and the whole nature of the sacrament; for at the Last Supper Christ instituted these words and nothing else. He intended them to have only a spiritual application, entirely devoted to the forgiveness of sin, to the operation of grace, and to the giving of divine help. He gave these words for our use, and in order that human hearts, depending on them by faith, might become strong to do everything good, and to resist sin, death, and hell. Christ intended His help to be, not temporal, but spiritual and eternal; and to operate through His word and work. Despite is done to God when the sacrament is misused and applied to temporal benefits.

10. Thus, when the priest administers the sacrament, he must be understood to be doing that of which Christ spoke when He said: "Take, eat", etc. And the communicant must take the sacrament conscious of the force and meaning of these words, never doubting but that all will take place in him according to the letter and spirit of Christ's own words; that Christ really did give His body for him and shed His blood for him; that he himself is an heir of the new testament, which is that of the grace and favour of God to eternal life. Of a truth, faith makes us godfearing and routs all sin; it always strengthens the weak, enlightens the blind, removes every evil inclination, shields from sin, and gives all that is good. In brief, the trust of faith is the end of sin once for all; for the Holy Spirit is given in that faith, and thereby a man wins the love of God. When God imparts His rich blessing to him in this way, he is joyful and glad to do every good thing without commandment or law.

11. Now consider how far the Romanists have travelled from the pathways along which we have learned how to take the sacrament properly. They teach: that we should be quite free from sin, and they have made us shy and bashful. In this way, they have converted the blessed holy sacrament into a terrifying and dangerous rite to which few can go happily and eagerly. They are always afraid that they are not sufficiently clean or meritorious. This fear or hesitation makes them most unfitted for partaking of the sacrament,

and yet deprives them of their hunger and thirst for it. Fear and desire are not mutually compatible. Thus we are held back, and thus also placed under the command. If you prefer not to come, you are quite blameless and commit no transgression. It is better for you to stay away. The sacrament is meant to cleanse and help you. If you prefer not to come, you have then no need at all of its help; you have already had your fill. It is just as if you had been invited to a rich banquet, but you ate and drank to repletion in advance. Then you could but sit at the table with indifference and aversion, and it would be useless to have the viands served to you. But how will that please your host?

12. Consider what happens when one attempts to use commands and laws to make the people godfearing and righteous. They only become worse, and the compulsion makes them unwilling. They find no pleasure in doing what they do. All this is a sheer barrier to God's grace and sacrament. God finds no pleasure in it, nor will He give His grace to those who are forced, and compelled, and required by command and law; but rather to the eager, to those who come voluntarily, to hearts thirsty and eager, as He says in Matthew 11; "The kingdom of heaven suffereth violence and the violent seize it for themselves from the time of John's preaching."[1] The point is that when Saint John (the Baptist) showed the people their sins and transgressions—as all preachers should—they became so eager for the kingdom and help of God that they pressed in forcibly, and made it their own. Men of that spirit are beloved by God, and very acceptable to Him; and thus they will be cleansed from their sins and trespasses, as Psalm 39 says: "Like as the hunted stag longs for a spring of water, so longeth my soul after Thee, O God."[2]

13. He draws us in the same way in Matthew 11: "Come unto me, all ye that labour and are heavy laden, and I will restore and help you."[3] This should not be understood to mean that the Lord is speaking of physical work or burdens. He gives spiritual help alone. Hence this word of His is to be understood of the labour of conscience and its burdens. This

[1] Matt. 11:17   [2] Ps. 42:2   [3] Matt. 11:28

is nothing else than an evil conscience, with sins committed, daily transgression, and inclinations to sin. God drives none of such persons away as are driven away by those who teach that we must be blameless and meritorious before going to the sacrament. Nor does He issue any command; neither compels anyone; rather He draws and lovingly attracts all who are sinners, who feel their burdens, and yearn for help in other ways. We must regard the blessed sacrament not as poison, but as a medicine of the soul; as Christ Himself says in Matthew 9: "The whole need not the physician, but the sick."[1] All that matters is that you should know your labour and feel your burdens and sincerely desire to be rid of them. Thus you will be made fit for the sacrament; then if you have faith, it will give you all that you need. But the majority go without this understanding of the case. They go with empty stomachs but with sated souls; offer many prayers in advance, but have no faith; partake of the sacrament, but gain no benefit from it. They do not know why they do it, except that they are obeying the command of the church, though unwillingly and in fear and trembling. Thus they are entirely unfit for the sacrament. Woe to all those teachers who not only say nothing about the benefit and power of the sacrament, but also prevent the right understanding with their witless compulsions and commands! God deliver us from them. Amen.

[1] Matt. 9:12

(ii) A SERMON PREACHED AT ERFURT EN ROUTE FOR WORMS LOW SUNDAY, APRIL 7, 1521

Introduction

O N March 29, 1521, Luther wrote to his friend John Lang in Erfurt that he expected to arrive as his guest on April 4 or 5. He set out from Wittenberg on Tuesday, April 2, on his journey to Worms, reaching Erfurt on Saturday, April 6. He was considerably excited, and was greeted with the greatest honour by the University where he had once been a student and, later, a teacher. The following day, Low Sunday, at the request of eminent and deeply learned men, he preached on the gospel passage set for that Sunday. Sharply polemical against the Romanists, against philosophy, and pulpit anecdotage, he emphasized the kernel of Christianity: faith in Christ, as taught by God's Word. Luther did not mention the serious mission that he was on, nor the enthusiastic reception accorded him *en route*. Nevertheless, this sermon reveals the Reformer's invincible courage in confessing his own faith: "Well do I know that I shall not be heard willingly. Nevertheless, I intend to speak the truth. I have no alternative, though it cost me my life twenty times."

Immense crowds gathered to hear him preach. Daniel Greser, who later became the superintendent of Dresden, was an eyewitness, and he described the scene in his *Curriculum Vitae*: "About that time, I heard Luther preach at Erfurt in his cowl; the church was so full that the gallery cracked, and all expected it to collapse. Some even knocked out the windows, and would have sprung into the campus. But Luther reassured them, and told them to stay where they were. He said it was an apparition of the devil; but they need only keep quiet and no harm would follow. And in fact no further incident took place."

The most detailed account of the impression made by Luther's sermon is preserved by Eoban Hesse in the third of his *Elegiae quaedam pro assertione Lutherani dogmatis* under the title of *de concione Lutheri ad populum Erphurdiensem honoribusque eidem exhibitis*. Of course, the sermon gave much offence, and much that Luther said was perverted by common gossip. This provided an opportunity, which was seized by "a layman", to print the hurriedly prepared sermon from some of his own notes. Cochlaeus's assertion, that Luther himself had the sermon printed, rests, without question, on a misunderstanding of the title which the first printed edition bears. In any case, the vivid style and the idiom of everyday speech, no less than the firmness of its tone and the simplicity of its spirit, make this sermon characteristic of Luther during his finest hours.

The original title-page reads:

> *A Sermon by Dr. Martin Luther at Erfurt when on his way to His Imperial Majesty at Worms; preached at the request of eminent and very learned men, without preparation or special study owing to the shortness of time. Published by a layman . . . and Printed by Matthes Maler in Erfurt.*

It was also included among *Etlich Sermones* published in August, 1521, by Adam Petri in Basle.

The present translation is based on the text printed in *W.*, Vol. VII, pp. 803-7, 808-13.

Text and Notes

[The gospel for the Sunday was John 20:19: "When the doors were shut where the disciples were assembled for fear of the Jews, Jesus came and stood in the midst, and saith unto them, Peace be unto you," etc.]

Dear Friends, I propose to pass over what is said about St. Thomas, and to deal with it on some other occasion. Rather I shall now consider Christ's words when He said, "Peace be unto you" (v. 19), and "Behold my hands and my side" (v. 20), and "as my Father hath sent me, even so send I you". Now, it is clear and requires no elucidation that we all like to think that we are religious and will attain eternal salvation. That is the question which I shall proceed to discuss.

You are also aware that all philosophers, doctors, and writers have laboured in teaching and explaining what attitude we ought to take to religion. They have given much attention to the subject, but, as is evident, without much success. But genuine and true piety consists of two kinds of works: those done for others, which are the right kind of works; and those done for ourselves, which are of smaller value. For the sake of getting some purchase on salvation, one man builds a church; another goes on a pilgrimage to

St. James (of Campostella) or St. Peter (in Rome); a third
fasts or prays, becomes a monk, walks barefoot, or does something else of that kind. These works, however, are quite
valueless, and ought to be discontinued. Remember that
nothing we do of ourselves is of any avail. God chose a man,
our Lord Christ Jesus, whose mission was to overcome death,
destroy sin, and shatter hell. Previously, there was no one
but belonged to the devil. The devil therefore thought that
Our Lord would fall a prey to him when He hung between
two thieves. These thieves were suffering only the first
foretaste of their punishment, and they were blaspheming
God and cursing man. But Christ's godhead was so mighty
that death, sin, and hell were utterly ineffective.

You should therefore mark well what Paul wrote to the
Romans: "Our sins spring from Adam",[1] and because Adam
ate the apple, we have inherited sin from him. But Christ
shattered the power of death for our sakes; I mean in order
that we might be saved, not by our own works, but by His
works; and these are works beyond our power.

But the papal authorities treat us quite differently.
They issue decrees about fasts, prayers, and butter-eating,[2]
to the effect that whoever observes these papal orders will be
saved, and that he who does not observe them will be seized
by the devil. Thus the people are led astray by the delusion
that their piety and salvation depend upon their own works. I
maintain, however, that none of the saints, no matter how
holy they may be thought, have attained salvation by their
own works. Even the blessed Mother of God was not made
godly, and did not gain salvation, on account of the fact that
her virginity was preserved throughout her motherhood;
rather it was by her faith, and by what God did—not, I
repeat, by her purity, or by her own works. Therefore, mark
me well: salvation does not depend on our works, no matter
of what kind; it can not and will not be effected apart from
faith.

If anyone should say, "Look, my friend, you are saying a
lot about faith, and claiming that our salvation depends
wholly and entirely on it. Now, tell me, how we can acquire

[1] Rom. 5:12ff.   [2] Cf. our Vol. I, pp. 140, 167, 176

faith?"—let me try to explain. The Lord Christ said, "Peace
be with you", "Behold my hands", etc. He said in effect,
"Consider, my friend, I am the only one who has taken your
sins away and redeemed you. Let your mind be at rest. When
you inherited Adam's sin, you did not commit it yourself.
You no more partook of the apple than I did." It follows
that we are not entoiled in sin; neither have we suffered
punishment. Rather, by what God has done, and not by our
own works, have we been set free from sin and (the terrors of)
death. That is why God says, "Behold, I am your redemption", just as Paul said to the church at Corinth, *"Christus
est justificatio, redemptio"*.[1]

Christ is our righteousness and redemption, as Paul explains in this passage. But the response of our Romish
masters is, "Yes, it is quite true that He is redeemer or
saviour, but that is not enough; so we repeat, as before, that
external works are required to make us godly." As distinct
from all this, however, the Lord Jesus says, "I am your
righteousness. I have destroyed the sins of which you were
guilty. Therefore, believe in me; believe that I have accomplished this; then you will be saved." The Bible also says
that *"Justicia est fides"*; righteousness is identical with faith
and comes through faith. Therefore, when we seek to possess
faith, we should believe in the gospel, in Paul, and the other
apostles, rather than in the papal briefs, or the Decretals.
Guard yourselves, indeed, as if from danger of fire; for every
word that comes from the pope cries out, "Give, give." But
refuse, lest you yield to the devil. It would be a small matter
if it were only a way of levying a tax. But it is of the greatest
possible evil to lead the people to believe that these outward
works can save us or make us godly. At the present moment,
the world is so full of wickedness that it overflows. It also
lies under a terrible judgment, a punishment that God
threatens to inflict. The people go astray, and deceive
themselves by their own ideas; they build churches, they
fast, they pray, and so on; they have all the appearance of
doing pious works. But we can deceive ourselves by our own
ideas; it is our duty not to give way to avarice, nor to desire

---

[1] I Cor. 1:30

worldly fame, nor indulge other vices; rather, we should lend what help we can to the poor round about us. God will then come and dwell in us, and we in Him; in other words, we shall be born again.

If we fall again into some sin, it will not be fatal unless we immediately fall into doubt; rather, let us say within ourselves, "O God, who ever livest, Christ my Lord is conqueror of sin." Then sin is at once overcome. The Book of Proverbs says,[1] *"Septies in die cadit justus et resurgit."* A just man may sin seven times in a day; yet he riseth up again. That explains why our times have become so grievously perverted and in error that there have been no genuine preachers for a very long while. In Germany, there may be altogether perhaps three thousand pastors, but not four men of the right sort—God have mercy on us in this woeful state of affairs! As soon as a good preacher appears, he deals briefly with the gospel and then follows it up with a fable of the old ass[2] or a story about Dietrich of Bern.[3] Or else, he dabbles in the pagan teachers, Aristotle, Plato, Socrates, and others, who are all quite contrary to the gospel. They are also contrary to God, for they have no knowledge of the light we possess. Yet one of these preachers will come along and say, "The Philosopher says 'Do plenty of good works, and you will acquire the habit and skill, and at last you will become godly.' "[4] But I say to the contrary, "Don't perform good works in the hope of becoming godly. If you are already of a devout mind, then what you do will be good, yet only passably so, and if done in faith!" All this shows how antithetic are the two points of view.

For a long time, the devil has been making fierce attacks on the people; the result of his attacks is that they have come to believe and have got it into their heads that, although Christ is there, He is of no avail. Then the devil invents another kind of sin, and infiltrates it into our youth; they are seized by it and begin a life of religious observances.[5]

[1] Prov. 24:16   [2] The reading is doubtful, the meaning obscure
[3] The name and description used in the Nibelungenlied for Theodoric, King of Italy, A.D. 493-526; cf. Russell, *History of Western Philosophy*, 1947, pp. 389, 392ff. Luther often refers to Theodoric in various ways
[4] Aristotle, *Ethics*, ed. Chase. 4th ed. Book II, chap. I, p. 34
[5] This seems to be the best translation of an obscure passage

Outwardly, all looks well, but all is poisoned within. The result is that young people grow up with certain delusions: they think that salvation consists in going to church, saying the prayers, fasting, attending mass. All this is the fault of our preachers, and none of it need have happened if only the right preachers had been there.

Our Lord addressed Saint Peter three times: "*Peter, amas me?*" etc.; "*pasce oves meas.*"[1] "Peter, shepherd, shepherd, shepherd my sheep." What is the meaning of *pascere?* It means to shepherd. How ought the sheep to be shepherded? Simply by preaching to them God's word, that is, faith. But then our Romish masters come along and say, *Pascere* means *leges dare*, to issue decrees; but with a subversive implication. The shepherding is attended to, forsooth! What they do is to shepherd the sheep in the same way as the butcher does on Easter Eve! And when the word of God plainly declares that the poor and helpless believers must be cared for, they mix in our friend Aristotle, whose teaching is contrary to the gospel. Paul makes this point in Colossians[2] when he says, "Beware of decrees and philosophy." What does philosophy imply? If we knew Greek and Latin as well as German, it would be quite clear what the apostle meant. Is not what he means the truth? I grant that we do not like listening to it and we are much annoyed: nor will I discuss it. But I will tell you this, whoever you are: do not become a priest or a monk if you have no intention of preaching, or of helping others to preach. For there is a passage in Ezekiel in the thirty-third and thirty-fourth chapter,[3] of a terrible kind; it reads "If you neglect to warn your neighbour, when you see him in error; if you do not help him, and do not preach the gospel to him, I shall call you to account for his soul." That verse is too often left unread. My point is that when you become a priest or a monk in order that you may observe the seven daily hours of prayer, and assist at mass, you do so because you believe that this shows you want to be a godly man. Of course, you will be a fine fellow; if you fall into sin, you will go through the Psalter and the rosary. You will make use of many other prayers beside, and keep on praying

---

[1] Cf. John 21:15ff.   [2] Col. 2:8   [3] Ezek. 33:8

for a long time. You will celebrate mass, kneel at the altar, confess, and mumble on. You will think all this makes you free from sin; and yet your heart may be so full of envy that you would like quietly to choke your enemy; and in that mood, you celebrate mass! It would not be surprising if a thunderbolt struck you to the ground. But if you have eaten three grains of sweet corn, or a piece of turnip, no one could drag you to mass with red-hot tongs. In this way, you gain in scrupulousness, but the result is that you will only go to heaven when the devil goes.

I am well aware that this is not nice hearing. Nevertheless, I shall and must speak the truth even if I were hanged twenty times to prevent my saying what I have said. Of course, you will object that there have been learned people for a hundred or at least for fifty years to tell you what is right.

Granted; still I am not concerned about length of time or number of scholars, but whether people have been aware that the devil is always putting in his fillings; and that he prefers the pagan authors to the holy gospel. I shall speak the truth and I have no alternative: that is why I am standing here without recompense or reward.[1] My purpose is to prevent any one from depending only on man-made decrees or what he himself does. Over and above all this I want people to have the right kind of faith, that is, the one that destroys sin. Then we shall find our faith has increased. In this way, everything is sweet that once was bitter. When that change has taken place, God will make Himself known to our hearts. Once we have been forewarned, we shall pay no attention to man-made decrees. Should the pope come and excommunicate us, then, if we are united with God, we shall pay no heed to any threat of hardship, or excommunication, or decree.

A further question may be raised, to the effect: Need we keep the man-made decrees at all? Can we not pray, fast, and so on, as well as follow the right way once we know it? My reply would be, if you have the true kind of Christian love and faith, everything you do is of service. We may all please

[1] This is meant literally, and describes Luther's practice. He accepted no royalties or fees, and no payment for any of his writings

ourselves what we do, so long as we understand that works are worthless, since they cannot gain salvation for us.

Now I come to a close. Every single person must understand and believe that it is not ourselves, but God, who is able to help us. Similarly, too, that although our works are of little value in themselves, we may yet possess the peace of God. Every one should so perform his works that they do not benefit himself alone, but also someone else, his neighbour. If he be rich, his wealth should be used to benefit the poor. If he be poor, his earnings should benefit the rich. If he or she is a workman or a maidservant, they must render proper service to their master or mistress. In short, no one's work should be of service to himself only. When you see that you are working only for your own advantage, then you are a bad worker. Have no fear as far as I am concerned, for I am well aware what man-made laws amount to. The pope may issue as many decrees as he likes, as is his wont; and I shall observe them if I feel so inclined. Therefore, dear friends, remember that God has risen from the dead. So let us also rise and be ready to speak about our faith to the weak, and let us do our work according to God's good pleasure. Then, we shall receive the peace which He has given us to-day; and may God grant us to keep it for ever. Amen.

(iii) A SERMON ON THREE SIDES OF THE GOOD LIFE

Introduction

JUST when this sermon was preached is unknown. It first appears in a volume of *Etlich Sermones* or Various Sermons published in August 1521. Luther is known, however, to have preached on his way from Wittenberg to Worms, in Erfurt, Gotha, and Eisenach. The first sermon has survived, but there is no evidence whether the Sermon on the Good Life was preached at Gotha or Eisenach. Luther chose no special text, but started from the idea of the three parts of the tabernacle described in the Old Testament and gives a threefold doctrine, with a very fresh treatment, especially of the temple court.

The translation follows the text printed in *W.*, Vol. VII, 792-94; 795-802.

Text and Notes

THE first point to note is that according to the Old Testament, Almighty God commanded Moses to make a tabernacle divided into three parts.[1] The first was the holiest of all, and was called the Holy of Holies. Its breadth, length, and height were each ten cubits and it was thus a perfect cube. The second apartment was called the Sanctum or Holy Place, and was of similar breadth and height, but twenty cubits long. The two apartments constituted a single building of wooden structure, and designed in such a way that you could pass from one apartment to the other as from one chamber opening out of another. The third was called the atrium or court. It was one hundred cubits long, fifty wide, and five high. And there was a white curtain, net-like and therefore transparent, round the tabernacle. This is doubtless the original form of our churches, which we also divide into three parts, viz.: the forecourt, the church, and the chancel; of these the chancel is the most sacred, then the church, then the forecourt. Dwelling-houses are similarly designed, with garden, living room, and then bedroom.

[1] Exod. 27:9-19, 38:9-20. Jos. *Ant.* III. vi. 2, cf. *Hastings' D.B.*, V, 656

The second point to note is that the Holy Spirit intends this
to be the figure of the threefold message or teaching regarding our threefold consciousness of sin, the threefold character
of a good life, or the threefold nature of good works. It is
both useful and necessary for a Christian to make these
distinctions lest he mix one with the other, and does nothing
properly. He must not regard the forecourt as if it were the
chancel, nor the nave as if it were the churchyard. In order
to make everything plain we shall keep to our custom and
call the Holy of Holies the chancel, the Holy Place the
church, and the atrium the forecourt.

In the third place, let us begin with the forecourt. Here,
firstly, are sermons or doctrines which deal entirely with
outer works, viz.: those that are conditioned by time and
place. These include ceremonies, outer conduct, and customs,
vestments and foods. Unless a minister watches over and
attends to his people, these things become, one might almost
say, dangerous and harmful to their consciences. It leads
men to become very conservative and blind, and they can
be taught nothing. By way of illustration, we would instance
a priest, monk, nun, bishop, or the whole of the clergy; they
wear clothes different from the ordinary man, and have other
habits. In church they wear sacred vestments, they pray,
sing and so on. All these matters are outer works, confined
to clothes and place. One whose practice this is, holds those
doctrines which pertain thereto, and calls these practices
good works, the good life, the spiritual office. This foundation
promises him (in advance) a good conscience, as having done
the right thing. On the other hand, if he overlooks or neglects
one of them, e.g. does not have the right garments, or neglects
his prayer time, he is conscience-stricken because he has not
kept the commandment.

Fourthly. We all do similarly when we keep or break the
prescribed fasts and feasts, until, because of some oversight
or slackness on our part, the preacher takes us to task. Then
it becomes more a matter of conscience whether one eats a
bit of bread on the evening of a fast than if one gets drunk,
or swears, curses, lies, deceives, commits adultery, or some
other mortal sin; that is because of the way these doctrines,

these customs, and this kind of life put their emphasis on food and outer things. Indeed how many priests are there to-day who are ten times as conscience-stricken if without their maniple, cassock, marble-slab[1] silver chalice, and the like for celebrating mass, than if they had defamed and slandered, lied, blasphemed, or perhaps spoken evil of their neighbour. This shows how much their consciences are concerned with outer things, and how little with questions of moral values. Moreover, what layman or average person would not have a sorer conscience, if, on the evening of our Apostle's Day or other fast, he were to eat eggs, or butter, or meat, than if he had struck someone a blow, or slandered him; or if he had made a suggestive glance, spoken a suggestive word, or done a suggestive deed? Nay, it has gone so far, on account of certain blind teachers, that no layman dare actually touch the chalice; and if one were to touch it by accident he would have a very uneasy conscience. Further, if an ordinary man should accidentally touch the holy sacrament with his finger, they would come and flay that finger. That shows how serious a matter they make of it, although, as far as I know, there is nothing commanded or forbidden in this respect.

Fifth. Listen: these scruples and errors arise from the fact that we have got everything mixed, and do not make the proper distinctions. Thus the true differences and the sound teachings vanish, and, before we are aware of it, we have got to the length of thinking the least is the greatest and the greatest the least. Then the fear of God departs, presumption enters, and men become too hardened and blind to look at their real sins. That is what is found almost everywhere. Everyone knows that all, whether clergy or laity, are full of deceit, pride, envy, hatred, uncleanness, and all sorts of sins. No one cares, no one continues in the fear of God, or even attempts to ask whether they can improve themselves in respect of these matters, not to mention being right and doing right in the sight of the Lord our God. They are

[1] Luther is probably referring to the marble-slab serving as an altar, which the clergy would carry round on a campaign as army chaplains in order to be able to celebrate mass anywhere, even when no bishop was near, who, according to canon law, was needed to consecrate an altar

content if they hold office, pray at the appointed hours, wear
clerical garments, or keep the canon law. The laity are likewise content, if they keep the fasts and feasts. As if it
matters to God whether you drink beer or coffee, eat meat or
fish, fast or feast! Christ speaks of these matters in
Matthew 23: "Woe to you scribes, clergy, and other hypocrites! You tithe mint, anise, and cummin, but omit the
important things commanded in the law: judgment, mercy,
and faith. These ought ye to have done first, and then not
left the other undone. O ye blind guides, which strain out a
gnat but swallow a camel!"[1]

Sixth. Has not Christ our Lord given a graphic picture of
those men of perverse consciences who make great things
small and small things great, whereby God is angered? Why
do they look so closely at the outer laws that they even
notice the gnat; but take so general a glance at the right
kind of works that they let a camel get by? The only reason
is that they make very great scruples and have very tender
consciences about things which matter little or nothing, but
are very easy-going and indifferent in the important matters
on which everything depends. All of them are *atrienses sancti*,
forecourt Christians. They are only five cubits high, i.e. the
height of the five senses, and an animal life is the whole of
their religion. Yet this is the very reason that religion counts
for more in the world than the true righteousness. There are
so many in the forecourt because it is three times as long as
the church, and ten times as long as the choir; and the crowds
find it a great attraction to go the way of mistaken and
perverse consciences, works, and life. The calling of preacher
or pastor is perilous because, at the Judgment day, they
will have to give an exact reckoning of their office, and
declare whether they have been wide-awake, whether
they laboured against these evils, and whether they taught
their people properly about them. On the other hand, if they
do their duty like this, they will have to suffer for it from the
pope, and bishops, and the spiritual prelates. For these same
persons are so penetrated with these forecourt evils and
serious sins, that they cannot tolerate it that anyone should

[1] Matt. 23:23

teach differently. They choose to remain gnat-strainers and camel-swallowers.

Seventh. Everybody knows and understands that this outer, forecourt way helps no one; and that no matter of clothes, food, places, or holy days makes anyone into a godly man. They all remain faithless, greedy, impatient, proud, impure, bad-tempered, and envious. Indeed no one is so deeply sunk in these vices as the very people who have found their religion in food and vestments, in holy places and holy days. When we notice this, we should take ourselves to task and say, That cannot be the right road or pathway to godliness and salvation; there must be some other. Just because these people greatly despise the great and serious transgressions, we must be very much on the alert to watch quite closely and notice how wrong is that outer ceremonial in which we see so many are lost. We must train ourselves to look in the right direction. Should you chance to see a back-biter, or one who tells dirty stories, on the one hand, and, on the other, someone who neglects a fast or a feast, or eats forbidden food, you should be ten times more indignant about the first than the second. Regard the latter as having swallowed a gnat, but the former a camel. It is regrettable and exasperating that the pope should be so strict about eating butter and eggs that we have to get a dispensation for them, that he is not stricter still lest we sin against God, and that bishops and prelates should aid and abet him in this regard. But if they themselves meddle in these things and pervert them, filtering gnats away and swallowing camels, then, of course, poor folk will wriggle themselves free, especially while their rulers and teachers lead them astray with their teaching, example, and authority.

Eighth. Now let us leave the atrium and go into the Holy Place, the church. This signifies the teachings, the works and the consciences which are genuinely good, namely, humility, gentleness, meekness, patience, peace, faithfulness, love, chastity, modesty, and the like. These things have no necessary connection with food, clothing, holy places, holy days, or personal position. Rather these qualities have to do with the layman more than the priest, the priest more than the pope, the wife than the husband, the child than the adult, the poor than the rich, the ill-clad than the richly clad, work in the field more than that in the house, your own room rather than the church. It is to these qualities alone that God attends. He who takes this path, walks on the straight road to heaven, irrespective of what he does or leaves undone in the atrium. God does not inquire about the latter, provided a man lives as he should in the sanctum. Further, we should be conscience-stricken when we curse, or swear, or speak, see, hear, do, or think anything unclean. That is the right kind of conscience. That is the way to filter off the camel and swallow the gnat. That is the way to keep the corn and let the chaff go. That is the way Abel offered a lamb whereas Cain offered straw.[1] That is the way to fight against pride, greed, uncleanness, ill-temper, hatred, and the like. This is the place where we work with both hands and all our lives, in order to forget the forecourt and feel no lack of it. We can see that this is the direct road to godliness and salvation. It is plain that those who practise these things become truly godfearing, and not those who stay in the forecourt. Hence this, and not that, must be the right way.

Ninth. But even works of this character may be done in two different ways. Some enter the church eagerly and voluntarily. Others enter backwards; they are carried in on another's shoulders like dead men and are buried there. I mean those who unwillingly keep up godly conduct on account of public opinion and because of fear of punishment or of hell. For many remain blameless only because of public opinion or fear of punishment; if these were removed, they would act just like those who have no respect for opinion, and hold the idea of punishment in contempt. So, too, many restrain their ill-temper or bold ways not because they wish to do so, or like to be gentle, but because they hate to apologize or make amends.[2] Many pay for divine services or make benefactions, but not from love of meekness, but for praise and personal pleasure. This evil motive is so profound that no saint has ever fully confessed it. He may have been perplexed and confused by it, and prayed, Psalm 50: "O

[1] Cf. Gen. 4:1ff.   [2] *nit fuglich kulen und pursen mag*

Lord my God, create in me a clean heart and renew a right spirit or will within me,"[1] and also, Psalm 18, "Who can understand all his own errors? Keep me clean from my secret sins."[2] It is not as if God wanted these works done for their own sake, but done gladly and heartily. If the gladness and willingness are absent, then, in God's sight, the works are dead. Such service is grudging, forced, constrained, reluctant; and displeasing to God. St. Paul says "God loveth a cheerful doer".[3]

Tenth. As far as human nature goes, this pleasure, love, joy, and willingness are to be found nowhere in the world in the human heart. Rather we are all reluctant and unwilling to serve God. But we are afraid of punishment or public opinion otherwise; or we seek our own advantage and satisfaction in this way. No one does it just for the sake of the will of God, or because it is right and devout. Human nature likes and needs to have some cause for being devout. It cannot and does not like to be devout for the sake of being devout. It is not satisfied with being devout, as it should, but seeks to gain some advantage or benefit from it, which is wrong in God's sight. St. Paul in Romans 3, referring to Psalm 13, says, "There is none righteous".[4] For we ought not to be devout in order to earn or to avoid something. All of that character are hirelings, servants, and paid workers; not willing children and heirs. These latter are devout and pure for the sake of godliness itself, for God's own sake. For God is the essence of righteousness, truth, goodness, wisdom, and sanctity. A man who does not seek the mere odour of religion, seeks and finds God Himself. But the man who seeks gain, or flees pain, never finds God. He makes a God out of his gains. For the very aim or ground of a man's action is, in itself, his god.

Eleventh. Hence we must lay hold on grace, and cease from our self-seeking. That is why God has built us the chancel and the Holy of Holies. For this reason also He has set Christ in front of us, and promised that whoever believes in Him and calls upon Him, shall soon receive the Holy Spirit. It says in John 16, "The Father will send the Holy Spirit in

---

[1] Ps. 51:12   [2] Ps. 19:13   [3] 2 Cor. 9:7   [4] Rom. 3:10 and Ps. 14:3

my name",[1] for it must be that when a man renounces
himself, and calls on Christ in true faith, he shall receive the
Holy Spirit. The Holy Spirit comes where the name of Christ
is. And whoever calls on Christ in faith, has His name, and
therefore the Holy Spirit will also assuredly come. But when
the Spirit comes, He makes a pure, free, glad, joyful, and
loving heart; and this heart is devout pure and simple. It
seeks no gain, fears no punishment. It is devout, and does all
it does gladly just for the sake of the godliness and the
righteousness. This is truly good doctrine, because it instructs
consciences and teaches the nature of works. This is what it
means to enter the chancel, the Holy of Holies. This is the
climax of what is possible for us on earth. This is the road to
heaven. It is clear that no evil person can journey on it, but
only the devout. It is the very opposite to the forecourt, for
in the Holy of Holies no one heeds outer things. Yea, those
in the forecourt seem to be the bitter foes of this way of life.

Twelfth. Christ speaks of it in Mark's gospel and says,
"He that believeth, shall be saved".[2] It is faith which saves.
Why? Because it conveys the Spirit which does all good works
joyfully and gladly; and that is what fulfils God's commandment and redeems us. That was the purpose when the church
was made a single building connected with the chancel, the
sanctum with the Holy of Holies. But the atrium, the
separate forecourt, signifies that there are no good works
apart from faith, and that faith without good works does not
last. A preacher ought not to separate these two elements of
teaching, although he should give faith the premier place.
Of course, faith and good works may remain at the stage of
those whose religion consists of outer things like food, and
garments, holy days, and personal status. Hence it says in
the book of Revelation that, in the new covenant, the atrium
is given over to the gentiles.[3] This is in order that, in the new
covenant, these outer things should be free and separate, and
at each man's choice. Then only will the Holy Place, and the
Holy of Holies, be rightly used. Unfortunately the present
state of affairs is such that never before, among many people,
has there been a larger forecourt or more of those whose

---

[1] John 14:26   [2] Mark 16:16   [3] Rev. 11:2

religion consists of food, garments, holy days, and status, than is now to be found among Christians. The blame is to be laid at the door of the papacy and the canon law. This latter contains so much that is useless, dangerous, and hurtful that it is indescribably detrimental to faith and good works, and beclouds them. May God in His mercy set us free from it, and watch over us. Amen.

5
LUTHER AT WORMS

1. D̲URING the *annus mirabilis*, 1520, when Luther published a large number of writings important at the time, and afterwards found to be classical for the Reformation as a whole,[1] he seems to have been preoccupied subconsciously with apocalyptic expectations. He felt himself to be living in the last days, those of the Final Judgment, and he spent much thought trying to understand the book of Daniel and its relevance to the prevailing situation. Fortunately, these inquiries and speculations never came to be more than flashes of sheet lightning which lit the horizon, gave an unaccustomed profile to persons and events, and then left one to find one's way by the usual means. Luther remained too realistic to be deflected from the path pointed out by the insight gained from the Bible.

Nevertheless, it must be granted that several movements were tending to a common assize, a far-reaching judgment, and the final division of western Christendom. History was moving to a moment which was to be the most dramatic for a millennium. Some men were crying, Lo here! and others, Lo there! but only a few were convinced that the kingdom was within as well as among them.

While Luther was busy writing his *Appeal to the Ruling Classes*,[2] Charles V of Spain set out on his first journey as German emperor. He left Spain on May 26, 1520, and spent most of the summer in the Netherlands in surroundings in the midst of which he had been brought up. On September 28, he gave the mandate, at Aleander's request, that the bull excommunicating Luther should become effective. In October Luther's books were publicly burned in Louvain and Lüttich, and similar bonfires were made in many towns during the next few weeks.[3] The young monarch was showing himself a faithful son of Holy Church. His coronation as king of the Romans took place in accordance with ancient tradition, and with great splendour, at Aachen on October 23; and on October 26 he assumed the title of German emperor with the agreement of the pope. He was twenty years of age. On November 1, the day when he took up residence in Cologne, he summoned his first imperial council to meet at Worms, 150 miles further up the Rhine.

The people of Germany set great expectations on the new reign, and Luther was very well disposed in favour of the highly-bred young man, with his deeply religious instincts.[4] Bishop Berthold

[1] *Vide* our Vol. I, pp. 16-17   [2] *Vide* Vol. I, pp. 103ff.
[3] Cf. *supra*, pp. 73ff.   [4] Cf. Vol. I, p. 111

I M L

of Chiemsen, a man of high principles, expressed his expectation publicly that Charles would do wonders in dealing with anti-Christian opponents in church and state. It would not have been strange if some people had regarded Charles as a kind of Messiah.

It says much for his character that Charles acted cautiously. At his court in Brussels, he was very "gracious" to Karl von Sickingen, and more so to Frederick the Wise. He even promised, when he met the latter in Cologne at the end of November, that he would command Luther to the imperial council at Worms. This promise was contrary to the requirements of the pope, whose nuncio, Aleander, had demanded that Luther should be outlawed immediately.

Aleander understood the situation thoroughly; he sought, on the one hand, to stiffen Charles's ancestral loyalty to the church; and, on the other, to prevent Luther's appearance before the council. But it was desirable to take into account numerous other persons of influence who reflected the humanistic trend of the times, like the High Chancellor, Gattinara, and, with a difference, Albrecht of Mainz; or who, like the fair-minded Henry of Nassau, were very conscious of widespread German ill-will towards Rome.

The situation was further complicated by the fact that the princes, including that loyal papalist, Duke George of Saxony, were concerned to restrict the emperor's power over the ruling authorities in the empire; but this was not so important a consideration as the restiveness of the populace which was felt to be greater than ever before. Even Aleander reported that nine-tenths of them raised the war-cry of "Luther!"; and that the other tenth, who might perchance care little for Luther, would shout, "Down with the Roman curia!"

It was while Frederick the Wise was at Cologne about this time that he asked Erasmus what was the complaint against Luther; and received the famous reply after a short pause that Luther had "attacked the crown of the pope and the bellies of the monks".[1]

In the end there was no alternative to commanding Luther's attendance at Worms, even if Charles had to tell the princes that he only wished to hear Luther for himself. The outlawry remained ineffective and, on March 6, the summons, accompanied by a "safe-conduct", was issued. On Tuesday April 2 Luther set out, and Sturm, who was the emperor's messenger, did nothing to hinder popular demonstrations. Luther's journey, far from being the furtive movement of an outlaw, became a kind of triumphal progress. He preached three times, once on setting out, and twice en route.[2] Public opinion in Worms itself was very unfavourable to

[1] Reported by Spalatin, who was present; cf. T.R., Vol. I, p. 55, par. 131; also H. P. Smith, Erasmus, p. 235, who gives the date as November 5
[2] Vide supra, pp. 101ff., 110ff., 117ff.

the Romanists. Indeed, the vicar, John Vigilius, an eminent humanist, had been in friendly correspondence with Melanchthon and the Wittenberg reformers since April 24, 1520. The group of humanists included Theobald Fettich—a medical man, Martin Butzer, and Hermann von dem Busche, a strong and active nucleus favouring reform and exercising much influence among the townspeople.[1] It is no wonder that Glapio, the emperor's confessor, tried to draw Luther aside into private conversations before he arrived in Worms itself; he arranged with von Sickingen to invite Luther to the castle at Ebernburg, but the latter refused to mix in politics. Even when he received hints about the fierce, hostile Spanish guards, he was undismayed; and tradition says that his response was, "Even if there were as many devils in Worms as tiles on the roofs, I would still enter the place."[2]

He arrived on Tuesday, April 16, having been just a fortnight on the way; and was now a very weary, indeed a sick man. He was brought into the council the following day. The brilliance of the assembly must have been as overwhelming as the close and heated chamber was stifling. The scene and the setting would remind Luther of the critical occasion, almost two years earlier, when he took part in the public debate at Leipzig which Duke George had mounted with all the splendour at his command. But now Luther faced the emperor, the greatest councillors of state, and the highest dignitaries of the church outside Rome itself, most of whom were eminent Frenchmen, Italians, or Spaniards, et al. A lesser man might excusably have wilted; and even Luther, though his answer had been prepared, in principle, for many months, felt compelled to plead for time on account of fatigue. It speaks for the grace of the young emperor that he granted the request and gave him one day.

By Thursday, April 18, Luther was much refreshed. He was summoned for four o'clock, but was made to wait for two hours before being admitted to the council chamber. His speech was manifestly the utterance of a man whose conscience was, as he said, in chains to the word of God.[3] The emperor himself, although he spoke no German, and understood Latin imperfectly, felt its power, for he declared obstinately, "That fellow shall not make me a heretic." The tension must have been well-nigh intolerable. The emperor had told the assembled princes, at an earlier stage of the negotiations, that he accepted his ancestral duty, and would defend accordingly both the Catholic faith and the Roman papacy against heretics.

Every effort was made to avoid a split. Yet, since the emperor kept to his purpose and his promise, the course of events was not

---

[1] Cf. Borcherdt and Merz, op. cit., Vol. 3, pp. 378f.
[2] Br. Vol. II, 455. Kooiman, op. cit. p. 100
[3] Infra, pp. 155, 157, 166f., 178

interrupted. The "Edict of Worms",[1] published in May, pronounced Luther an outlaw within the empire, and forbade the
printing and reading of his books.

Luther left Worms on April 26, and travelled by way of
Frankfort-am-Main, Friedberg, and Eisenach, to Mohra, the home
of his ancestors. At Friedberg, he said goodbye to Sturm, the
imperial envoy who had escorted him thus far; his only companion
was now John Petzensteiner, an Augustinian monk. Having
visited his relatives at Mohra, and having gone a short distance
from the village, he was set upon, taken prisoner, and brought
to the castle at Wartburg, where he arrived on the evening of
Saturday, May 4. Here he was kept in "protective custody" for
ten months.

On the way he had written two fairly long letters, to the
emperor,[2] and to the princes;[3] letters which reveal how he construed the events in Worms. "My conscience is in bonds and fetters
to Holy Scripture; I have expounded it in my books. Hence,
unless bidden by the Holy and divine Scriptures, I am unable to
retract anything whatsoever." He devoted most of his labours at
Wartburg castle to the Holy Scriptures themselves, and it was
here that he translated the New Testament into German.

According to all the extant records, Luther spoke at Worms
first in Latin, then in German; and all the records agree that, in
any case, his last sentence was spoken in German.

The extant records do not originate from Luther himself,
except for a fragmentary note in German[4] setting down a preliminary draft of his proposed speech on the morrow, April 18.[5]
Very shortly after the council, editions of his speech were published in German and also in Latin. Some of the editions appeared
as special leaflets, some as part and parcel of the records of the

[1] Cf. Mirbt, *Quellen zur Geschichte des Papsttums.* 2nd ed., pp. 186f.;
also Borcherdt and Merz, *op. cit.,* Vol. III, pp. 380f., "The edict was
drawn up on May 8, and passed through a hastily called meeting of the
imperial council on May 25th, at which only a part of the nobility were
present. It was not brought forward as a motion, but only read aloud;
whereupon the archduke, Joachim of Brandenburg, expressed his agreement, and no one had the courage to say, Nay. Yet the edict speaks of
'unanimous opinion and desire.' This misrepresentation angered Luther,
and rightly so; he declared, 'I was not condemned by the imperial council
as a heretic.' He hewed his way through the diplomatic phrases and cried
to the noble lords, 'You ought to be ashamed that you had not the courage
to listen to a poor, lone beggar like me.' The emperor (falsely) regarded
Luther as the dupe of hypocrites." Cf. *op. cit.,* Vol. III, p. 64, and *W.,*
Vol. XIX, pp. 275ff.

[2] Cf. *infra,* pp. 176ff.

[3] *Br.,* Vol. II, 314-17, and cf. *W.,* Vol. XIX, 275ff. *Unterricht u. Warnung
wider . . . Ratschlag . . . Pfafferei,* 1526; *Br.,* Vol. III, pp. 41, 74ff.; *W.,* Vol.
XII, pp. 61ff., *Widder die Verkerer u. felscher Keyserliches Mandats,* 1523

[4] *Infra,* p. 136   [5] Cf. *W.,* Vol. VII, p. 815

council.[1] The German version, made, probably by Spalatin, from the Latin form, was published substantially by Luther in the earliest edition of his collected Works.

2. The Accounts of the Negotiations with Dr. Martin Luther at the Imperial Council at Worms in April, 1521[2]

Innumerable accounts of the events in Worms were circulated either at the time, or only after many years, by persons of different standing and reliability, and everything of this kind has been assembled and published by Wrede and Bernay, *Deutsche Reichtagsakten unter Kaiser Karl V*, Gotha, 1896, Vol. II. Of these accounts, only few can claim to have great historical value; namely, (*a*) what Luther himself wrote at the time, whether in preparation for his speech, or immediately afterwards to various persons, especially during the week of negotiations before he again left Worms; (*b*) those records that give Luther's speech and other matters in relatively their best tradition.

The first document strictly *ad hoc* is the fragment of a speech which Luther sat down to write on the evening after his first and brief appearance at the council on Wednesday, April 17. The original is in Luther's own handwriting and is preserved in the archives of Ernestine Saxony at Weimar. This is to be found *infra*, p. 136.

Whether Luther thought this first draft unsatisfactory, or what other considerations caused him to break off, must remain unknown; but Luther now proceeded to work out the whole of his speech in Latin. In this draft he refused to make the recantation which had been put to him, in accordance with his frequent earlier declarations of firmness[3]—with due allowance for minor variations in the actual delivery of his answer which he had been ordered to make by word of mouth.

Afterwards, he added to this draft his account of the discussion which took place between him and John von Eck of Trier, and which the latter ended by asking for a reply "without horns and teeth". The ancient handwritten copy is in the Königliche Offentliche Bibliothek in Dresden. This final record made by Luther was expanded by others in various ways, but always retained Luther's first person singular in the original parts. The various sections are only loosely conjoined, as will be seen in the translations given herewith, e.g. pp. 151ff.

3. The Expanded Records

(*a*) *Acta et res gestae D. Martini Lutheri. etc.*, at Worms 1521.

[1] *Acta et res gestae D. Martini Lutheri Augustiniani in comitiis Principum Vuormaciae*, and cf. *W.*, Vol. VII, pp. 814-87
[2] Cf. *W.*, Vol. VII, pp. 814-87
[3] Cf. *Br.*, Vol. II, Nos. 339, 341, 347, 351, and oft. It follows that he had really committed himself before he ever met the council

The author of this compilation is unknown. Jerome Aleander
feared as early as the end of April, 1521, that Luther himself had
published an account of his arrival in Worms and of his process
before the council in order, in his view, "to rouse the people by
suggesting that he had not been allowed a public discussion, and
had not been heard at all".[1] As early as May 8, he was speaking
of a certain unrest among the German people caused by "the
Akta which Luther had written in his familiar way omitting the
answer (given by von Eck)".[2] It is thus confirmed that the *Akta*
were published by the beginning of May, but it is only a surmise
that Luther was their author.[3] This accusation of Aleander's,
however, may really have to do with the publication of Luther's
own draft of his speech, which seems to have been in print between
April 29 and May 8; and by May 5 a German translation of this
(Latin form of the) speech seems to have been issued. But a letter
of Jerome Vehus composed on June 3 shows that the complete
Akta had been published during May.

Writing on that date in early June to the Margrave Philip
of Baden, Vehus described the full contents of the *Akta*; he said
that it was "published by an unknown author anonymously",
and tried to show that, in some respects, the account was untrue.
John Cochlaeus, writing in 1549, however, asserted that Luther
himself had prepared the *Akta*, the proof of the assertion being the
use of the first person singular in the passages which had been
copied from Luther's own record. But critics have not upheld this
view.[4]

(b) *Acta comparationis Lutheri in daeta Wormatiensi.* While
Luther and his friends were busy setting down their records and
preparing their accounts, Aleander, the papal nuncio, was working to provide a counterweight; and he wanted it printed with a
lawyer's accuracy,[5] but it is not known why his project mis-
carried. Meantime, von Eck of Trier described the events, and
made use of Luther's own edition of the speech, of which he had
been handed a copy. The speech, as edited by von Eck, therefore
appears in two forms: (a) the brief version as provided by Luther;
(b) that which included both what von Eck had said, and also
records on which Aleander placed the greatest value.[6] Finally, a
list of Luther's condemned works was added to this form of the
Acta.

In harmony with the conclusions of A. E. Berger and the editor
in the Weimar Edition of these records, in the present translation we shall give first place to the anonymous record. This was
hastily printed in Wittenberg, and subsequently corrected.
Naturally, it includes Luther's speech in the first person singular.

---

[1] Brieger, *Aleander und Luther, 1521.*, p. 169   [2] *Ibid.*, p. 193
[3] *W.*, Vol. VII, p. 819   [4] *W.*, Vol. VII, p. 820
[5] Brieger, *op. cit.*, 216   [6] Cf. *infra*, pp. 151ff., 158ff.

Next in importance is the Eck-Aleander account referred to above, in the midst of which is the same version of Luther's speech. This account contains the additional records stressed by Aleander,[1] and there is appended a list of Luther's works "exhibited" to the council. All this is followed by a German account of the latter part of the proceedings.

No records survive of the speech that Luther made in German; but one known as the Erfurt version and another as Spalatin's were made from the Latin speech. The latter is by far the better known, and contains a brief account by Spalatin of the events immediately preceding and succeeding. It was probably done at once in order to send to the elector Frederick.[2] We have printed this report below in parallel to the anonymous record.

Certain ancient MSS. include an account of events at the brief hearing before the council on April 17,[3] and others give a short account of the conclusion of the session.[4]

On May 3, 1521, Luther wrote to Albert, count of Mansfeld, at the request of Rudolf von Watzdorf, and gave a summary account of the events in Worms, and, later in the year, a more or less exact copy was sent to Duke George of Saxony, who had heard of the letter and believed it maligned him; he therefore requested to see it, and, after various evasions and some delay, Count Albert complied. The letter has survived in two somewhat different German versions and a Latin translation.[5] Minor references and some pointed comments are to be found in the Table Talk.[6]

W., Vol. VII, p. 887 lists various contemporary records which were however, only published at a much later date; including those of Luther himself,[7] Spalatin, Spengler, Fürstenberg, Krel, Bock and Duntzenheim, Köllner, Vehus, Cochlaeus, *et cetera aliorum.*

[1] Cf. *infra*, pp. 151ff., 158f.   [2] *W.*, Vol. VII, pp. 865-879
[3] *W.*, Vol. VII, pp. 880f.   [4] *W.*, Vol. VII, pp. 881f.
[5] *Br.* Vol. II, pp. 319-29   [6] *T.R.*, pars. 357, 3,474, 3,480, 3,724
[7] Luther published an account in the first edition of his collected Works: this is in substantial agreement with that published in the year 1521, the differences being almost purely verbal, and of negligible importance. The version of Luther's speech contained in this account is the one which gained the widest currency. Cf. Borcherdt and Merz, *op. cit.*, Vol. III, pp. 11ff.

The fragment, in German, of the draft of Luther's speech written by him at the inn after his first, brief appearance before the emperor, and in preparation for the morrow, April 18.[1]

A T the desire and command of his Majesty, the Roman emperor, I came here yesterday,[2] and I now appear again. I am at peace with God, and I am a dutiful subject of his imperial, Christian Majesty. I came here under a safe-conduct to hear obediently and to grasp what was addressed to me in accordance with the emperor's mandate and intention.

But, when I appeared here yesterday, two questions were put to me: whether I acknowledged as mine a list of books whose titles were read out, and which had been published in my name; and, then, whether I wished to stand by them or to renounce them. I gave a plain answer to the first question: I acknowledged that the books were by me, and I shall always acknowledge it.

As to the second question, which raised issues of the highest importance in heaven and on earth, namely, about God's Holy Word, and about faith, I humbly asked for postponement to give me time to think. This was because I had to answer orally, and I did not wish to risk blundering by lack of caution; to say too much or too little, to the hurt of my conscience. Hence I requested this (kindness)[3] of his Majesty.

And, besides what I said, there was the implication, when . . .

[1] Cf. *supra*, p. 123
[2] From the time of the actual delivery of the speech; hence Wednesday, April 17
[3] Not in the original, but apparently omitted by accident

COLUMN A

Anonymous Latin record[1]

IN THE NAME OF JESUS

M.D.XXI.
Records and Reports
of Dr. Martin Luther
Augustinian
at the council of princes at
Worms

Four days after the Sunday of Misericordia Domini,[2] doctor Martin Luther, a professing Augustinian monk, journeyed to Worms in A.D. 1521, in response to the command of the emperor, Charles V, king of Spain, archduke of Austria, etc., who was holding his first council at the royal city of Worms in the first year of his reign. Three years earlier, Dr. Martin had propounded unusual theses for discussion at Wittenberg, a town of Saxony. The theses were directed against the oppression of the bishop of Rome; and meanwhile, there had been exhaustive discussion by many without proving the theses contrary to Scripture or reason. The affair began to tend towards unrest, the populace regarding it as a case of the gospel against the clerics. On this account, it seemed

[1] Cf. *W.*, Vol. VII, pp. 825ff.
[2] April 18

COLUMN B

Spalatin's German record[1]

Doctor Martin Luther, an Augustinian monk, arrived here in Worms with the emperor's envoy[2] on the Tuesday[3] following the feast of Misericordia Domini shortly before ten o'clock in the morning. He remained here eleven days, till the Friday[4] after the feast of Jubilate or St. George. Crowds of people did him honour, welcomed him, and made his acquaintance. He was sought out and greeted by princes, dukes, barons, knights, gentry, citizens, and all, whether ecclesiastics or laymen. Some had travelled many miles to see him. He was held in such regard that it was the widespread opinion that, if he were made to suffer injury, much harm would result.

It was comforting and encouraging to many a deeply Christian heart, that Martin, the Christlike doctor, appeared quite calm and confident. They were aware that, although he had received the emperor's safe-conduct, a decree had nevertheless been issued against him in the emperor's name.[5] This decree was intended to compel him to retract—or so

[1] *W.*, Vol. VII, pp. 865-79
[2] Casper Sturm   [3] April 16
[4] April 26   [5] On March 10, 1521

advisable that the Roman legates should take the initiative, and that Luther should be commanded to attend the imperial court; he was to be provided by the emperor and the princes with a safe conduct for this purpose. He was summoned. On his arrival, he was directed to the jurisdiction of the Rhodians, where he lodged in the inn. Far into the night, he was sought out and greeted by many counts, barons, gilded knights, and nobles, both ecclesiastical and secular.

his enemies hoped; and then they would have grounds for dealing with him as a rebellious outlaw.

But he came, good Father that he was, and showed himself to be so truly a Christian that it was plain he feared nothing on earth, but would risk his neck and venture life and limb a hundred times, rather than withdraw a single letter without proof from the Word of God.

i. *Luther's first appearance*

On the day after his arrival, Ulrich von Pappenheim, a nobleman who was master of the imperial knights, was sent by the emperor. He called before lunch, and showed Charles's command to doctor Martin; he was to appear at four o'clock in the presence of his imperial Majesty, the electoral princes, the dukes, and the other orders of the empire, when it was arranged to give a hearing of the case for which he had come. Dr. Martin was happy to agree, as was right.

Immediately after four o'clock that day, there came Ulrich von Pappenheim and Caspar Sturm, the imperial herald for Germany, by whom Dr. Martin had been summoned and escorted from Wittenberg to Worms. These two made their request to him, filed through the garden of the inn of the Rhodians, and into

On Wednesday the day after Misericordia Domini,[1] his imperial Majesty commanded the presence of doctor Martin with the princes and dukes and noblemen of the empire. The time set was four o'clock in the afternoon, and the place was the palace or bishop's court, which was the lodging of his imperial Majesty and his brother, the grand-duke Ferdinand.

[1] April 17

COLUMN A—*cont.*   COLUMN B—*cont.*

the assembly hall of the Pala-
tine counts. In order that they
should not suffer from the
crowd, which was very great in
the narrow street that led to
the emperor's residence, they
made their way furtively by
side streets, and entered the
auditorium. Yet they had not
escaped the notice of many,
who could scarcely be
prevented by force from push-
ing in.

When Dr. Martin was act-   When doctor Martin appeared,
ually standing face to face
with his imperial Majesty, the
electoral princes, the dukes,
and, in short, all the orders of
the empire, who were then in
attendance on the emperor, he
was admonished by Ulrich von
Pappenheim not to speak without being requested.

It was then that John von   the secretary[1] of the archbishop
Eck, the speaker of his im-   of Trier, at a sign from his imperial Majesty, and general   perial majesty, required doctor
secretary of the bishop of   Martin to declare whether he
Trier, spoke first in Latin, then acknowledged authorship of
in German, but with the same   the books published in his
substance, as follows: His im-   name; and whether he wished
perial Majesty has brought   to retract them or not.
you here, Martin Luther, for
two reasons; firstly, to know   [1] John von der Eck (to be care-
whether you publicly acknow-   fully distinguished from John Eck
ledge here the books so far   of Ingoldstadt). See *infra*, p. 151, n. 1
published in your name, and
say that they are yours; secondly, after it is known that all
are to be held as yours, whether
you wish to retract anything in
them.

At this point, Dr. Jerome
Schurff, a Swiss from St.
Gallen, who was standing by
Martin's side, cried, "Let the
titles of the books be read out."

COLUMN A—*cont.*

Then the secretary from Trier recited the names of those books which had been printed at Basle. These included commentaries on the book of Psalms, a monograph on Good Works, a commentary on the Lord's Prayer, besides other volumes on the Christian religion, of a non-contentious character.

At this point, Dr. Martin replied to these questions in German and Latin as follows: Two propositions have been put to me by his imperial Majesty; firstly, whether I am willing to acknowledge as mine all the books that bear my name; secondly, whether it is my intention to stand by, or to retract any of those already published by me. To these questions my reply shall be as brief as possible. In the first place, I cannot deny that I am the author of the books named a moment ago, nor shall I ever deny any of them. As to the next question, whether in the same way, I would stand by all, or whether I would retract what seemed to have been said beyond the testimony of Scripture: because this is a question concerning faith and man's salvation, and because it has to do with the word of God, than which there is nothing more important in heaven or on earth, and which it rightly behoves us all to hold in reverence, it would be bold of me, and perhaps perilous, to make any unpremeditated assertion. If I had not thought

COLUMN B—*cont.*

Doctor Martin acknowledged the books; but, as to the second question, whether he regretted having written them or not, he begged time for consideration.

The question had to do with the word[1] of God, and this was the highest of all things in heaven or on earth. He did not wish to fall under the condemnation which Jesus, our Lord, had pronounced: For whosoever shall be ashamed of me and of my words, of him will I be ashamed before my heavenly Father and His angels.[2]

[1] Cf. *supra*, p. 131, n. 3 [2] Luke 9:26

COLUMN A—*cont.*

the subject over, I might maintain, on the minor issue of
substance or the major issue
of truth, a view in either case
leading me away from what
Christ meant when He said,
Whoever denies me before men,
I will deny before my Father
who is in heaven.[1] For this
reason, I do beg and beseech
your imperial Majesty for time
to think, in order that I may
give a satisfactory answer to
the question, an answer that
will do no wrong to God's
word and avoid peril to my soul.

The princes thereupon went
into council; of which, later,
the secretary of Trier reported
as follows: Martin, you are well
enough qualified to understand
from the nature of the emperor's command why it is
that you were summoned here.
It is therefore quite plain
that you do not deserve to
be granted longer time for
thought; nevertheless, by his
characteristic clemency, his
imperial Majesty will grant
one day for deliberation; you
will appear before him to-
morrow at the same hour, it
being understood that you do
not proffer your opinions in
writing, but by the spoken
word.

Doctor Martin was then
taken back to his lodgings by
the herald. It should be said
that, while on his way to the
audience at the emperor's command, and even when he was
in the assembly of the princes,

COLUMN B—*cont.*

His imperial Majesty granted
him time for consideration till
the following day, Thursday,
again at four in the afternoon.

[1] Cf. Matt. 10:32

COLUMN A—*cont.*

Luther was continually urged by first one voice and then another to be brave; to play the man; not to fear them who could kill the body, but not the soul; rather he must revere him who was able to cast both body and soul into Gehenna;[1] and again, When you stand before kings, do not deliberate what you shall say, for it will be given you at the time.[2] One of the bystanders shouted, Blessed is the womb that bore you.[3] Thus that day came to an end.[4]

ii. Luther's second appearance

On the morrow, the fifth after Misericordia,[5] about four in the afternoon, the herald came and fetched Dr. Martin, and led him into the emperor's court. The princes being engaged, he remained in attendance until six o'clock among a great bustle of people, and felt tired on account of the crowd. But when the assembly was seated, and Martin stood in front, the secretary began as follows: His imperial Majesty appointed this hour for you, Martin Luther, when you publicly acknowledged as yours the books which we yesterday mentioned by name. You asked for time to consider your answer to the second question,

[1] Cf. Matt. 10:28
[2] Cf. Luke 12:11   [3] Luke 11:27
[4] For what Luther did that evening, cf. *supra*, p. 133
[5] Thursday, April 18

COLUMN B—*cont.*

Consequently on Thursday, doctor Martin went to the palace shortly after four o'clock, but the hour had turned six before his case came on to be heard. He made a speech which was that of a Christian; it was at once a reply and a defence; he spoke first in Latin and then in German. He explained why he had written and acted as he had done; and concluded by saying that he would have no objection to retracting anything once he had been corrected out of Holy Scripture. And, although his imperial Majesty had threatened to proceed against him in the manner appropriate to such cases, doctor Martin stood his ground firmly, and begged him in God's name not to compel him against his conscience, against God's word; but if and when it was proved

namely, whether you wished any of them to be withdrawn, or whether you stood by all those which you had published. That time has now ended, although by rights you ought not to have asked for a further space for deliberation, for you have known long enough why you were commanded here. Moreover, the question has been certain to all men for so long that anyone, if questioned at any time, could give an assured and trustworthy response, especially one like you, a well-versed professor of theology. You perceived his Majesty's clemency when you asked time for deliberation. Well, now, answer his Majesty's question, Is it your will to defend the books acknowledged as yours, or to retract any of them? The secretary said this in Latin and in German, but more sharply in Latin than in German.

Dr. Martin then replied in Latin and in German, humbly, quietly, and modestly, yet with Christian courage and firmness. But they looked forward with the greatest expectation to his revocation, some hope of which they had conceived from his request for time for deliberation.

from God's word that his writings were erroneous, he would readily retract, and would be the first to burn them and tread them underfoot.

N.B. I shall now give a German translation of the speech delivered by doctor Martin when he appeared before his imperial Majesty on the said Thursday.

The Declaration made by Dr. Martin Luther before the Emperor, Charles, and the princes at Worms on the fifth day after Misericordia Domini

Jesus

Your serene Highness the emperor, most illustrious princes, and most gracious lords, I have come here obediently and by God's mercy, at the time fixed for me yesterday evening. I beg your most serene Majesty and your most illustrious lordships to be willing of your clemency to deign to hear my case which, so I hope, is both just and true. If through inexperience I do not give the proper title to anyone, or by manners and gestures act in any way contrary to the usage of courts, I beg you of your benevolence to pardon me as a man unversed in courts, and knowing only monastic cells. I can only give my testimony with the same straightforwardness as I have hitherto used in my lectures and writings, when what I have had in view was the glory of God and the true upbuilding of those who believe in Christ.

Most serene emperor, most illustrious princes; two questions were put to me yesterday by your serene Majesty, namely, whether I acknowledged certain books written and published in my name, and whether I persisted in defending them or wished to revoke them. I gave a

Doctor Martin's address to his Majesty, the Roman Emperor, the Electors, Princes, and Ruling Classes of the Empire

Most illustrious and most mighty emperor, very illustrious princes, most gracious and gracious lords, I have come here obediently at the date and time set and prescribed to me yesterday evening. I pray by the mercy of God that your imperial Majesty and gracious princes will, as I hope, graciously listen to these questions of righteousness and truth. And if, through my lack of experience, I fail to give anyone his correct title, or act in bearing or manner contrary to the custom of the court, I trust that you will graciously forgive me. I have not been brought up in the courts of princes, but bred and trained in the seclusion of a monastery. The only thing I would wish to say about myself is that, up to the present moment, I have set forth my writings and my teaching with such singleness of mind that my only object has been the glory of God and the much needed instruction of Christian believers.

Most gracious emperor, very gracious and gracious electors, princes, and lords, there were two questions which your imperial Majesty and your graces put to me yesterday, namely, whether I acknowledged as mine certain books, whose titles were read out, and which had been published in my name; secondly, whether I persisted in defending them or

COLUMN A—*cont.*

plain and ready answer to the first question, an answer to which I now, and shall always, adhere. I agree that those books are mine, being published by me under my own name, unless perchance an exception must be made of anything changed in them by the cunning or the incongruous opinions of my enemies. Otherwise I am quite unaware of anything that is not mine alone, written by me alone, except when I have expounded the writings of some one else.

In respect to the second head, I beg that your serene Majesty and your lordships would deign to note that my books are not all of the same sort.

In some of them I have dealt with the faith and morals of the religious life, with the result that even my opponents can do no other than agree that they are valuable, harmless, and obviously worthy, Christian literature. Even the bull, although harsh and hard, grants that some of my books are innocuous; nevertheless it condemns these also—an utterly monstrous judgment. If I were to begin revoking these books, what, I beg you, should I be doing? Should I not be alone among mortal men in condemning that which my friends and my enemies alike acknowledge to be true? should I not be alone in striving against what all have agreed to confess?

K_{ML}

COLUMN B—*cont.*

wished to retract them. I then made a ready and clear answer to the first question; I stand by it and shall always do so. Those very books are mine and are published in my name. It may well be that some of the contents have been changed or twisted, perhaps on account of my faulty style of expression, or misapplied information. I acknowledged nothing as mine except what is entirely mine and wholly written by me. I do not accept any explanation or interpretation put on it by someone else, no matter how carefully done.

As to the second point, I would most respectfully beg your imperial Majesty and your graces, please to note that my books are not all of the same kind. There are some in which I have dealt simply and evangelically with the value of faith and morality; and my worst enemies must grant that these books are useful and innocuous, and that it would be a good thing on all counts for Christian people to read them. Even the papal bull, although otherwise hard and harsh, grants that there is no harm in some of my books, although, inconsistently, it goes on to condemn them. If I were to retract these books at the present juncture, what should I be doing? I should be alone among all men in condemning truths which friends and foes alike acknowledge; I alone would be against, and hostile to, what is universally and rightly accepted.

COLUMN A—*cont*.

A second kind consists of those books in which I have used invective directed against the papacy and the system[1] of the papists; for example, against those who by their most evil doctrines and examples have done great harm to Christendom in both body and soul. Nor can anyone deny or dissemble these facts, for they accord with the experience of all, and are the complaint of everybody. By papal laws and human doctrines, the consciences of Christians are ensnared, tormented, and excoriated. The German nation,[2] as to both its goods and wealth, is especially included here, for they have been eaten up with incredible tyranny, and are being ruthlessly despoiled at the present time in grievous ways. The papists' own decrees, make a proviso that (as in distin. 9 and 25, q.1 and 2[3]) the laws and doctrines of the pope which are contrary to the gospel or the opinions of the fathers, are to be regarded as erroneous and reprobate.

[1] Lat: *res*

[2] Cf. this page, col. B, n. 1

[3] Cf. this page, col. B, n. 3

COLUMN B—*cont*.

There is a second group among my books in which I have attacked the papacy and papal policy and practice; attacking them where their very false teachings and examples have harmed, harassed, and destroyed Christian people in both body and soul. No one can deny it, or pretend that the case is otherwise, because it is common experience and deplored by all men. The papal decrees and other merely human doctrines of theirs hold Christian consciences fast to a most painful degree, oppressing, tormenting, and grieving them. Moreover, goods and possessions are drained away and swallowed up; and this is especially the case with the splendid German nation[1] who are oppressed and ravaged to an incredible extent. To this very day there is no halt in the work of plundering without excuse. The Romanists' own decrees and regulations,[2] e.g. the ninth and the twenty-fifth paragraphs of the first and second sections, say that an ordinance or a doctrine of the pope's which is contrary to the gospel or the opinion of the canonized fathers, must be regarded as erroneous and without effect.[3]

[1] Germ.: *nation*—an early use of the word, and not quite in the modern sense; perhaps *people* would be more accurate

[2] In the canon law

[3] This statement is usually said to be based on the passage in the *Decretum Gratiani*, dist. 9, can. 8, where a person in a spiritual office is referred to the limit of authority given by the word of God

COLUMN A—*cont.*

If, therefore, I revoke these books, I should guarantee nothing except that strength would be added to tyranny, and both the windows and the doors would be opened to this great evil, which would ravage with less restraint and more freedom than it has dared to use till now. The consequence of my revocation would be to strengthen and stabilize that order of things in which their wickedness is quite dissolute and unbridled, and which has long been felt most intolerable by the wretched populace. In particular, if I were to act like this, it would seem to have been done by me with the authority of your serene Majesty and of the whole Roman empire. What an act of wickedness and oppression should I do, O my God!

A third class of these books consists of those which I have written against certain ordinary people thought to be of consequence; in particular those who strove to defend the tyranny exercised by Rome and to undermine the religion taught by me. In these books, I confess myself to have used a sharper tone than accorded with religion or my monastic profession. But I am not excusing myself, nor defending my life; on the other hand, I am discussing the teaching of Christ. Yet I am not fully at liberty to revoke these books because, once again, the

COLUMN B—*cont.*

If I were to revoke these books of mine at the present juncture, I should only be adding force to the Romanist tyranny, and opening, not only the window, but also the door and the gate to a gross and unchristian state of affairs; and this would spread much further, and grow rampant more readily, than has been possible till now. Calling my recantation to witness, the Romanists would exercise, quite unreproved, all their resources of evil arrogantly and impudently against ordinary, defenceless men, and would feel themselves strengthened and justified in so doing. It would be made a particular point that I had recanted at the orders of your imperial Majesty and of the entire Roman empire. O God, what a shameful cover I should then be for wickedness and oppression!

The third group of my books consists of those in which I have attacked certain private and particular individuals, who have taken it upon themselves, on the one hand, to maintain and defend the tyranny of the Romanists; and, on the other, to stamp out the godly way of life which I have been teaching. I freely confess that I have expressed myself rather more vigorously against these people than was appropriate in a religious issue and to one of my profession. I do not pretend that I am a saint; on the other hand, I am not arguing to defend my life, but the consequence of that revocation would be that oppression and impiety would reign in my native land, and would be more rampant among godly people, and rule with greater violence than ever before.

Yet because I am a man and not a god, I can only invoke that protection for my books which my lord, Jesus Christ, himself adduced to His own doctrine. When He was examined about His doctrine in the presence of Annas, and was struck by a servant, He said, If I have spoken evil, testify to the evil.[1] If the Lord himself, who knew He could not err, was not unwilling to listen to views against His own doctrine, even those of a mean slave, how much more should I, a worthless person and unable to avoid error, beg and desire that someone should be willing to bear his witness against my teaching? I therefore pray your most serene Majesty and your most illustrious lordships, by the mercy of God, to let someone, whether of high or low estate, bear his witness, show my errors, and vanquish me by the prophets and gospels of the Bible. When that proof has convinced me, I

[1] John 18:19ff.

teachings of Christ. I find again, therefore, that I cannot retract these books; such a retraction would only mean once more that oppression, cruelty, and all sorts of wickedness would enjoy authority with my consent, my help, and my inaction;[1] they would flourish and exercise power, and treat godly people cruelly and unmercifully, in a manner far worse than they have behaved up to now.

Since I am merely human and not divine, the only way in which I can defend my little books is that which our Lord and Saviour used for His own teaching. When He was questioned by Annas, the high priest, about His teaching, and when He had been struck in the face by the high priest's servant, He replied, If I have spoken wrongly, bear witness to the wrong.[2] Our Lord knew that He could not err, but He did not refuse to hear testimony against His teaching, even though by a base underling of little account. In the same way, I myself, who am but dust and ashes, and cannot avoid error, ought only to be anxious to hear whatever testimony any person may wish to make against my teaching.

Therefore, by the mercy of God, I beseech your imperial Majesty, and your graces, and whoever is of high or low

[1] Germ.: *ruckhaltung*
[2] John 18:23, R.S.V.

COLUMN A—*cont.*

shall be most ready to revoke whatever error I have made, and I shall be the first to fling my books into the fire.

These words are, I believe, a clear answer; and I think I have sufficiently dealt with and assessed the warnings and the perils, the difficulties and dissensions, excited in the world by the spread of my teachings, things for which I was yesterday taken to task seriously and firmly. Yet, from my point of view, it would be a most happy turn of events if the word of God were to become the subject of inquiry and argument. That is but the way and work and consequence of the word of God, for we read: I have not come to bring peace, but a sword; for I have come to set a man against his father, etc.[1] Hence, if we perchance begin by condemning the word of God, we must beware lest what now is most firmly believed does not issue in a flood of intolerable evils, because God is marvellous and terrible in His counsels. Furthermore, care must be taken lest the reign of Charles, this young man who is the best of princes and on whom high hopes are set, become unhappy and inauspicious.

COLUMN B—*cont.*

estate, that you would bear testimony and prove, out of the writings of the prophets and apostles, where I have gone astray. As soon as I am shown, I shall be only too willing and ready to renounce all my errors; and I shall be the first to want to consign my little books to the flames.

From what I have said, it should be obvious and clear that I have properly considered and weighed the danger of quarrels, uproar, and rebellion aroused by my teaching; of all this I was firmly and definitely reminded yesterday. In fact, it gives me the profoundest pleasure and the greatest joy that differences and disagreements have arisen as to the word of God; indeed Christ our Lord Himself said, I have not come to bring peace but a sword; for I have come to set a man against his father, and so forth.[1] We must therefore take into account how wonderful and terrible is God in His counsels, purposes, and plans. Otherwise, if we begin by condemning the word of God, perhaps that which is put forward in order to do away with party spirit and disunity will end with a world-wide flood of intolerable evil. We must take care lest this very religious-minded young man, the emperor Charles, on whom, under God, great hopes are set, makes an inauspicious

[1] Matt. 10:34f.

COLUMN A—*cont.*

I could cite numerous examples from Scripture, for example, Pharaoh, or the king of Babylon, or the kings of Israel, and explain why they foundered completely at the very time when they endeavoured, with the aid of sagest counsels, to rule and establish their kingdoms in peace; "For God it is who ensnares the cunning with their own guile", "and moves mountains before they are aware."[1] God is therefore to be feared. I do not say this because my doctrine or advice are needed for these great problems, but because I ought not to do anything to lessen the loyalty due to Germany, my country. With these remarks I pay my respects to your serene Majesty and to your lordships; and I humbly pray, owing to the zeal of my enemies, that you will not allow me to be regarded as an enemy to yourselves without good cause.

That is all.

When this speech had been delivered, the speaker for the emperor, as if in reproach, said that my answer was not to the point. It was not for me to call in question things which had already been condemned and defined in church councils. He therefore made request for a

[1] Cf. Job 5:13, 9:5

COLUMN B—*cont.*

beginning of his reign as emperor.[1]

I could easily explain and underline many examples drawn from Scripture, and cite Pharaoh, the king of Babylon, the kings of Israel, who wasted much of their time and effort. All they wanted was to pacify and strengthen their kingdoms by very clever plans and projects of their own devising. For God it is who takes the crafty in their craftiness and cunning, and overturns mountains before men are aware how needful it is to fear God.[2]

I speak in this fashion not because I am of the opinion that great rulers such as you need instructing or reminding by me; but because I ought not, and will not, avoid the duty which I owe to Germany, my homeland.

At the same time, I wish to commend myself obediently to your imperial Majesty and your graces. I humbly pray that you will not allow the unpleasantness and disagreeableness of my views to disparage me in your eyes, and bring me into disgrace.

After this utterance, the speaker representing the em-

[1] This last sentence is the reading of the original text, and corresponds well with the Latin version of Al. But the MS. shows signs of an incompleted change to "an unfortunate imperial reign"; cf. *W.*, Vol. VII, p. 873, note on lines 2-3

[2] Cf. Job 5:13, 9:5

COLUMN A—*cont.*

simple reply without horns, whether I would revoke or not.

(Without horns=without ambiguity; cf. "the horns of a dilemma")

COLUMN B—*cont.*

pire[1] interposed as if addressing one who should be rebuked,[2] and declared that I had not answered properly; nor was it permissible to question or to discuss anything which had already been defined, decided, or condemned by councils. Wherefore I was requested to give a simple and straightforward answer: Did I wish to recant or did I not?

[At this point, the Eck-Aleander record makes a fairly extensive addition to what is found elsewhere, an addition consisting of observations to which Aleander seems to have attached much importance as an essential part of the proceedings. It reads as follows:]

When Luther had finished speaking, the secretary, at a nod from the emperor, began:

By rights, Luther, you might well think yourself favoured in that you have been allowed to speak in the presence of a very gracious emperor. He has listened with greater self-restraint while you were speaking than you yourself used in the course of your utterance. Do you think that this very devoted prince was indifferent, or was glad to hear you make charges against the supreme pontiff, and this in a more violent and harsh manner than beseemed one of your religion and profession? Beware lest this habit should grow upon you, and overrule those qualities of moderation and modesty which should govern your conduct.

You were commanded to speak after deliberation on the proposition whether you wished to revoke and retract the books which you have acknowledged, together with their contents. You complain that you will be treated unfairly if

[1] Johann von der Ecken (also called Eck) who was the official representative of the archbishop of Trier; and who was a lawyer and a nobleman. He must not be confused with John Eck of Ingoldstadt, Luther's opponent in the public debate at Leipzig in the summer of 1519

[2] Germ.: *der eyn straffen wolt.* But the whole passage is obscure

all your books are dealt with together in one group without distinction, since they are not all of the same sort and kind. You divide them into three classes, and say that in some you have dealt simply, sincerely, and evangelically, with questions of faith and morals. You say that even your enemies hold that these books are innocuous; moreover, that the apostolic bull, severe and harsh in other respects, attaches no blame to some of them; that if you were to revoke them, you would, in fact, condemn what friends and foes alike approve. Other books are of the kind in which you say that you attacked the pope and the papacy, and tore to shreds their habits, vices, abuses, acts of oppression, and things of that kind; and that you are not free to recant these lest you seem to increase the force of the tyranny.

In the third group are books which you have written against those who defend the oppressions of Rome while weakening and undermining your own religious teachings. But this is why they have been put in as evidence in your cross-examination. You say that if you were to revoke these, then Rome would exercise greater violence in her oppression by virtue of your support than at any earlier period.

Yet in these distinctions, Martin, you have not made a satisfactory classification of your opinions and your books; for those which you have published since the pope's decree are far more inexcusable and deplorable than those which you wrote earlier and which merited condemnation. In them you assert the catholic truth of the heresies already condemned in John Huss; and, equally, you gravely undermine and weaken the entire authority and majesty of councils. Further, in what you said, you did not give a satisfactory answer to my questions. Even granted that some of your books contain nothing harmful, a point that we do not concede; but cut out your pernicious and poisonous dogmas, cut out the blasphemous passages, cut out the heresies and what savours of heresy, cut out the passages hurtful to the catholic faith; then no danger will arise from what is right and proper. His sacred and imperial Majesty is prepared to deal very leniently with these matters; and, if you alter your views, will prevail upon the supreme pontiff not to destroy and blot out the good with the bad. If, however, you obstinately persist in your notorious errors and heresies as up to the present, most certainly all memory of you will be wiped out, and everything, whether right or wrong, together with their author, will be condemned. Nor will this be an innovation or a thing unheard of, seeing that men of old burned the books of the Arians, the Montanists, the Photinians, the Nestorians, and also the Eutichians and other heretics, although they contained much that was devout, catholic, and religious; for there is no doctrine better calculated to deceive than one which mingles a little that is false with much that is true.

Moreover, Martin, you are one who, in the end, retreats to and takes refuge in the place where all the heretics are accustomed to retreat and find refuge. Of course, since you are human and liable to slip and fall, you are ready to be instructed by anyone, whether eminent or humble, on the basis of sacred Scripture; yet to the present time, I think none have tried to do what you say except heretics, and they have always followed the same practice; like them, you want Holy Scripture to be understood according to your own will and wish; and also you have come as the defender of new kinds of heresy, and not those already condemned. Most of the things that you adduce are heresies of the Begards,[1] the Waldenses, the Poor Men of Lyons, of Wyclif, Huss, and others; heresies already exposed by the synods. It is not fitting to reopen questions, and again argue matters upon which the church has pronounced judgment in due form; matters which have to do with its usages, rites, and observances, which the fathers of the church held as the assured faith, and for failure to observe all of which, due penalties and pains are provided.

[1] A medieval religious society founded about 1180 by Lambert of Beghe of Lüttich. After having gained a considerable following, especially among women, it was condemned at the Council of Vienne in 1311 because of its unorthodox doctrine of the Holy Trinity. Many members were burnt by the inquisition, more particularly after 1366; but after the council of Constance in 1415, it was regarded more favourably. The order did not survive after the Reformation, but traces still remain in Holland and Belgium though with meagre prospects

Nay, they would rather undergo a thousand deaths than depart from them in any way. And do you want us to deviate from the narrow path in which our fathers faithfully trod?

If the Jews, Turks, Saracens, and other sects which are hostile to our faith were to hear of all this, what would they say? Surely, they would break into laughter! Surely they would mock when, now at length, we Christians debate whether we have hitherto believed aright. I beg you, Martin, do not claim that you, I mean you alone, one man, know the Scriptures; that you alone grasp the true sense of sacred Scripture, the sense to which the most consecrated doctors have devoted great efforts and assiduity by day and night in expounding the Scriptures. Do not rate your opinion before that of so many, very eminent men. Do not think that you know better than they all. Do not throw doubt on the most holy, orthodox faith, the faith which was founded by Christ the perfect legislator, and preached by the apostles throughout the world; which miracles illuminated, and martyrs confirmed with their red blood. Moreover, sainted doctors have discussed the obscure passages of the prophets, and disclosed the greatest mysteries of both the Old and the New Testaments; discussed the reasons with heretics, and shed on them the light of day. The faith has been confirmed by the definitions of sacred councils; and what the learned have discussed as doctrines, the church has defined as decisions. It is the faith in which the fathers and our ancestors trusted when they died, and which they transmitted as our heritage. We are prohibited from disputing it by the laws of the emperor and the pontiff; and, since no amount of argument or discussion leads to a final conclusion, they will condemn those who, in their impudence and temerity, refuse to submit to what the church has determined; and will impose the penalties which are provided and have been published.

As for the rest of your remarks, Martin, partly to save time, and partly because they are irrelevant to the business in hand, I purposely ignore them.

It is therefore useless, Martin, for you to expect a discussion of those subjects which you hold and believe to be assured and certain faith. For this reason, I must again and again insist and demand that you give your answer sincerely, frankly, unambiguously, and without horns. Do you choose, or do you not choose, to revoke and retract your books and the errors that they contain and that you have disseminated?[1]

COLUMN A—*cont.*   COLUMN B—*cont.*

My reply.

Since then your serene Majesty and your lordships request a simple reply, I will give it without horns and hoofs, and say: Unless I am convinced by the testimony of Scripture or by plain reason (for I believe in neither the pope nor in councils alone, for it is well-known, not only that they have erred, but also have contradicted themselves), I am mastered by the passages of Scripture which I have quoted, and my conscience is captive to the word of God.[2] I cannot and will not recant, for it is neither safe nor honest to violate one's conscience. I can do no other. Here I take my stand, God being my helper.[3] Amen.[4]

The princes proceeded to discuss the speech made by doctor Martin. When they had examined it, the secretary from Trier began to pull it to pieces in the manner agreed on. He said, You have not answered as modestly as beseemed one of your standing, and, moreover,

[1] At this point, Aleander's account resumes its close similarity with the anonymous record

[2] Cf. *infra*, pp. 179f. and 180, n. 3

[3] The last clauses, from "I can do no other", were said in German

[4] Aleander's second main variant occurs at this point, when he gives a brief conclusion, followed by a list of the books which served as exhibits. This variant will be given *infra*, pp. 158ff.

COLUMN A—*cont.*   COLUMN B—*cont.*

not to the point. You have classified the books in such a way that none of them contribute anything to the issue. However, if you were to revoke those which contain a large proportion of your errors, no doubt his Majesty, by his natural clemency, would not take proceedings against you in regard to the rest which are unexceptionable. It is a further point that you have brought up subjects condemned by the general council of Constance which represented the whole German nation; and you ask to be convinced by Scripture. Here you have gone seriously astray. It could be of no value to debate anew subjects condemned by church and council throughout the world, unless perchance every single thing must be defended to any upstart. If the point were to be granted that whoever denies the opinion of council or church, must be refuted by Scripture, we should have nothing certain or settled throughout Christendom. This is the reason why his Majesty the emperor asked for a plain and straightforward reply from you, either positive or negative. Now, do you wish to defend all your books as catholic? or, on the other hand, to revoke any of them?

But doctor Martin put no further question, lest his Majesty should allow him to be compelled to revoke contrary to his conscience, which was

COLUMN A—*cont.*

bound and fettered by the Holy Scriptures; and without the advantage of having heard clear arguments from those who spoke against him.

He replied that he had been asked for a simple and direct answer without horns, and that he could give no other reply than that which he had already given: unless his adversaries could bring sufficient arguments to bear, and could free his conscience from what they called his errors, he would be unable to escape from the toils in which he was involved. Moreover, councils had not always reached true decisions, and had often reached conclusions at variance with previous decisions. Hence the arguments of those who contradicted him were of no avail. He could show that councils had erred. He could not recant what Scripture repeatedly taught. At this point, he cried finally, May God help me.

The secretary made no reply to this except to say very briefly that it was impossible to prove a council to have erred; but Martin maintained that he was both able and willing.

Since darkness had by now fallen on the whole auditorium, each went off to his own home. Luther, that man of God, left the presence and tribunal of his imperial Majesty, and was followed by a good part of the Spaniards with cries of indignation, much derision, and prolonged protest.

COLUMN B—*cont.*

To this I rejoined, Since your imperial Majesty and your graces desire a simple answer, I will give an unobjectionable and inoffensive answer on this issue. My position is then that I must be overmastered by the testimony of Holy Scripture, or overmastered by self-evident reasoning—for I believe neither in the pope nor in councils alone, because it is as clear as the day that they have often erred and contradicted themselves. I am overmastered by the Scriptures adduced by me, and my conscience is prisoner to God's Word. The result is that I neither can nor will revoke, because it is hard, hurtful, and dangerous to do anything contrary to conscience. God help me. Amen.[1]

[1] A rather later edition of Spalatin's version gives the concluding words as "There is nothing else I can do. Here stand I. God help me. Amen."

Other forms, rather later again, give the whole paragraph from "I am overmastered by the Scriptures adduced by me . . ." in the following form: "The fact is that I am bound by the writings which I have published and written. And, because my conscience is held prisoner by the word of God, I neither can nor will alter or retract a single word; and a further reason is that it is dangerous and hurtful to act against conscience:" Von der Ecken, "Martin, if you refuse to retract anything, his Majesty will let the good and the evil remain together, and suppress both, lest anything at all survive. For

[After Luther had said, Here I take my stand, God being my helper (see p. 155, *supra*), the Eck-Aleander account has the following brief conclusion, together with a list of the books used as exhibits.]

When Luther had made this reply, and the whole assembly, fatigued by the crowd and the heat, were preparing to depart, the secretary already mentioned[1] cried out in a few words because of the shortness of time, Depose the conscience, Martin, which you claim to dispose, because it is in error, and you will be on safe and sound ground if you revoke. When you say that councils have erred, you will never be able to prove it, especially as regards the faith; and even in morals I think it will be very difficult.

To this Martin rejoined that he could prove his contentions.

Then the assembly dispersed.

The Exhibits

Martin Luther's books written in German[2]

Of Good Works
Of Christian Liberty
To the German Nobility
Of the New Testament and the Mass
Defence of the Articles, in German
To the Secretary at Stolpen
An Appeal to a Council
A Booklet designated J. G.[3]
What Readers are to Reply when Accused of Reading Martin's Books
A sermon on the Picture of a Man with a Shepherd's Staff

---

what has formerly been condemned by councils, must never be called in question. You would not wish to assert that councils have erred." Luther, "It is possible for councils to err, and they have erred. That is as plain as the day, and I am willing to prove it, God being my helper. Amen. That is my position." It will be noticed that in only one version does the famous phrase occur: Here I stand. The revised version says: *Da bin ich*, with the meaning given in the translation, cf. *W*, 877n.

[1] von der Eck of Trier   [2] The list gives brief titles in Latin

[3] John Grunenberg

A second quarto volume entitled, *To the Goat.*
A certain book of eight quires against the Pope[1]

In Latin

A large folio volume printed at Basle[2]
On the Pagan Servitude (De captivitate babylonica)
A Defence of the Articles
Of Good Works
A Commentary on the Lord's Prayer
An Appeal to a Council
Why the Pope's Books were Burned
A Sermon on Preparing for Death
A Commentary on the First Thirteen Psalms[3]
Against the Execrable Antichristian Bull

COLUMN A—*cont.*

*(Continuation of the anony-
mous Latin account from the end
of the Aleander-Eck addition.)*[4]

On the sixth day after
Misericordia Domini,[5] when the
electoral princes, the dukes,
and the nobility of whatever
rank who were accustomed to
be present at consultations, had
assembled, the emperor sent a
document, written with his own
hand and having the following
contents:[6]

Most of us, including the
Christian rulers, shall be as
faithful as ever to the Roman

COLUMN B—*cont.*

[1] Cf. *W.*, Vol. VI, 281, A

[2] *M. Lutheri lucubrationum pars una. Basilae in aedibus Adae Petri
M.D. XX Mense Julio*

[3] Cf. *W.*, Vol. V., 13, B

[4] At this point a similar account begins from an unknown source in
German; cf. *W.*, Vol. VII, pp. 841ff., *infra*, pp. 161f.

[5] Friday, April 19

[6] This declaration, dated April 19, 1521, was written by the emperor himself in French. It was often reprinted in a Latin translation, but the original
French document was first published in *Reichtagsakten*, No. 82, pp. 595ff.

church which doctor Martin has recently impugned. Since he is unwilling to depart a hairsbreadth from his errors, we ourselves are unable with self-respect to depart from the example of our ancestors in maintaining the ancient faith and affording help to the see of Rome. We shall prosecute with excommunication Martin himself and his adherents, and whatever else may seem to require bringing to an end.

But the agreement which he had signed and sealed, the emperor refused to break; and he would in fact take care that Luther returned safely to the place whence he had set out.

The electoral princes, the dukes, and the estates of the empire discussed Charles's communication all that afternoon, and so, too, for the whole of Saturday, the day following. The result was that Dr. Martin remained without an answer during this time.[1]

Meanwhile, he was seen and visited by many princes, counts, barons, knights, noblemen, priests, both secular and religious, to say nothing of numerous ordinary people. These last always crowded the court and could not gaze enough.

It should also be said that two placards had been posted up, one against the doctor, and the other, it seems, favouring

[1] The German version says that no reply was received by Luther even on the Sunday (of Jubilate, April 21)

COLUMN A—*cont.*   COLUMN B—*cont.*

the doctor.[1] But the latter was considered by many people, including persons of under-standing, to have been done cunningly by his enemies, in order to afford an excuse for breaking the safe-conduct, an excuse which the Roman legates were not actively seek-ing.

[At this point, the German account, which has so far resembled the Latin version, preserves two paragraphs recording the events on Monday, April 22. Nothing of this appears in the anonymous Latin version. The two para-graphs are as follows:]

On Monday, the day following Jubilate, his imperial Majesty sent to the imperial council a message[2] to this effect: After his Majesty had thought over the Luther affair, his Majesty regretted having put forward his earlier suggestion, which he had recently placed before them in accordance with the copy in his own handwriting, because Luther's will remained obstinate. Nevertheless, his Majesty commanded that certain persons should negotiate with him, and test whether he was, or was not, willing to recant the condemned articles; and further, in order to keep the business within bounds, that Luther should not remain more than three days in Worms; and, in case he did not wish to recant, care should be taken that he left immediately.[3]

The princes and noblemen took careful note of his imperial Majesty's command, and had no wish to raise any objection, except that, if doctor Martin was unwilling to recant, the ban of excommunication should not be published before the

---

[1] *Pro* Luther was the placard beginning "Down with the nobility . . ." and ending with "B.B.B." i.e. *Bundshuh, Bundshuh, Bundshuh* (i.e. wooden shoe, or sabot, as worn by the peasantry; the word was later of immense significance in the Peasants' War of 1525). This placard was posted on several public buildings during the night of April 19-20, see references in *W.*, Vol. VII, p. 843, and *RA.*, pp. 559, 28ff.

[2] Or: written communication—on a variant reading

[3] The actual wording of the emperor's message on April 22 is unknown. Cf. Brieger, *op. cit.*, 159ff. Kalkoff, *Wormser Reichtag*, 82ff., and note in *W.*, Vol. VII, p. 842

time when he arrived home again. Although it was opposed by a few who were unfriendly to doctor Martin, the motion was agreed. It was then decided to send him a deputation consisting of an elector, a duke, a representative of the town, and several doctors, to negotiate with him as to whether he would recant the condemned books or not.[1]

COLUMN A—*cont.*

On the second day after Jubilate[2] before breakfast, the archbishop of Trier sent word to doctor Martin that he must appear before him on the fourth day at six o'clock before dinner in a place which would be told him in the meantime. On St. George's day,[3] the messenger returned by order of the prince archbishop of Trier to say that he should come next day at the hour specified to the quarters of his principal.

On the fourth day following the feast of St. George, as appointed, doctor Martin was conducted by a priest and a herald of the empire and brought into the quarters of the archbishop of Trier. The herald was followed by the counts of Thuringia and Saxony, beside some others who were exceedingly friendly. Then, in the presence of the archbishop of Trier, Marquis Joachim of Brandenburg, duke George of Saxony, the bishops of Augsburg,[4] and of Brandenburg,[5] the Master of the Teutons,[6] Count George Würtheim,

COLUMN B—*cont.*

After this, they let doctor Martin alone till the Wednesday[7] after St. George's day, and had no negotiations at all with him during this time. Meanwhile, his imperial Majesty gave stern orders that he, and all his adherents, should be under the closest surveillance,[8] and that the empire should be advised accordingly.

On the said Wednesday, in the presence of the archbishop of Trier,[9] the grand-duke Joachim of Brandenburg, electors, *et al.*, duke George of Saxony, the bishops of Augsburg[10] and Brandenburg,[11] Graf

[1] At this point we return to the anonymous Latin document, which is again in general followed by the account in German by Spalatin
[2] Tuesday, April 22   [3] April 23   [4] Christopher von Stadion
[5] Jerome Scultetus   [6] Order of Knights: Dietrich von Cleen
[7] April 24   [8] By his declaration of April 19   [9] Richard von Greiffenklau
[10] Christopher von Stadion   [11] Jerome Scultetus

COLUMN A—*cont.*

doctor Bock of Strassburg, and doctor Peutinger, doctor Vehus,[1] the confidential adviser of the Marquis of Baden, began to speak and put the following case: That he had not been called there to engage in controversy or debate, but that, solely by the Christian charity and clemency of his imperial Majesty, the princes had been asked to entreat him in a kindly and fraternal way. Moreover, although they had promulgated varying views, councils had not promulgated anything self-contradictory; and even if they had erred very seriously, that did not detract from their authority to the extent that anyone might lean on his own opinions contrary to them. He introduced many remarks on the centurion[2] and Zaccheus,[3] and also about human institutions, ceremonies, and statutes; and affirmed that all these were devoted to reprehending evils according to their degree and the changes due to time. Nor could the church do without human institutions. A tree was known by its fruits,[4] and it could be said that many good things had been born of the laws. He granted that St. Martin, St. Nicolas, and many other saints had been put to death by councils; but he went on to say that his books would excite great commotions, and incredible tumults; that the

COLUMN B—*cont.*

George of Wertheim, *et al.*, the chancellor of Baden[1] read out a long memorandum in German in the lodgings of the archbishop of Trier, with the object of inducing doctor Martin to modify what he had said.

[1] Jerome Vehus

---

[1] Cf. his letter to Philip of Baden, *R.A.*, 86, pp. 611ff.
[2] Matt. 8:8ff   [3] Luke 19:6ff
[4] Matt. 12:33

populace had made wrong use
of his booklet, *The Freedom
of a Christian,*[1] in throwing
aside their yoke and in con-
firming their disobedience. Far
otherwise was it now than when
believers had one heart and
one mind.[2] Here was the place
of laws. Moreover, it should be
remembered that, while he had
written many things that were
in an unexceptionable spirit,
as his *De Triplici Justitia,*
and similar works, the devil was
using this fact now to set
hidden snares in order that all
his works might be condemned
in perpetuity. For he was to be
judged by the most recent of
his writings, just as a tree is to
be judged, not by its blossom,
but by its fruit. At this point,
he added remarks about the
demon at midday, and the go-
between carrying through business in the shadows, and the
arrow flying in darkness.[3]

The speech as a whole was
admonitory, with rhetorical
passages on the usefulness and
benefits of the laws; on the
other hand, it was full of the
perils of conscience, and of well-
being, whether public or
private. Both at the beginning,
in the middle, and at the end,
he made the same point, that
this exhortation was due to the
most propitious goodwill and
the very singular clemency of
the princes. Coming to the
peroration, he added threats
and said that, if Luther should
persevere in his propositions,

[1] Cf. our Vol. I, pp. 349ff.
[2] Cf. Acts 4:32   [3] Cf. Ps. 91:5f.

the emperor would take action;
he would expel him from the
empire, and would confiscate
his possessions. He urged him
to think over and weigh these
and the remaining considerations.

Dr. Martin replied: Most
gracious and most illustrious
princes and lords, I give you
my most humble thanks for the
most gracious and most kindly
intention on which your admonition is based. I recognize
that I am a person far too
humble in station to be worthy
of the admonitions of great
princes like you. I did not
condemn all the councils, but
rather that of Constance; and
this one chiefly because it
condemned the word of God,
as in the case of the article
where it condemned John Huss:
"The church of Christ is the
community of those predest-
ined." This the council condemned, and similarly this
article of faith, "I believe in the
Holy Catholic Church." He did
not refuse to give his life and
blood, provided he were not
constrained to the extent of
being compelled to revoke the
plain word of God; for one
ought to obey God rather than
man in defending it. There was
a twofold difficulty: the first,
that of Christian virtue, and
second, that of faith; Christian
virtue having to do with
morals and life; and the other,
of faith or doctrine, where the
word of God could not be dis-
regarded. According to that
word, it was inevitable that

Without hesitation doctor
Martin gave a Christian's
answer.

COLUMN A—*cont.*   COLUMN B—*cont.*

Christ would be a rock of offence.[1] If the faith were truthfully preached, and if the magistrates were good men, one law, that of the gospel, would be enough, and human laws would be unprofitable. He was aware that we must obey magistrates and those in authority, even if their lives were evil and wicked. He knew that he must yield to what was right and proper, and that was what he had taught in his own writings. So long as he was not driven to deny the word of God, he would show himself most obedient in all other respects.

When Dr. Martin had retired, the princes discussed what they should order to be done with this man. He was then called back into the room, and doctor Vehus of Baden recited the main points, and urged that he should submit his writings to the adjudication of the emperor and the empire.

Doctor Martin then withdrew. When his presence was further required, the above mentioned chancellor again urged him to modify what he had said, and surrender his writings to the adjudication of his imperial Majesty and the empire.

Dr. Martin answered modestly and submissively that he did not grant, and would not grant, that the truth could be determined by the emperor, the leaders, and the ruling ranks of the empire; but he was far from fearing investigation by them; and he would allow his works to be tested most minutely and examined most narrowly, always granted that the basis was the authority of sacred Scripture and the

Doctor Martin then answered in a modest manner, and said that he was prepared and pleased to surrender his writings into the hands not only of his imperial Majesty and the empire, but also of the lowliest person; and that he himself would make the sharpest of attacks on those writings, always provided that what he did was in accord with God's word. All this took place before noon on that Wednesday.

[1] Luke 2:34

word of God.[1] The word of
God, indeed, was so clear to
him that he was unable to
make concessions unless better
instructed by the word of God.
St. Augustine had written and
taught, however, that this
weight attached only to the
books that were canonical, and
to be believed as true. Other
doctors, no matter how great
their sanctity, were to be
believed according as they
wrote what was true. St. Paul
wrote to the Thessalonians on
this point when he said, Prove
all things, hold fast to what is
good,[2] and to the Galatians,
Even if an angel came from
heaven, and preached otherwise, let him be anathema,[3]
and not be believed. So much
the more did he beg that they
would not constrain his conscience, which was bound and
fettered to Scripture and the
word of God;[4] and that both for
themselves and to the em-
peror they would hold him in a
favourable light. No matter
how submissive he was, there
was nothing further he could
do.

When he had said this, the
elector of Mark Brandenburg
asked whether his point was
that he would not give way
unless convinced by Holy
Scripture. Dr. Martin's answer:
That is so, most gracious lord,

[1] This phraseology implies the
vastly important distinction between the text of the Bible and the
word of God. Cf. *infra*, p. 170

[2] 1 Thess. 5:21   [3] Gal. 1:8f.

[4] Cf. *supra*, p. 131, n. 3

COLUMN A—*cont.*   COLUMN B—*cont.*

or by the clearest and plainest reasons.

The meeting then closed, and while the other princes went out into the court, the archbishop of Trier called Dr. Martin into his dining room, together with his secretary, John von Eck, and Cocleus.[1] With Martin were Jerome Schurff and Amsdorf.[2] The secretary began to plead like a barrister, and said, Almost always heresies derive from the Holy Scriptures: for example, Arianism from the verse, My Father is greater than I[3] and, secondly, from this passage of the gospel, Joseph knew not his wife until she gave birth to her first-born son.[4] From that he went on to try to prove that the catholic church was the communion of the saints. He even endeavoured to make wheat out of weeds, and limbs from the excrement of the body. Dr. Martin and Dr. Jerome twitted and reproached him for these remarks and other foolish talk. John Cocleus broke in noisily, trying to persuade him to abandon his thesis, but without effect. At length they separated. The archbishop asked them to come back in the afternoon, but his secretary and Cocleus did not agree.

After dinner, Cocleus cunningly waylaid Dr. Martin in his lodgings with very odious suggestions (for which he was

[1] Often spelt Cochlaeus
[2] Cf. Vol. I, p. 109
[3] John 14:28   [4] Matt. 1:25

COLUMN A—*cont.*

suitably reproved by Jerome, John, and Tilemann Conradi); he even dared to suggest that Dr. Martin should renounce his safe-conduct and engage in public debate with him, and, after being urged to do so, that he should revoke. Dr. Martin, however, with remarkable gentleness and frankness, dealt with him in a kindly manner and urged him to depart in order that he himself should not be carried away too much by his own feelings; and when he wrote, he would bring to bear against him the authority of Holy Scripture; otherwise, Cocleus would effect nothing.

In the evening the archbishop of Trier informed Dr. Martin, Amsdorf acting as go-between, that the safe-conduct had been extended by his Majesty to them both, in order that he might be able in the meantime to negotiate with him. With this object, doctor Peutinger and Dr. Vehus of Baden would come to him on the morrow; and, indeed, he himself would negotiate with him.

On the fifth day of the week, St. Mark's day,[1] in the forenoon, Peutinger and Vehus of Baden tried to persuade Dr. Martin that he should frankly and fully submit his writings to the adjudication of the emperor and the empire. He replied that he would do and allow anything and everything, if only those things rested on the authority of Holy Scripture;

COLUMN B—*cont.*

On Thursday, St. Mark's day,[1] the chancellor of Baden and doctor Peutinger visited doctor Martin, and tried to persuade him to surrender his books to the judgment of his imperial Majesty and the empire, and to make no conditions. Then doctor Martin responded that there was nothing he desired from his imperial Majesty and the empire, except

[1] April 25

COLUMN A—*cont.*

in no case would he agree to anything less. For one thing, God, speaking through the prophet, had said, Put not your trust in princes, nor in the sons of men, in whom there is no help;[1] for another, Cursed be the man that trusteth in man.[2] When they pressed him more urgently, he replied, Nothing is less subject to man's judgment than the word of God.[3] They then left him, but asked that he would consider giving a more favourable reply, and that they would return after dinner.

They came back in the afternoon, and attempted to persuade him in the same manner as had been useless in the morning. They begged that he would submit his case at all events to a future council. He agreed on the condition that they showed him the passages culled from his books that they proposed to submit to the council, and also that they should bring the meaning drawn from these passages to the testimony of Scripture and the word of God. Then they drew aside from Dr. Martin and suggested to the archbishop of Trier that he should promise to submit his points

COLUMN B—*cont.*

that they should pronounce on his books on the basis of Holy Scripture. In this, they had no hope of succeeding.

They came again, nevertheless, in the afternoon and made the following proposal: that he should submit the whole matter to the judgment of a council. Doctor Martin agreed, but on the understanding that they drew up the agenda beforehand and let him see it, and also that the council should reach a verdict based on God's word.

[1] Ps. 146:3   [2] Jer.: 175
[3] Obviously, L. is being hard pressed and has his back to the wall. As far as his adversaries are concerned, he very closely identifies the word of God with the text of Scripture, or with certain passages of Holy Writ. But the distinction is again clear in the following paragraph

COLUMN A—*cont.*

under a few heads to the council, but that in fact, he should say nothing about them.[1] This was a suggestion that was not for a single moment entertained by Dr. Martin, who up till then had constantly set his face against the slightest detraction from or modification of anything appertaining to the word of God.

The outcome, by the gift of God, was that the archbishop of Trier summoned Dr. Martin for a personal hearing. There he made a different assertion from what he understood the doctors to say. He declared that it would not easily have been put right unless he had heard him for himself. For otherwise, he would have gone immediately to the emperor and repeated what the doctors had reported.

The archbishop dealt very gently with doctor Martin, in the first instance without the presence of any witnesses, about the adjudication both of the emperor and the empire on the one hand, and on the other, of a council. During this conversation, Dr. Martin concealed nothing from the archbishop; he showed how very unsafe it would be to surrender a matter of this importance to men who condemned, and attacked with new demands, one summoned under a safe-conduct, and men who approved,

---

[1] Whether this suggestion was ever made is a point which Vehus afterwards vehemently denied. Cf. *W.,* Vol. VII, 853, footnote 1 on this passage

COLUMN B—*cont.*

Later on, my lord of Trier[1] sent for doctor Martin, spoke in a friendly way, warned him that perhaps the very articles would be selected which the council at Constance had condemned. Dr. Martin then replied that those articles must not be touched.[2] Since that very council had condemned the word of God, he neither could nor would keep silent about it.

---

[1] The archbishop
[2] *mugen keyn handlung leyden*

COLUMN A—*cont.*

moreover, of the opinions and the bull of the pope.

When a friend of his had been admitted,[1] the archbishop asked Dr. Martin what means he could suggest for meeting the present situation. Luther replied that there was nothing better than what Gamaliel had advised in the fifth chapter of Acts, on the testimony of St. Luke, namely, If this plan is of men, this affair will come to nothing; but if it is of God, you will not be able to destroy it.[2] The emperor and the orders of the empire could write and say this to the Roman pontiff. For he knew that if what he had advanced was not from God, within three years, if not two, it would perish of itself.

The archbishop asked what he would do if the heads which were to be submitted to the council were chosen out. Luther replied to this that he did not mind provided that they were not those which had been condemned at the council of Constance. The archbishop said he feared those would be the very articles. To this Luther rejoined that, about those particular heads, he could not and would not keep silence, because he was positive that the word of God had been condemned by the decrees issued at Constance, and that he would rather lose his life and his head than depart from the utterly clear word of the Lord.

[1] George Spalatin; cf. *W.*, Vol. VII, p. 854, note 1
[2] Cf. Acts 5:38f., R.S.V.

COLUMN B—*cont.*

Further, doctor Martin answered a question put by my lord of Trier, and said that he knew of no better way of settling the affair than following Gamaliel's advice in Acts, chapter 5. For, when the high priests of the Jews planned to prohibit and forbid the holy apostles from preaching Christ, Gamaliel said, Leave these people in peace; for if their undertaking is human, it will fail; but if it derives from God, you will be unable to hinder or uproot it.[1]

[1] Acts 5:38ff.

COLUMN A—*cont.*

When the archbishop saw that Dr. Martin would never submit the word of God to the adjudication of men, he dismissed him in a kindly manner; and when Martin inquired whether he would kindly obtain from his Majesty consent to go unhindered, he replied that he would attend to it carefully, and let him know.

Thus a short time later, the archbishop's secretary, in the presence of the chancellor of Austria[1] and of Maximilian,[2] one of the confidants of the emperor, spoke to Dr. Martin in his lodgings; and, as commanded by the emperor, said, Although he had often been admonished, but in vain, by the emperor, the electors, the princes, and the orders, he refused to return to the fold[3] and to the unity, it remained for the emperor as the legal defender of the catholic faith to take the next step. Accordingly the emperor commanded that within twenty-one days he should return to the security of his home under the safe-conduct guarding his freedom; and that, on the journey, neither by preaching nor by writing should he rouse the people.

The Father, that most Christian of men, began his reply as follows: All has taken place according as it pleased the Lord. Blessed be the name of the Lord.[4] Before anything

COLUMN B—*cont.*

About six o'clock that evening, von Eck of Trier with the chancellor of Austria and Maximilian, the emperor's secretary, gave notice regarding doctor Martin that he must be home in Wittenberg within twenty-one days. His safe-conduct would hold good, etc. There was subjoined an order that he was not to preach *en route*, not to write, nor to do anything that would rouse the people.

Doctor Martin's response began with the words, "All has happened according to God's will. Blessed be the name of the Lord."[1] He then expressed his most humble thanks to his imperial Majesty and to the whole empire for all the grace

[1] Cf. Job 1:21

[1] John Schnaidpeck
[2] M. von Sevenberghen
[3] *ad cor*   [4] Cf. Job 1:21

COLUMN A—*cont.*

else, I humbly thank his serene Majesty, the emperor, the electoral princes, and the other orders of the empire for hearing me with goodwill and clemency, and for keeping, and promising to keep the freeconduct. I have never desired anything in these proceedings beyond a reformation in accordance with Holy Scripture as warmly urged by me. In other respects, I am willing to suffer anything for his imperial Majesty and the empire, life or death, fame or disgrace; and the only reservation I shall make is freedom to confess and testify to the word of the Lord. I commend and subject myself to his imperial Majesty and the whole empire.

On the morrow, therefore, namely the sixth day after Jubilate, on April 26, he said farewell to his protectors and friends who gathered to him in great numbers. After breakfast, he left there about ten o'clock in the morning accompanied by those who had attended him on his forward journey, and by doctor Jerome Schurff, the Wittenberg lawyer. Caspar Sturm, the herald, followed a few hours after he had set out, found him at Oppenheim and, with an oral order from the emperor Charles, bade him farewell.

And so may God preserve to His church and His word for a very long time this most devout-minded man, born for defending and teaching the gospel. Amen.

COLUMN B—*cont.*

which they had shown him; also for having maintained the safe-conduct and proposing to extend it. He submissively expressed his intention of showing humble obedience at all times to his imperial Majesty, and to allow nothing on earth to weigh more with him except only the free word of God, and his right to confess it and testify to it. He then paid his dutiful respects to his imperial Majesty and the whole empire.

The next day, Friday,[1] he set out at ten o'clock in the morning and reached Oppenheim that day.

God grant grace and firmness in His holy Word to all Christian people for their comfort, salvation, and happiness. Amen.

Among[2] all the hostile people, doctor John Cocleus, otherwise Schneck of Nüremberg, was the harshest, most begrudging, and adverse to the pious-minded and kindly doctor Martin. He is now dean to our dear women at Frankfort-am-Main, and he even ventured to suggest that he should blot

[1] April 26
[2] This final paragraph, in the original document, is separated from the preceding by a line, apparently to show that it was a postscript.

COLUMN A—*cont.*

COLUMN B—*cont.*

out[1] the safe-conduct and that he would publicly debate with him, etc.

[1] The wording of the suggestion is obscure: *ausschreiben* usually means something like *write out*, but in this context, *delete* seems possible. But who is meant by the "he" after "suggest that"?

A LETTER FROM LUTHER TO THE EMPEROR, CHARLES V, WRITTEN ON SUNDAY, APRIL 28, 1521

Introduction

THIS letter was written in Latin on Sunday April 28, 1521, two days after Luther had left Worms and while he was still on his way back to Wittenberg. He had now reached Friedberg in Hesse, near the river Nidda, about sixty miles from Worms, and forty miles from Oppenheim where he had lodged the first night.

The purpose of the letter was to explain in writing and to defend his attitude in Worms; it is a recital of the main points that he had tried to make. The chief importance of the letter is that this comes from Luther's own hand, and is thus a valuable check on the other accounts that have survived and especially those that we have reproduced.[1] In general, the letter agrees with the account in the anonymous Latin record, and with that made by Spalatin which was printed in haste in Wittenberg as soon as the MS. arrived there.[2] But the differences are instructive: they give some additional details, throw light on Luther's feelings, and stress what he regarded as the essentials which Charles would be likely to accept. The tone of the letter as a whole is, however, the most revealing feature, for it betrays the almost intolerable strain of the past months and especially the last few days, a strain which was even now by no means over. He holds tenaciously, but rather plaintively, to his main points. Probably this is the only document which reveals this mood, in which he had hopes (although tinged with a certain fear) that he would get safely back to Wittenberg.

Secondly, it shows that Luther attached as much importance to the stand he took in the subsequent negotiations as he did to his speech in the imperial council.

Thirdly, it is of great value on account of its clear, if brief, statement of his doctrine of the word of God.[3]

Immediately after completing this letter, he wrote to the princes in German a letter which is a close translation of the present, but which appears to show traces of Spalatin's handiwork. It adds nothing of substance to the Latin text of the present letter; but that it should have been written at all, proves how anxious Luther was that the princes, some of whom understood very little Latin, and many of whom may not have grasped what was said on April 18, should be clear about the essential issues.

[1] Cf. *supra*, pp. 137ff.   [2] *Supra*, p. 135   [3] Cf. *infra*, p. 180 and n. 3

He also wrote much in the same terms, and much to the same purpose, the following Friday, May 3, to Albert of Mansfeld at the instance of Rudolf von Watzdorf, by which time Luther had reached Eisenach.[1]

The following translation is based on the text printed in the Weimar Edition of Luther's correspondence, Vol. II, No. 401, pp. 306ff.

THE LETTER

To the most serene and invincible doctor, Charles V, the elected emperor of the Romans, Caesar Augustus, king of the Spains, of both Sicilies, and of Jerusalem, etc., archduke of Austria, duke of Burgundy, etc., and my most gracious lord.[2]

Jesus

May grace and peace be given you, with due submission, in Jesus Christ our Lord. Most serene and invincible emperor, and most gracious lord, when your Majesty gave me a safe-conduct and a free pass, and commanded me to come to Worms in order that you might examine what I had in my mind regarding the books which I had published, I came[3] with due humility and obedience, and appeared before your sacred Majesty and all the orders of the empire. The first proposition that your sacred Majesty ordered[4] should be put to me, was whether I acknowledged as mine certain books whose titles were read out; and whether I was willing

[1] Cf. *Br.*, Vol. II, No. 404, pp. 319ff.

[2] In the original MS. preserved in Leipzig, following the address, a note in Spalatin's hand reads: "1521 This letter to the emperor was never sent because, in the difficult times, there was for a long while no one who could deliver it." On the inside of the page, near the top on the left, another note in Spalatin's hand says; "Dr. M. Luther to the Roman emperor, Charles V, regarding the council at Worms." To the right it reads: 1519—an obvious oversight

[3] Luther's coming had been greatly doubted before he actually set out; it was not thought he would dare to leave the safety and security of Wittenberg and the protection of the elector Frederick there

[4] These questions had been agreed in advance after long and strenuous debates, cf. Kalkoff, *Wormser Reichstag* pp. 50ff., and cf. the same author's *Briefe, Depeschen, und Berichte über Luther vom Wormser Reichstage, 1521*, esp. pp. 40ff., Aleander to John Mayr von Eck, February 17, 1521; etc.

to retract them, or wished to stand by them. I first acknowledged that the books were mine except insofar as my enemies might have altered anything by cunning glosses or other devices. With much respect and with a humble mind, I made clear what was my view. My books had been buttressed by me with plain and straightforward passages of Scripture. I could not, in honesty and fairness, run any risk of denying the word of God, or revoke my books, or be thought to have done so. I humbly prayed that your sacred Majesty would in no way allow me to be forced to a revocation of this character; but, on the contrary, that your own self, or some other person of whatever rank, and however lowly, if one could be found suitable for the task, would examine my books and refute by Holy Scripture, in particular by the gospels and the prophets, those errors which, it was pleaded, they contained. For my part, if I were refuted, and convicted of error, I declared that, as a Christian, I would be ready to revoke everything, and would be the first to fling my books into the fire and trample them underfoot. I was further prayed and urged to give a simple and direct answer to all the questions at issue, and say whether I was prepared to revoke or not. For the second time, with all the humility I could command, I replied: since my conscience is held prisoner by all the passages of Holy Scripture which I have quoted in my books, it is impossible for me to revoke anything before being better taught.

Then certain electors, princes, and other orders of the empire negotiated with me, and urged that I should submit my books to the examination and adjudication of his sacred Majesty and the imperial orders. This is what doctor Vehus, the chancellor of Baden, and doctor Peutinger urged upon me; and, as before, I said I was ready to be corrected by Holy Scripture or by plain reasoning. It was then suggested that I should agree to entrust selected articles to the adjudication of an ecumenical council. For my own part, I have always been prepared, and this very willingly, to do and agree to everything that was possible for me; but I could not obtain the concession of this simple and most Christian request, namely that the word of God to me should remain free and unfettered; and that were I to submit my books to your sacred Majesty and the orders of the empire, or even entrust them to the judgment of a council, it would be on the understanding that nothing contrary to the gospel sent by God should be held to have been subjected by me and left to be construed by them.

Here was the very crux of the controversy. For God, who searches the heart, is my witness that I am most ready to bow to and obey your sacred Majesty, whether in life or death, in glory or disgrace, in advantage or condemnation, as I have often said and still affirm. I make no reservations apart from the word of God, that word which not only man lives by—as Christ teaches, Matthew 4,[1]—but which the angels also desire to look into, 1 Peter 1;[2] that word which, since it is above all things, is of necessity quite free and unbound—as Paul teaches.[3] And in no circumstances is it left to human choice whether to belittle and jeopardize the word of God, no matter how far men may excel in eminence, numbers, doctrine, and sanctity. So truly is this the case that St. Paul ventured to cry and protest in Galatians 1, Though we or an angel from heaven should preach another gospel to you, let him be accursed;[4] and David says, Put not your trust in princes, the sons of men, in whom there is no help.[5] Nor, according to Solomon, can anyone give way to his own self, for he says, He that trusteth in his own heart is a fool;[6] while Jeremiah 17 avers, Cursed is he that trusteth in man.[7]

Things material have nothing in common with the word of God and the eternal blessings. In material things we should deal with one another in good faith. In subordinating these things, or leaving them out of account, we do nothing that imperils our salvation, whenever it is fitting to relinquish things that we have conserved. But as regards the word of God and the things that are eternally good, God does not suffer that word to be so imperilled that one man should subject it to another man. He commands that everyone and everything should be subject to Himself alone, as the One to whom belongs the splendour of the truth and who is the truth

[1] Matt. 4:4   [2] 1 Pet. 1:12   [3] 2 Tim. 2:9   [4] Gal. 1:8
[5] Ps. 146:2f.   [6] Prov. 28:27   [7] Jer. 17:5

itself; whereas every man is a liar and inconstant, as Paul argues outstandingly in Romans 3.[1] Nor is it wrong to have faith in God and to be subject to Him. This is indeed that true worship and adoration of God which St. Augustine teaches in the *Enchiridion* I[2] and which ought not to be offered to any creature. St. Paul, therefore, vigorously denies that angels or himself and, surely, any of the saints in heaven or on earth, are worthy of this faith; they themselves would not tolerate it, much less demand it. Indeed to trust in man in matters pertaining to eternal salvation is to give the creature the glory due to the Creator alone. Hence, I beseech your sacred Majesty, with the utmost humility, not to regard this prejudice in favour of the word of God as born of a wrongful mistrust, and not to interpret it harshly. It was born in me by what the Scriptures preached, by that to which every creature rightly submits.[3] St. Augustine declares that the authority of these Scriptures goes beyond the reach of the understanding of the whole mind of mankind. I have shown my true opinion and belief to your sacred Majesty. Your sacred Majesty will be easily able to perceive from what I have said, that, under the safe-conduct, I duly appeared in all obedience before your sacred Majesty quite undaunted, although I knew that my books had been burned by my enemies, and that meanwhile an edict in your name against my person and my books had been publicly posted up in

---

[1] The precise reference cannot be determined, but cf. Ps. 116:11 and Rev. 2:2

[2] There is no such passage in *Enchiridion ad Laurentium* (ed. O. Scheel, 1903); the true reference appears to be *de Civitate Dei*, X, I. 2; Tauchnitz, Vol. I, pp. 279ff.

[3] This passage is definitive and crucial in Luther's doctrine of the word of God, and for understanding the freshness and vigour of the first decades of the Reformation movement. The word of God, according to Luther's doctrine, is not identified with the *ipsissimis verbis* of sacred Writ, and to identify Luther's doctrine with a hard and naked literalism such as reached its apotheosis in (say) Quenstedt (1617-88) e.g. "The Holy Spirit inspired and dictated . . . the very sentences and all the words severally", is to make the Bible a fetish. Rather the word of God is what the Holy Scriptures *preach* to the heart; and this Luther felt to be in harmony with what "plain reason" on other occasions would teach the intellect. The word of God derives from the action of the Holy Spirit, on the one hand, and on the other, the receptivity of Christian faith, a process which is closely linked step by step with what the Scriptures preach. Cf. further, *supra*, p. 131, n. 3; K. Holl, *Ges. Aufs.* I, pp. 291f., 431f., 436, 557, and E. Brunner, *Philosophy of Religion*, E.T., 1937, chap. 2

many places;[1] it is not true that these things would not unreasonably have frightened such a poor little monk as I, and caused him to draw back, unless I had anticipated from the good God, and from your sacred Majesty and the orders of the empire, that all would be well—which is what I still look for.[2]

Being therefore unable to obtain my request and have my books shown false from Holy Scripture, I was compelled to depart without being refuted. The whole matter under debate issued, as I have said, in this one point: it was not agreed to refute from Holy Scripture the erroneous passages contained in my books; nor was any hope held out, or promise given, that at some future time my books would be examined and tested by the word of God.[3] But nevertheless I offer your sacred Majesty my most humble thanks for having strictly upheld the safe-conduct even at Worms, and promising that it would be kept to the time of my return to the safety of my own quarters.[4] Yet I pray your sacred Majesty once more, do not permit me to be oppressed, constrained, and condemned by my enemies, seeing that, as beseemed a Christian and an obedient subject, I have said all I can say. I am, of course, fully prepared, still trusting in your Majesty, to stand before impartial, erudite, and free judges, whether secular or religious, and be set right by your sacred Majesty, the orders of the empire, councils, doctors, or by whoever can or will. I am ready to submit my books and teaching freely for examination by all, and accept their judgment, with the sole condition that it should be by the plain, clear, and utterly free word of God which, as is its due, is superior to all else and remains the judge of all men.

Wherefore, not for my own sake (I am of no account), but

[1] According to the *Table Talk*, *T.R.*, Vol. V, pp. 65 and 68, Luther first heard of the excommunication when he had reached Weimar, whereas in *T.R.*, Vol. III, p. 282, his condemnation was posted on the doors in every town "before he had reached Erfurt" on his way to Worms; cf. *Br.*, Vol. II, p. 297, note 4

[2] Luther's construction here is greatly overloaded and far from clear; what he means to say is that he came obediently, but that in fact nothing would have frightened him enough to prevent the journey

[3] Here almost but not quite the text of the Bible; rather it is still the word that that text "preaches"

[4] Cf. *supra*, pp. 173, 132; and *W.*, Vol. VII, p. 841; and *R.A.*, p. 595, 35ff.

in the name of the whole church, I beg and pray, what is only right and proper, that I may be allowed to send this letter to you back in Worms.[1] I desire with all my heart to be wholly acceptable to your sacred Majesty, to the whole empire, and to the most noble German people; and I pray that all may continue to enjoy the grace of God.

Hitherto, I have never sought anything else than the glory of God, and the common salvation of all, without taking thought of what would be of advantage to myself, or whether my enemies would condemn me or not. For if Christ, my Lord, prayed on the cross for His enemies, how much the more should not I pray for your sacred Majesty, your empire, my own beloved superiors, and all my motherland of Germany? All these have my best hopes. Relying on the explanation which I have now set forth, and moved with joy, and with faith in Christ, I beg to offer my prayers and petitions. And so I would commend myself to your sacred Majesty under the shadow of the wings by which the Lord our God guides us, and keeps us in health and happiness. Amen. Written at Friedberg, Cantate Sunday, 1521

To your Serene Majesty,

Yours most sincerely,

Martin Luther.

[1] *Ut has literas post tergum mitterem*

6

THE MAGNIFICAT
TRANSLATED AND EXPOUNDED
BY
DR. MARTIN LUTHER,
AUGUSTINIAN

Introduction

AFTER it became known that the bull excommunicating Luther and banning his books was coming into force in certain places in November, 1520, duke John Frederick wrote to his uncle, Frederick the Wise, and declared himself on Luther's side; and he sent a copy of this letter to Luther to make plain where he stood. Meanwhile, there was much strenuous discussion among the various princes about Luther; but, on December 20, John Frederick was able to write and inform the latter of the Elector's promise to support him as far as he was able and the nature of the case allowed.[1] John Frederick added several kindly and encouraging remarks, and asked for Luther's prayers.

Luther's exposition of the Magnificat was intended to express his appreciation of the young prince's attitude, as is shown in the dedication of the work. He also mentioned this fact when he wrote to Spalatin on February 27, 1521.[2] He began the work in November, 1520, and sent the first batch of pages to the press on March 17. The work was interrupted soon after by the emperor's command to go to Worms, but he sent John Frederick the first three printed sections on Easter Sunday, March 31, just before his departure. By this time the fourth section was already in the press. Hence, March 1521 may be regarded as the date of the work, although it was only completed at Wartburg castle after Luther's appearance before the emperor at Worms. He was again busy on the MS. by May 14, and finished it on June 10, when he sent the parcel to Spalatin to be printed.[3] But the press in Wittenberg was "snowed under", and the work was not finally published till the end of August or the beginning of September, a delay which made Luther quite restless.

By way of conclusion, Luther had specially translated king Solomon's prayer from 1 Kings 3, for the benefit of John Frederick, and as an example of how a prince ought to pray. He emphasized the fifth and sixth verses of the Magnificat, too, on account of their importance to one who was destined to be a ruling prince.

As in other writings and sermons of his at this period, Luther had much to say in praise of Mary. Her chief virtues were humility and the complete tranquillity with which her soul rested in God, for whom she abandoned every other desire. Luther's attitude to the worship of the Virgin seems to have reached its turning point in his exposition of the Magnificat. At the beginning and also at

[1] *Br.*, Vol. II, pp. 237f., No. 363   [2] *Br.*, Vol. II, p. 270, No. 378
[3] *Br.*, Vol. II, p. 354, No. 417

the end, he calls her the blessed mother of God, and prays for her intercessions; but he says elsewhere in the course of the work,[1] "she does not want you to come to her, but through her to God." There is also a touching passage[2] where he depicts her work about the house as that of a serving maid or a working woman like a multitude of others; all this was conceived much after the manner of Albert Dürer's famous woodcuts of his *Life of Mary*, which was first published between 1503 and 1510. But from now onwards, Luther abandoned his Mariolatry, and even warned his followers of its dangers in distracting them from the true worship of God and from full faith in Christ.[3]

It should be understood that this is not a literary but a devotional exposition, and that its great value lies in the profound and subtle religious insight, and in its minute analysis of the deepest emotions. All this is presented with a remarkable simplicity and directness of language, very difficult to translate into English, but very suitable for the personal instruction of a devout young prince such as John Frederick, or any other young person, at the time when the significance of evangelical faith was just beginning to be perceived in its true proportions.

The present translation is made from the Weimar Edition of Luther's Works, Vol. VII, pp. 538-604.

[1] Cf. *infra*, p. 219; also pp. 210f.   [2] *Infra*, p. 226
[3] Cf. *W*. Vol. X, ii, 338, and the numerous references there

Text and Notes

THE MAGNIFICAT TRANSLATED AND EXPOUNDED BY DR. MARTIN LUTHER, AUGUSTINIAN

𝕵𝖊𝖘𝖚𝖘

To the Illustrious, Right-Honourable Prince and Lord Lord John Frederick,[1] Duke of Saxony, Landgrave in Thüringia, and Margrave in Meissen, my gracious Lord and Patron from his humble chaplain

D. MART. LUTHER

ILLUSTRIOUS and right-honourable prince, gracious lord, my humble prayer and service do ever attend upon your Highness.

Gracious lord, I have humbly received the answer which your Highness has recently written[2] and its contents have encouraged me and given me much pleasure. It is now a long time since I faithfully promised your Highness to expound the Magnificat, but unfortunately I have often been turned aside, and compelled to deal with various enemies. I have tried to answer your Highness's letter with this booklet; a longer delay would make me blush for shame, and would not chime with the help it is intended to give. I have no wish to do anything that would discourage your Highness. Already in your tender youth, you have shown an eager love for the word of God, a love which further study will stimulate and strengthen. To this end I pray for God's blessing on your Highness, and that His help may ever be sufficient for your needs.

A person of high and princely rank promotes the

---

[1] Born in 1503, he was now eighteen years of age, and already a devout and eager follower of the Lutheran way. He succeeded his father, Duke John, as elector of Saxony in 1532, and became one of the principal members of the League of Schmalkalden. He was largely responsible for the first publication of Luther's collected Works. He died in 1554

[2] Dated December 20, 1520; cf. *supra*, p. 185

well-being of many people if he himself is ruled by the grace
of God. On the other hand, many would suffer harm if he
should grow slack or become harsh in spirit. For, although
all men's hearts are in God's hands, there is point in saying
of kings and princes alone, that the king's heart is in the
hand of the Lord; He turneth it whithersoever He will.[1]
God's purpose is to put the fear of Himself into the hearts of
great lords in order that they may learn that they cannot
possess a single thought not specially given to them by God.
What other men do brings bane or blessing only on themselves and a very few others. But when they are rulers, *eo
ipso*, they are helpful or harmful to others, and this in
greater numbers according as their sway is of greater extent.
Here is the reason why Scripture calls devout, God-fearing
princes God's angels, and even gods; on the other hand, it
calls wicked princes lions, dragons, or savage animals.[2]
Such are the names that God gives to one of His four
calamities when He enumerates plague, war, famine, and
savage animals. The human heart is by nature only flesh and
blood, and therefore it easily becomes over-bearing; and
when power, possessions, and prerogatives are also at its
disposal, these exercise a strong influence and readily dispose
it to become arrogant and far too greatly self-assured. The
result is that a prince with such a heart forgets God and pays
no regard to his own subjects; and because he has the
opportunity to do evil and go unpunished, he sets off on this
course and acts like a wild beast. He does only what pleases
himself; he is a lord in name, but a disgrace in fact. So also
Bias the sage[3] has well said that *Magistratus virum ostendit*,
or "authority reveals the man", and his subjects dare not
speak a word for fear of those in power. Therefore, all rulers,
just because they are not in fear of other men, should fear
God more than others do. They should know Him and His
works well, and be on their guard about the way they

---

[1] Cf. Prov. 21:1

[2] Cf. 1 Sam. 29:9; Ps. 82:6; Zeph. 3:3; Jer. 51:34; Ezek. 14:13ff.

[3] Bias of Priene, sixth century B.C., one of the seven sages of Greece. Cf.
Erasmus, *Adagia*, which seems to have been Luther's source for this quotation. Erasmus, however, adds that others attribute it to Pittacus or Solon;
so Brieger, Vol. III, 335

themselves live their lives. It is as St. Paul says in Romans 12, He that ruleth, let him exercise care.[1]

There is nothing known to me in all Holy Scripture so appropriate in this connection as this holy hymn sung by the mother of God when she felt herself greatly blessed. All rulers who want to be good and beneficent lords over their people might appropriately learn it and live according to it. The main points of the hymn sung by Mary are: the fear of God; the sort of lord God is; and, particularly, His works on behalf of high and low. Let others listen to a common slut singing a ribald song; but a prince and ruler would do well to listen to this modest maiden as she sings a spiritual hymn of pure adoration.

It is a goodly custom to sing this hymn daily at vespers in church, and it is well suited for other times. May the tender mother of God endow me with a spirit by which I may give a practical yet penetrating exposition of her canticle. May your Highness and indeed all other men find here sound instruction for a praiseworthy life; and may we sing our praises in this eternal Magnificat in eternal life. May God help us, Amen. I send your Highness my humble greetings, asking that your Highness will graciously accept what little I have been able to do.

Wittenberg, on the tenth of March, 1521.

The Magnificat[2]

   i My soul magnifies the Lord

  ii and my spirit rejoices in God my Saviour,

 iii for he has regarded the low estate of his handmaiden.
For behold, henceforth all generations will call me blessed;

 iv for he who is mighty has done great things for me, and holy is his name.

  v And his mercy is on those who fear him from generation to generation.

 vi He has shown strength with his arm, he has scattered the proud in the imagination of their hearts,

[1] Rom. 12:8   [2] Following the R.S.V., Luke 1:46-55

vii he has put down the mighty from their thrones,
     and exalted those of low degree;
viii he has filled the hungry with good things, and the rich
     he has sent empty away.
 ix He has helped his servant Israel,
     in remembrance of his mercy,
  x as he spoke to our fathers,
     to Abraham and to his posterity for ever.

PREFACE AND INTRODUCTION

To understand this holy hymn of praise, we must first grasp the fact that the Blessed Virgin Mary is speaking from her own experience, an experience in which she has been enlightened and instructed by the Holy Spirit. No one can rightly understand God's Word without the help of the Holy Spirit. And we can only receive anything from the Holy Spirit according as we experience it, test it, and grasp it. By that very experience, the Holy Spirit teaches us as if in his own school-room, a school-room outside of which we learn nothing but hollow words and empty talk. When the holy virgin learned in her experience that God was performing a very great work in her, although lowly, unpretentious, poor, and despised, the Holy Spirit taught her this rich piece of knowledge and wisdom: namely, that God is the sort of lord whose one work is to exalt what is lowly, abase what is exalted; and, in brief, to break down what has been built up, and build up what has been broken down.

For example, at the beginning of all creation, He created the world out of nothing. Hence He is called Creator and Almighty, and He continues unchanged to work in this way. Indeed, that is the way in which He does all His work and will do so to the very end of the world: out of what is as nothing, lowly, despised, poor, dead, He makes something precious, splendid, full of joy and life; and again, everything that is costly, splendid, holy, and alive, He makes as nothing, lowly, despised, poor, and dying. He does it in a way that no creature can do, for no man can make something out of nothing. He sees into the depths as well as into the heights. Thus Daniel 3 says, Thou sittest upon the cherubim, and seest into the depths, or the abysm.[1] Similarly Psalm 137, God is on high, but He looks below, and sees the humble; but the proud He knoweth from afar;[2] and again, Psalm 111. Where is there a God like our God, who sitteth on high, and looketh below to see the humble in heaven and earth?[3]

[1] The Song of the Three Men, verse 32   [2] Cf. Ps. 138:6   [3] Cf. Ps. 113:5f.

Because He is the highest of all, with nothing above Himself, there is nothing to see above Himself, nothing beside Himself. Because no one is His equal, it must needs be that He looks within Himself and beneath Himself; and the lower anyone is beneath Him, the better He sees him.

But the eyes of the world and of mankind work in the opposite manner; men see what is above them, and want to fly high; as it is written in Proverbs 30, There is a people whose eyes look up on high, and their eyelids are lifted high. It is our daily experience that all people are self-centred, and care only about honour, power, wealth, ability, good living, and anything large and exalted. Where such people are to be found, everyone else becomes a hanger-on, rushes into their presence, serves them with pleasure. Everyone wants to be present with, and share in their eminence. It is not without reason that so little is said in Scripture about devout kings and princes. On the other hand, no one wants to look into the lowly places: at poverty, shame, distress, sorrow, and pain; each man turns his eyes away. And wherever such people are to be found everyone runs from them, flees, avoids, and neglects them; no one thinks of helping or standing by them, or improving their condition. They are compelled to remain abased, and stay in the midst of the lowly and despised. Among all mankind, there is no one who can make something out of nothing. Paul therefore teaches us in Romans 12, and says: Beloved brethren, do not be haughty, but associate with the lowly.[1]

We must understand that God alone sees things in this way: He sees into the depths of distress and woe, and is near to all who are in the deep places. It is as Peter says, God opposes the proud, but gives grace to the humble.[2] And this is the spring from which flow our love and praise of God. No man can praise God without first loving Him; and, similarly, no one can love Him unless God is his best beloved and his nearest friend. Further, He is known to us by His own work felt and perceived within us. But when our experience is that He is a God who sees into the depths, and gives help only to the poor, the despised, the pitiable, the sorrowing, the

---

[1] Cf. Rom. 12:16; cf. R.S.V.   [2] Cf. 1 Pet. 5:5, R.S.V.

forsaken, and those of no account, then we come to love Him
with our whole heart. Our heart overflows with joy; it leaps
and bounds with the sheer delight which it has found in God.
And there, in the experience of a single moment, is the Holy
Spirit, and it has taught us the supreme art of life and
happiness.

Here, too, is the reason why God has laid death on us all,
and given to His dearest children the cross of Christ, and
unnumbered sufferings and distresses; and even sometimes
allows them to fall into sin. Then there is much in the depths
for Him to see, many to help, much to do. He shows Himself
to be a real creator, and in this way makes Himself known,
loveable, and praiseworthy. At the same time, unhappily,
men of the world, whose eyes are on high, ceaselessly strive
against Him, to prevent His seeing, working, helping; and His
being known and loved and praised; and to rob Him of all
this kind of honour, as well as their own pleasure, joy, and
happiness. So too He surrendered His own well-beloved Son,
Christ himself, to the deepest sorrow; and to Him supremely,
God did show how He sees, works, helps, plans, counsels
and wills; how the whole is directed to Himself. And because
Christ was versed outstandingly in this knowledge, he
continually confessed Him, loved Him and praised Him.
Accordingly, it says in Psalm 15, Thou hast made him
rejoice with pure joy before Thy face;[1] in other words, He
sees you and knows you. Similarly, it says in Psalm 44, All
the saints shall continually praise God in heaven because
He has looked into their hearts, and there made Himself
known, loved, and praised.[2]

It is in this way, too, that the tender mother of Christ
teaches us—by the example of her experience and also by
her words—how we ought to confess God, and love and
praise Him; for because she was glorified and praised God
with a glad and joyful spirit, and He watched to see if she
was indeed humble and lowly, we are led to think that her
parents were poor, despised, and of low estate. That is the
picture presented to our eyes and to those of simple people.
Without question, there were in Jerusalem the daughters of

[1] Cf. Ps. 21:6   [2] Perhaps cf. Ps. 145:10ff.

NML

the high priests and of the rulers, rich, pretty, young, educated, very highly esteemed, looked up to by the whole country, just like the daughters of kings, princes, and wealthy people to-day; and so also in many other places. Even in her home town of Nazareth, Mary did not belong to the upper, ruling classes, for she was the daughter of an ordinary, poor citizen whom no one regarded as important or noteworthy. And in the eyes of her neighbours and their daughters, there is no doubt that she was but a simple girl who looked after the cattle and the house. To-day she would have been a poor servant-girl doing what was required of her in the house.

This is what Isaiah had prophesied, Isaiah 11, A shoot shall grow out of the stem of Jesse, and a blossom out of his roots, on which the Holy Spirit shall rest.[1] The trunk and root are the tribe of Jesse or David, in particular, the virgin Mary; the rod and the blossom are Christ. Now it is not to be expected, indeed it is incredible, that a lovely branch and blossom should grow from a dry, worthless stem and root. And, similarly, it was not to be expected that Mary, the virgin, should be the mother of such a child. I am of the opinion that she was not called a stem and root simply because she, of her supernatural and undefiled virginity, had become a mother, just as it would be supernatural for a shoot to grow from a dead stump; rather, the reason was that the royal stem and tribe of David were even then, so to speak, blossoming and blooming in greater glory, power, and richness even than in the times of David and Solomon, and were also of outstanding importance for the world. But, to the end that Christ should come, the priests had made this glory subject to themselves, and they alone exercised authority. The royal line of David, by its poverty and contempt, was like a dead tree-stump; there was no longer any hope or expectation that there should ever again come from it a king who would rise to great honour. And yet, all un-expectedly, at the last moment, Christ came and was born from the despised stem, from the poor little maiden. The shoot and the blossom then grew from the person whom

[1] Cf. Isa. 11:1f.

the daughters of my lords Annas and Caiaphas would not have thought worthy of being their meanest maidservant. That is how God's work and sight plumb the depths; man's work and sight seek only what is exalted. And that was the reason for Mary's song of praise, which we shall now listen to word for word.

(i) *My Soul Magnifies God the Lord*[1]

This sentence expresses great fervour and overflowing joy, for her whole outlook and life were exalted by the spirit within her. That is why she says, not "I magnify God", but "My soul magnifies God"; as much as to say, My life and all I am conscious of are borne up by God's love and praise, and by intense joy. Though weak, I am more led to praise God than if I were strong. This is the experience of all who are suffused with delight in God and His spirit; they feel more than they can express. To praise God joyfully is not a man's own doing; rather he is glad to be the instrument, and God alone does the work. It cannot be taught by words, but only learned from one's own experience. Accordingly, David says in Psalm 33, O taste and see how sweet is God the Lord; blessed is the man who trusts Him.[2] The tasting comes first, afterwards the seeing . . . in order that He may not let Himself be known without personal experience and feeling, things to which no one attains of himself. But a man will trust God with his whole heart when he is in the depths or in distress; and that is why David joyfully adds, Blessed is the man who trusts in God, for he will experience God's work in his own self; hence the sense of delight, which will also lead him to full understanding and knowledge.

Let us consider the words of Mary one at a time. Firstly, My soul. Scripture divides man into three parts. Accordingly St. Paul, in 1 Thessalonians 5, says, May God, who is a God of peace, make you holy through and through; and may your whole spirit, soul, and body be kept sound and healthy at the coming of our Lord Jesus Christ.[3] This threefold nature, and so the entire man, is divided up in another fashion, into two

---

[1] Luke 1:46   [2] Cf. Ps. 34:8   [3] 1 Thess. 5:23

elements called flesh and spirit. This is not a division of our nature, but of our qualities. That is to say, human nature consists of three elements, spirit, soul, body; all three of these may be either good or bad, or to put it otherwise, spirit or flesh; but we are not using this nomenclature at the moment. The first element, the spirit, is the highest, deepest, noblest part of a man, and with it he is able to lay hold of the incomprehensible, the invisible, and the eternal. In brief, it is the house in which faith and the word of God dwell. David speaks of it in Psalm 50, and says, Lord create in my inmost self an upright spirit;[1] in other words, an exalted, resolute faith. He speaks of the unbelieving, on the other hand, in Psalm 77, Their heart was not right with God, and their spirit had no faith in God.[2]

Secondly, the soul: this is the same thing as the spirit in its nature, but in another kind of activity, namely, its work in making the body alive and in operating through the body. Scripture often calls it "the life", for, while the spirit may indeed live without the body, the body cannot live without the spirit. We are familiar with the way this element works during sleep, and without cessation. It is its nature to comprehend, not the incomprehensible, but what reason knows and measures. In particular, it is here where reason is at home; and, where the spirit is not illumined by faith as by a higher light, and this light does not control reason, reason is always subject to error; and indeed, reason is too lowly a thing to deal with the divine. Scripture ascribes to these two elements of spirit and soul many things, such as *sapientiam* and *scientiam*, wisdom to the spirit, and knowledge to the soul; and similarly hate, love, pleasure, horror, and the like.

In the third place is the body with its organs, whose function is confined to movements and habits, following on which the soul knows and the spirit believes. We can find a parallel to this in Scripture. Moses made a tabernacle with three different chambers. The first was called the Holy of Holies; God dwelt within, and it was without light. The second was called the Holy Place, and within it stood a

---

[1] Cf. Ps. 51:10   [2] Cf. Ps. 78:37

candlestick with seven branches and lamps. The third was called the atrium or forecourt; it was open to the sky, and its light was the sun. This figure portrays the Christian man. His spirit is the Holy of Holies, God's dwelling place in the darkness of faith, without light, for he believes what he neither sees, nor feels, nor understands. His soul is the Holy Place; here are seven lights, namely, all the different ways of understanding, distinguishing, knowing, and recognizing corporeal and visible things. His body is the atrium or forecourt, open to everyone; it is what can be seen, what he does, and how he lives.

Now Paul's prayer is, May God, who is a God of peace, make us holy, not in one part alone, but altogether, through and through, that spirit, soul, body, and all may be holy. Much could be said of the ground for such a prayer, but in brief it is this: if the spirit is no longer holy, nothing is any longer holy. The greatest struggle and the greatest danger has to do with the holiness of the spirit, because the spirit does not consort with tangible things, as I have explained. Then false teachers appear and seduce the spirit; one inclines to works, and another to devices for being godly. If the spirit is not on the alert and wise in these matters, it goes astray; soon it comes to outward works and wisdom, thinking to become godly thereby. All too quickly, faith is lost, and the spirit is dead in the sight of God.

This explains the origin of the various sects and orders; one becomes a Carthusian, another a Barefoot; all expect to be saved, one by fasting, another by prayer, some by one sort of works, and some by another. Yet taken altogether, they are works and rules of their own choice, not commanded by God, but conceived by man alone. Moreover, they no longer pay attention to faith, but always teach a man to depend on works; they keep this up so long and drive it so far, that they part company. Each wants to be the best, and despises the others . . . like the brag and bounce of our present-day Observants.[1] It is against such teachers, holy by works and

[1] These comprised the ardent members of the Order, who aimed at strict observance of its rules; the Conventuals, on the other hand, were inclined to a milder discipline

saints on the surface, that Paul prays when he says, God is a God of peace and unity; but these disunited, discontented "saints" have no place for Him, and they will find none unless they change their policy. They must all come together in one spirit and one faith, and recognize that works only breed differences, separations, dissensions; whereas only faith makes men godly, united, and peaceable. Thus it says in Psalm 67, God brings it about that we live in unity in the house,[1] and Psalm 129, Behold how good and pleasant it is for brothers to dwell together in unity.[2]

Peace never issues, as is taught, from works, from anything outward, but only from faith. Faith means sound confidence in the promise of God's invisible grace; and that grace is what makes us godly, righteous, and holy, as I have explained at length in my book on Good Works.[3] When there is no faith, many works are required followed by discontent and disunity; with the result that God is no longer present. Hence St. Paul in this connection is not content with saying: your spirit, your soul, or the like; but your whole spirit, which shows the real point at issue. The expression he uses here in Greek is the spirit which possesses your whole heritage.[4] It is as if he intended saying, Do not let any doctrine of works lead you astray; the whole matter depends on having a believing spirit. I pray by this same all-possessing spirit that God will guard you from false teachings, such as would rely on works to win trust in God. These teachings are false because they do not build their trust on God's grace alone. But if the spirit takes entire possession, then, at once, both the soul and the body will abide free from error and evil works. On the other hand, when the spirit lacks faith, it is impossible to prevent wrong-doing and error from entering the soul and permeating one's whole life; and this in spite of the fact that the soul, full of good intentions and good nature, has its own devotional life and its own satisfactions. The consequence of error and wrong ideas in the soul is that all the works of the body are evil and

---

[1] Cf. Ps. 68:6   [2] Cf. Ps. 133:1
[3] Cf. *W.*, Vol. VI, p. 196, and Vol. IX, p. 329
[4] τὸ ὁλόκληρον πνεῦμα ὑμῶν

MY SOUL MAGNIFIES   199

vain, even though a man fasts till he dies, or performs all the holy works. Our first need, therefore, is that God should guard our spirit, and only afterwards our soul and body; and then we shall avoid working or living to no purpose. In this way, we shall live uprightly, and be saved, guarded not only from open sins, but much more also from specious good works.

For the time being, I have said enough by way of explaining the two words, soul and spirit, especially as they occur very frequently in the Bible. We now come to the word *magnificat* or "magnify", meaning make large, lift up, hold in high esteem; and it refers to one who feels that he can do many great and kindly things, and he means to do them, as this hymn goes on to say. Like the title of a book, the word *magnificat* or "magnify" describes the subject-matter. When Mary used this word, she indicated the subject of her praise, namely, the great deeds and works of God. She did it to strengthen our faith, to comfort all who are of low estate, and to frighten the great ones of the earth. These are the three uses or services by which we must see to it that the song of praise is judged and understood. Mary sang not for her own sake alone, but for us all; and that we might sing like her. But let us see to it that no one takes fright, and also that no one builds on these mighty works of God. Let no one be content with believing that God is able, or has power to do great things: we must also believe that He will do them, and that He delights to do them. Nor indeed is it enough to think that God will do great things with other people, but not with you, and thus leave you without the benefit of works like these; for then you will perform godly deeds of the kind done by those people who, when prosperous, have no fear of God, and who forsake Him in times of distress.[1]

Such faith amounts to nothing; it is exactly like the fancy suggested by a fairy tale. Rather, what is needed is that, without any faltering, without any doubting, you envisage God's will for you; you must believe firmly that He wills

---

[1] This sentence is obscure, but the insight is obvious

great things, and will do great things, for you. This kind of
faith is alive and active; it penetrates and transfuses the
whole self; it makes you afraid because you are on a height,
and it comforts you because you are lowly. The higher you
are, the more must you fear; the deeper you are made to
sink, the more you can take comfort; which no one does
whose faith is of the other kind.[1] And what are you to do in
the dread hour of death? Then you must not only believe
that God can help you, but also that it is His will to help
you; nay, that for you to be redeemed from eternal death,
and become an eternal heir of God's own, a work must take
place too great to be told. This is the faith that can do all
things, as Christ said.[2] It is something unique; it enters into
our experience of God's work, and then of God's love.
This leads us to sing God's praise. We have received great
things from God, and accordingly we magnify Him very
greatly.

Yet we do not make God great in His nature, for He is
unchangeable. Rather we make Him great in our knowledge
and perception of Him. In other words, we reverence Him
highly and fear Him greatly, especially for His goodness and
grace. That is why the holy mother does not say, My voice
and my mouth, my hand and my thoughts, my reason and
my will, magnify Him. In her view, there are many who
praise God loudly, preach with fine words, speak, argue,
write, or paint much about Him, meditate much on Him,
and seek after and speculate about Him with their reason;
also many who exalt Him with shallow devotions and
intentions. Rather, her words are, My soul magnifies Him;
meaning, my whole life, all I do, all my character and
strength, hold Him in great reverence. She feels herself caught
up in Him and uplifted by His gracious goodwill, as the next
verse shows. Similarly, when some person does us a special
kindness, we find our hearts respond to him, and we say, I
hold him in very high esteem; really meaning, I truly
magnify him. But much more will our life be stirred when we
become aware of God's goodness. His goodness is so over-
whelmingly great in His works, that every thought and word

---

[1] *Wilchs ihener glawben keiner thut*   [2] Cf. Mk. 9:23

of ours shrink into insignificance. When everything that is within us would joyfully sing and be glad, we must let the emotion stir all our heart and soul.

At this point, we should take note of two wrong kinds of spirit in which to sing the Magnificat: the first is that of the man who does not praise God before being blessed. David says, They praise Thee when Thou dost bless them.[1] Such men have every appearance of praising God highly. But, because they are never willing to suffer oppression and sorrow, they can never experience the true works of God, and so they never truly love Him or praise Him. To-day the whole world is full of services of worship and praise with singing, preaching, organs, and pipes. The Magnificat is splendidly sung but, the pity of it, entirely without heart and life. We do not sing it unless all goes well, and if things turn out badly, we do not sing it at all. When we cease receiving benefactions from God, we say, as it were, God is unable or unwilling to do anything for us, and therefore the Magnificat must wait.

The second spirit inclines in the other direction, and is more dangerous. It belongs to the people who prosper under God's blessings, but do not ascribe the gifts to God alone. They want to establish their own claims, seeking to be honoured and favoured in the sight of other men. They look at the great wealth with which God has prospered them, grab at it, and preen themselves on it as if it were their own; they think themselves different from those people who have not been favoured in the same way. This is a very smooth and slippery position. God's blessings, when regarded in the ordinary way, make our hearts haughty and self-content. We must therefore take note of the last word of the text: God. Mary's words are not, My soul magnifies my own self, or holds my own self in high esteem. She does not want any regard to be paid to her. Rather she magnifies God alone, and attributes everything to Him alone. She puts aside everything of self, and then lifts everything up simply to God from whom she had received it. Then, in spite of her personal experience of a transcendent act of God, she

[1] Cf. Ps. 49:18

remained quite lowly, and never set herself above the
lowliest person on earth. If she had done so she would
have fallen with Lucifer into the depths of hell.

She would still have had the same cast of mind if another
maiden had received a like blessing from God; she would have
rejoiced equally, and would have been as glad for her sake as
if it were for herself. Indeed she would have thought herself
unworthy of the honour, and the other worthy. Nay, she
would have been content if God had taken the blessing
away from her, and given it to another under her very eyes.
In the fullest sense, she claimed nothing at all for herself;
she left every blessing freely and entirely at God's disposal.
She had become altogether the joyous lodging and the
willing hostess of such a guest; and so she has kept everything
for evermore. And that is what it means to magnify God
alone, to reverence Him alone, and to think nothing of oneself.

All this shows that she had much occasion of falling and
sinning, for it is no small marvel that she avoided pride and
hauteur when she was filled to overflowing with such a
blessing. Can you understand what a wonderful heart she
had? She found herself to be the mother of God, exalted
far above all mankind; and yet she remained so simple and
submissive that she did not despise a humble serving maid.
But what poor sorts of men and women are we, for when we
receive some small gift, a little authority, or honour, or
merely to be better-looking than our fellows, we cannot
keep to the level of one of the lowly sort; and there is no
limit to our pride. What would we do if we were to come
into great possessions?

Perhaps the reason why God lets us remain poor and
unhappy is because we do not keep His tender mercies unsoiled, and are unable to retain our equilibrium as before.
We let our spirits rise or fall as our possessions come or go.
But Mary's heart remained firm and unchanged all the time;
she let God work His will in her, and received from it only
good courage, joy, and trust in God. Were we to do the same,
that would be to sing a splendid Magnificat.

(ii) *And my Spirit rejoices in God my Saviour*[1]

First, as to what the spirit is. The spirit is that which, through faith, sees the incomprehensible. Mary called God her saviour or salvation; she neither saw nor comprehended Him, but she trusted Him with a firm confidence. He was her saviour and salvation; and she received this faith from the work of God which she had experienced in herself. Of course she saw things in sequence. She first called God her Lord, and afterwards her Saviour; and her Saviour before telling of His work. Thereby she teaches us that we ought to love and praise God simply, and in the normal course, without seeking any advantage to ourselves from Him. To love and praise God with a pure and upright heart is to praise Him just because He is good, and to have nothing else in mind than His perfect goodness, and to have joy and gladness in that fact alone. This is a noble, pure, and tender way of loving and praising, very appropriate to the noble and tender spirit such as this maiden possessed.

Those whose love is impure or debased, who are merely self-seeking and eager for benefactions from God, do not love and praise His perfect goodness. With an eye to themselves, they look only for the blessings God shows to them; in other words, for the way in which He gives them tangible things and prospers them. Then they exalt Him highly and are happy in singing His praises as long as the experience lasts. But when God hides Himself, and takes away the glory of His goodness, so that they are left alone and in distress, then fail both their love and their praises. They have neither the will nor the ability to love and praise the quite intangible things which lie hidden in God. This shows that their spirit does not rejoice in God as saviour; there is no generous love and praise for His perfect goodness. Nay, rather they take more pleasure in the help than in the Helper, more in the gift than in the Giver, more in the creature than in God; for they cannot remain the same in prosperity and in adversity, in wealth and in poverty. Yet the right attitude is as is expressed when St. Paul says: I have learned how to abound, and how to be in want.[2]

[1] Luke 1:47   [2] Phil. 4:12

It is of this sort of thing that Psalm 48 speaks: They praise Thee as long as Thou dost prosper them.[1] Much as if the Psalmist had said, Their mind is on themselves and not on Thee; they seek only pleasure and blessing from Thee; they sacrifice nothing to Thee. Similarly in John 6, Christ said to those who sought Him, Verily, verily, I say to you, you seek me, not because you saw the signs, but because you ate your fill of the loaves.[2] Unclean and false spirits of this kind soil all God's gifts and prevent His giving them much; nor can He effect their salvation. Here is a vivid illustration: Once on a day, a devout woman had a vision, in which she saw three maidens seated by an altar. During mass, a pretty little boy ran from the altar, and went up to the first maiden. He was friendly with her, hugged her, and smiled lovingly at her; then he went up to the next maiden, was not so friendly with her, nor did he hug her; but he lifted her veil and smiled at her in a friendly way. To the third, he made no friendly gestures, passed her by without a friendly sign, ran quickly to the altar, and disappeared.[3]

The vision was then explained to that woman, and she was told that the first maiden meant the impure, pleasure-seeking spirit, which expected many benefits from God, and wanted her own way rather than His. She was unwilling to endure hardship, always wanted the help and happiness which God gave, and was not content with His goodness. The second maiden signified one who had begun to serve God, and who could endure a certain amount of hardship, yet was not quite without self-seeking and the desire for enjoyment. She needed God sometimes to give her a loving glance, and let her feel His goodness; by this means she would learn to love and praise His perfect loving kindness. But the poor Cinderella endured nothing but hardship and affliction, sought no pleasure, was content that God was good, even though she never experienced it (an impossible supposition), remained serene and equable either way, loved and praised God's goodness just as much when she received no benefits as when she did receive them. Nor did she snatch at them when they came, or droop when they were lacking. Here was the very

[1] Cf. Ps. 49:18   [2] Cf. John 6:26   [3] The origin of this story is unknown

bride to say to Christ, I do not want Thy gifts, but Thine own self. Thou art not dearer to me in good times, nor less dear in hard times.

Such a spirit fulfils the passage which says: You must not depart from the smooth, straight pathway of God, neither to the left side, nor to the right.[1] In other words, you must love and praise God always uprightly and in the same way, not seeking your own interests and pleasure. David had such a spirit when he was driven from Jerusalem by his son Absalom; he was sure that he was finally cast out, and would never again be king and receive God's favour. He said, Behold, if God will have me, He will surely bring me back again; but if He says, "I want you not", I shall content myself therewith.[2] O what a pure spirit was that which, even in the deepest distress, did not cease to love, praise, and cling to God's goodness! In our text, Mary, the mother of God, when she was inundated with a great and overflowing blessing, nevertheless did not snatch at it, nor seek her own pleasure. Rather she kept her spirit undefiled as she continued in her love and praise of God's bountiful goodness; ready and willing to accept, even though God should will to take it away again, and leave her a poor, naked, and needy spirit.

It is much more dangerous and difficult to maintain self-control in the midst of wealth, and great importance, and much power, than in poverty, ignominy, and weakness, because riches, honour, and power, give rise to strong incentives to and occasions for evil. All the more praiseworthy, then, is Mary's marvellously pure spirit; she was in a position of the highest honour, and yet did not let herself be tempted; she acted as if she did not perceive it, but held unswervingly to the right path. She clung to God's goodness alone, although she could neither see it nor grasp it. She paid no heed to tangible benefits, took no delight in them, nor sought her own pleasure. Therefore, she had sure and sound reasons for singing, My spirit rejoices in God my saviour. In truth, this is a spirit that leaps and dances only through faith. She did not rejoice in those blessings of God

---

[1] Cf. Isa. 30:21   [2] Cf. 2 Sam. 15:25f.

of which she was aware, but only in a God who was beyond her immediate experience, and yet was her salvation; and this she knew only in faith. O these are the genuine lowly, free, hungry, god-fearing spirits—of which more later.

From what I have said, it is possible to know and judge how full the world is to-day of hollow preachers and holy men, who preach so much to needy people about good works. Although it is true that there are a few of them who preach how one ought to do good works, the majority of them preach man-made doctrines and works which they themselves have thought out and set forth. The result is, unfortunately, that the very best of them are still so very far from the straight road that they continually drive people into the wrong side of the road.[1] They never teach them to do good works and to live the good life just for the sake of God's sheer goodness, but only for their own enjoyment. If there were no such places as heaven and hell, and if they were unable to enjoy God's benefits, they would let His goodness go unloved and unpraised. They are only self-seeking hirelings, servants and not children of the house, strangers and not heirs, making idols of their own selves. They hold that God ought to love and praise and do for them exactly what they ought to be doing for God. Such people do not possess the true spirit; God is not their saviour; His good gifts are their saviour, through which God is expected to serve them like a lackey. Such were the children of Israel in the desert, when they were not content with manna, but wanted to eat meat and onions and garlic as well.[2]

To-day, unfortunately, all the world, all the cloisters, all the churches, are full of such people. All of them alike live with a false, perverse, and unrighteous spirit. They put so much stress on good works that they believe they serve heaven thereby. Nevertheless, the perfect goodness of God ought to be preached and known as prior to all else. We ought to understand that just as God, of His goodness alone, saved us apart from any merit due to works, so our response ought to be that we do the works without greedily seeking any

[1] *Das sie das volck ymmer. auff die rechten seiten treiben*
[2] Cf. Num. 11:4ff.

reward, just for the sake of the goodness of God. We should desire nothing more than His good pleasure, without caring for any reward. The reward will look after itself, and come about without our seeking. For, surely, it is impossible for the reward not to come if we do good with an undefiled and upright spirit, without looking for reward or pleasure. Nor will God accept that pleasure-seeking, unclean spirit, nor will it earn any reward. A child serves his father willingly and freely because he is the heir, and for his father's sake. When a child serves his father only for the sake of the heritage and the property, it is surely a hateful child, whom the father might worthily disown.

(iii) *For He has regarded the low estate of His handmaiden,*
For behold, henceforth all generations will call me blessed[1]

Some people have translated the Latin word used here, *humilitas,* by humility, making the virgin Mary proudly claim humility. In the same way, many prelates have called themselves humble, when the appellation was far from the truth; for in God's eyes no one can boast of any good thing without sin and hurt. Since God's pure goodness and grace show us to be unworthy, we must never again boast about ourselves in His sight. Not our own, but only God's love and praise must keep and uphold us, as Solomon says, Proverbs 25, You must not come in pride before the king, nor stand (meaning: claim to be somebody) before great lords; it is better to be told, "Come up here", than that you should be put lower in the presence of the prince.[2] How can one then ascribe pride and haughtiness like this to the pure and guileless maiden, and imply that she boasted of her humility before God? Humility is the greatest of all virtues, and no one can boast of or take pride in his own humility, except one who is haughtier than anyone else. God alone recognizes humility, justifies, and reveals it only where the[3] person concerned is

---

[1] Luke 1:48 [2] Cf. Prov. 25:6f.

[3] At this point we reach the end of the three printed quartos that Luther sent to the young prince John Frederick; but a fourth was already in the press when Luther set off to Worms. The rest of the monograph was written only after he was safely ensconced in Wartburg castle. Cf. Introduction, *supra,* pp. 185

never less aware of his humility than when he is truly
humble.[1]

The idiom of Scripture requires that what is usually
translated as "to be humble", should be translated as "to
abase oneself", "to make oneself of no account". Many
passages term the Christians *pauperes, afflicti, humiliati*;
the poor, the afflicted, the despised. Thus Psalm 115, I am
become almost entirely of no account, or abased.[2] The word,
humiliatas, or "low estate," simply refers to a despised,
negligible, lowly person of a poor class such as the indigent,
the sick, the hungry, the thirsty, those in prison, the sufferers,
and the dying; like Job when he was tempted; like David
when he was deposed from his kingdom; and like Christ and
all Christians suffering hardship. These are the deep places of
which I have already said that God's eyes look only into the
depths, but men's eyes into the heights.[3] In other words,
men only look for those of consequence, the conspicuous, the
men of splendid style and rank. Hence, Scripture calls
Jerusalem a city which God's eyes see, meaning that the
Christian state is to be found in the lowly places, in-
conspicuous to the eyes of the world. So God looks at it, and
keeps it ever in His eye, as He says in Psalm 31, I will keep
you always in My eye.[4]

Similarly, St. Paul says in 1 Corinthians 1, God chooses all
that the world thinks foolish, in order to bring to shame what
the world thinks wise; He chooses the weak and the inept in
order to bring to shame everything that is strong and powerful. He chooses what the world counts as nothing, in order to
bring to nought what the world counts important.[5] In so
doing, God makes folly of the world and all its wisdom and
power; instead, He gives another sort of wisdom and power.
Because it is His way to look into the low places and see
things that are despised, I have translated *humilitas* by
low estate, or despised person; for what Mary meant was,
"God has looked on me, a poor, lowly, despised maiden,
although He could have found an exalted, noble, and powerful
queen, princess, or the daughter of some great lord. He

---

[1] Another proverbial saying   [2] Cf. Ps. 116:6
[3] Cf. *supra*, p. 192.   [4] Cf. Ps. 32:8   [5] Cf. 1 Cor. 1:27f.

could have found a daughter of Annas or Caiaphas who are the highest in the land; but in His perfect goodness, He cast His eyes on me, and so made use of a lowly and despised girl, in order that no one should boast before Him of being worthy. I must confess that it is pure grace and goodness, and not in any sense my merit or worth."

We have now said enough about the tender maiden, despised and lowly, who quite unexpectedly received this honour, and who found God to be overflowing with grace. She did not take pride either in her merits or her demerits, but only in God's regard, which so overflows with goodness and grace that He took notice of such a lowly maid, and that He was willing to regard her noble and honourable character. It is therefore wrong to say as some do that she took pride, not in her virginity, but in her lowliness. She took pride neither in her virginity nor in her lowliness, but only in God's grace and notice. It follows that the emphasis lies, not on the term *low estate*, but on *regarded*. What merited praise was not that she was of no account, but that God should have noticed her; just as if a prince had given his hand to a poor beggar, the praiseworthy thing would not have been the beggar's insignificance, but the prince's grace and goodness.

So in order to drive away any such false ideas, and to distinguish true humility from false, we shall digress for a little and discuss humility, a subject on which many have gone sadly astray. We use the term humility where St. Paul uses the Greek word *tapinophrosyne*, in Latin, *affectus vilitatis*, or *sensus humilium rerum*. It means an inclination to, or an interest in, things lowly and despised. In a case like this, there are many who seek to gild refined gold;[1] that is to say that there are people who parade shabby clothes, associate with humble people, adopt simple habits, move in lowly surroundings, use simple language, and generally adopt practices of that kind. They adopt practices of this sort with the notion that they are giving to the high, the rich, the learned, the religious, and even to God, the impression that they like associating with lowly things. But when they discover that no such impression is created they

[1] *Das wasser ynn den brunn tragenn*—a saying

cease the practice. That is an artificial humility. Their cunning
eyes look for the reward and profit of humility, and not at the
lowly things apart from reward or result. And in circumstances where reward and profit do not accrue, they have no
place for lowliness. Such people cannot be called *affectos
vilitate*, of humble feelings, with a will and a heart set on
humble things, but only having that kind of notion, speech,
action, clothing, and bearing; whereas at heart they look
above themselves to things high and great. That is the goal
they think of reaching by this kind of humble attitude;
yet people of this sort consider themselves humble and
saintly.

Those who are truly humble never think of the fruits of
their humility, but look at lowly things with simple hearts,
and are glad of the association without any self-consciousness
of being humble-minded. Water gushes from such a spring;
and the result, all unsought and of its own self, is that they
are unassuming in word, place, person, and clothing; where
possible, they avoid high and imposing things. That is what
David meant in Psalm 129, My heart is not haughty, nor my
eyes lofty, etc.[1] So, too, Job 22, The man who abases himself
shall come to honour; and he who has a humble mien shall
be saved.[2] The result is that such people continually meet
with unforeseen honours, and advancement comes to them
unexpectedly. They frankly let themselves be content with
simplicity, and are never ambitious. But those who are only
seemingly humble wonder that honour and advancement
delay in coming; and their secret, dissembled pride does not
let them be content with low estate, but only spurs their
ambitions.

Therefore, as I have already said,[3] genuine humility is
unaware of being humble, and if it were aware it would be
proud in the possession of this fair virtue. The truly humble
person cleaves with heart and mind and every feeling to
lowly things, and keeps his attention always fixed on them.
This picture is in his mind as he goes about his work; and,
because it is always in his eye, he never sees himself, is never
self-conscious, still less is he set on ambition. When honour

---

[1] Cf. Ps. 131:1, A.V.   [2] Cf. Job 22:29f.   [3] Cf. *supra*, p. 208

and advancement come, they are therefore always unexpected, and they awaken thoughts strange to honour and
advancement. This accords with Luke 1, which says that the
angel's greeting seemed marvellous to Mary, who wondered
what kind of a greeting it was, since she had never expected
it.[1] If the greeting had been addressed to Caiaphas's
daughter, she would not have wondered[2] what kind of
greeting it was; she would have accepted it at once, thinking
it right and appropriate.

Secondly, dissimulated humility is never aware that it is
really pride (if it were aware, it would immediately become
ashamed of the looks of the hateful and evil thing), and it
clings with heart and soul and mind to exalted things and
keeps them always in sight. It is with such ideas that it goes
about, and because they are ever present, it can never
become conscious of its real self. So, too, honours never come
unexpectedly or with surprise to a mind shaped in that
mould. On the other hand, ignominy and abasement come
with a shock, and to a mind filled with very different ideas.

For these reasons, it is useless attempting to teach humblemindedness by presenting the eyes with the image of lowly
and despised things; just as no one becomes proud by being
presented with the image of exalted things. What must be
done away with is not the image, but the vision.[3] We have to
live our lives in the midst of things both high and lowly; but
Christ said it is the eye that must be plucked out.[4] In
Genesis 3, Moses says that, after the fall, Adam and Eve saw
things otherwise than before. He says that their eyes were
opened, and they saw that they were naked. They had been
naked before, but were not aware of it.[5] When Esther, the
queen, wore a costly crown on her head, she said that it
seemed like a dirty cloth.[6] But they did not take these lofty
emblems away; rather they gave masses of gifts to her as to
a mighty queen who had no desire for lowly things. Yet her

---

[1] Cf. Luke 1:29

[2] This is the end of the quarto which was in the press before Luther set
out for Worms

[3] In the sense that everything depends, not on the outward impressions,
but on the mental attitude

[4] Cf. Matt. 18:9   [5] Cf. Gen. 3:7   [6] Cf. additions to Esther 3:11

outlook was humble; her heart and mind were not set on lofty things; therefore God could do mighty acts through her. Similarly, in our own case, what needs changing is not our surroundings, but our very selves, in mind and thought. Then we shall at once learn to despise and avoid exalted things. We shall respect and seek out whatever is lowly, because our mind is essentially humble and guarded on every side; for it is never self-conscious. Then all goes happily, and our heart abides equable and at one with itself, no matter how things ebb and flow, rise and fall, increase or decrease.

How great is the pride that can be clothed in humble words and lowly bearing, pride of which the world is now full. It is found in people who despise themselves in such a way that they resent it if anyone shows them disrespect; who flee from honour in the hope of being pursued by it; who avoid exalted things in order to be raised on high, to be praised, and not allowed to remain in the lowest place. But the virgin Mary showed her humblemindedness best by gladly living and remaining in a humble condition, never thinking of advancement and honour, and never being aware that she was of a humble mind. Lowliness is so tender and precious that it cannot bear to look at its own self; this searching glance is only for God's eyes, as it says in Psalm 112, He regards the humble in heaven and earth.[1] For if anyone could see his own humbleness, he would be able to pronounce himself saved, and the divine judgment would be inapplicable. Since we know of a truth that God saves the humble, it must be reserved to God to recognize and mark humility, and preserve it to us by instruction and exercise in lowly things, in the course of which we forget to think of ourselves. Many things on earth are directed to this end, such as suffering, death, and affliction. We have to contend with them, and take care and trouble to pluck out the evil-seeing eye.

The word *humilitas* makes it clear that the virgin Mary was a lowly maiden of little consequence. She served God unaware that her unimportant status was of great consequence

[1] Cf. Ps. 113:6

in God's sight. This fact should comfort us with the thought, even when we are willing to be abased and despised, that we must not lose heart as if God were wrathful towards us; but, rather, we must hope that He will show His grace to us. Yet we must watch that we are quite willing and glad to be in such a lowly state; otherwise we shall be deceiving ourselves once more, and be on the watch for exalted things, or our own good pleasure. Humility is very subtle.[1] What use is it to the damned to be flung into the bottom of the abyss if they do not accept it gladly and willingly? And what harm is it to any of the angels to be raised to the greatest heights as long as they take no wrongful delight in it? In short: this verse teaches us the true understanding of God; it points out that God watches the humble, the despised; again, that we know God rightly when we understand that His eye is on the lowly, as I have already said. Such knowledge leads us to love God and trust Him, and then we surrender ourselves willingly to Him and follow Him.

On this point, Jeremiah 9 says, Let no one boast of his strength, wealth, or wisdom; but, if any would boast, let him boast of knowing and understanding Me.[2] So, too, St. Paul teaches in 2 Corinthians 10, Let him who boasts, boast of God.[3] The mother of God had praised her God and saviour with a pure and unalloyed spirit; having not yet received any of His blessings, she sang of His goodness in the right way. Then it was that she went on to praise His works and bene-factions; for, as I have said, we must not first delight in, and lay hold of God's blessings, but through these reach up to God Himself, cling to Him alone, exult in His goodness. After that, we may praise Him for His works also, through which He has so shown us His lovingkindness that we love and trust and praise it. In this way, His good works are simply good reasons for loving and praising the sheer goodwill in which He rules over us.

When first Mary began to sing, it was about what God had done for her; and this fact teaches us two lessons: firstly, that each should look at what God has done for his own self, before looking at what He has done for others. Your own

---

[1] *Gar zu drummern gaht*   [2] Cf. Jer. 9:23f.   [3] Cf. 2 Cor. 10:17

salvation does not consist in what He does for others, but what He has done for you. Hence the last chapter of John's gospel tells how St. Peter asked, regarding St. John, What shall this man do? Christ answered What is that to you? Follow me,[1] as if He had said, What John does will not help you. Wait and see what I shall do with you. A very serious abuse dominates the world at the present moment, with the buying and selling of good works, by which certain persons with an excellent motive seek to help other people, especially those living and dying without doing God's work themselves. These excellent people act as if they had a superfluity of good works; but St. Paul clearly says in 1 Corinthians 3, Each shall receive his wages according to his labour,[2] undoubtedly not according to the labour of someone else.

It could be understood if they were to pray for others, or discharged their duty of offering intercession to God. But when they simply come to God with a present, it is deplorable; and worse still, when they offer their works as gifts, without knowing how they stand before God; for God looks, not at the works, but at the heart and its faith. He does His work in us by the latter, a fact of which these formalists have no suspicion. They build only on outward works, deceiving themselves and everyone else. They even go so far as to put monks' hoods on the dying, and declare that whoever dies in such a sacred garment, will receive indulgence for all his sins and be saved. In this way, they think to save people, not only with the works performed by others, but even with the garments worn by others.

I fear that no one suspects that the devil is leading them on to think that they can get people into heaven by means of the cloisters and their meals, lodgings, and funerals. Tell me how thick the darkness is when one believes that a monk's hood can give godliness or salvation. What is the place of faith in such a case? Let us all turn monk, and die in hoods! According to this way of thinking, all cloth should be made up into monks' hoods. Beware, beware, of this kind of sheep's clothing. These people will rend you, or deceive you. Remember, God also is at work in you, and He effects your

[1] John 21:21   [2] 1 Cor. 3:8, R.S.V.

salvation only by His operation in your own self, not in anyone else—as is plain in the case of the virgin Mary. It is right and good for you to have the benefit of the intercessions of another person, since we should all pray and labour for one another; but none should rely only on another and his works independently of what God Himself does. Let each man consider carefully his own relation with God, exactly as if he and God were alone in earth and heaven, and God were dealing exclusively with him. There is time to think of the works of others after that.

The next lesson that Mary teaches is that we should all make it our first duty to praise God and the works He has done in us; then we may go on to praise what God has done for others. Paul and Barnabas related to the apostles the works that God had done through them, and they in turn told theirs.[1] The same order is followed in the last chapter of St. Luke when the appearances of Christ after the resurrection are recounted.[2] They all rejoiced together and praised God, for each praised the grace shown to his fellow, but gave first place to his own, even if it were less than another's. They had no wish to be first and foremost in the blessings received, but only in loving and praising God. They were content with God and His sheer goodness no matter how small the gift to themselves might have been, for their hearts were of quite a noble simplicity. But the hirelings and the self-seeking look askance and are jealous when they find that their own blessings are not the highest and the best. They do not praise God, but grumble at being made only equal with or even less than others. So, too, the men spoken of in the gospel of Matthew, Chapter 20, murmured, not because the vine-dresser had done them wrong, but because he had paid them the same daily wage as the rest.

At the present time, many do not praise God's goodness, because they see that they have received less than St. Peter or some other saint, or than this or that man whom they know. They are such that, if they had been equally blessed, they too would praise and love God. They little heed that God's good things have been heaped on them, without their

---

[1] Acts 15:12   [2] Luke 24:34f.

recognizing it,—such things as body, life, reason, property, esteem, friends, the services rendered by the sunshine, and all created things. Even if these people had had all the blessings that Mary enjoyed, they still would not have known and praised God's handiwork therein. It is just as Christ said in Luke 16, He who is faithful in a very little, is faithful also in much; and he who is dishonest in very little is dishonest also in much.[1] Then what happens is that many important things never come their way, because they despise the little and the few.[2] If they were to praise God for the little things, they would soon have an excess of the big. But they admired exalted things, and not the lowly. As things are, if they were to look at humble people, they would see where their plenitude lay; these are perhaps not half up to their level, yet they are content with God and praising Him.[3] A bird sings and rejoices in what it can do, nor does it complain because it cannot speak. A dog jumps with joy and is happy, though not gifted with reason. All animals are content to serve God with love and praise, and lack the wily, self-seeking outlook of some men. It is on account of our ingratitude and pride that we are dissatisfied and discontented because we have not everything. We want to sit in the uppermost seat and be the foremost; we wish, not to honour God, but to be honoured by Him.

We read that, at the time of the council of Constance, two cardinals who were riding out in the country saw a shepherd standing and weeping. One of the cardinals, a kindly man, unwilling to ride past, wished to comfort him. He rode up and asked what was his trouble. Since the shepherd went on weeping bitterly and was unwilling to speak, the cardinal was perplexed. At length the man began to speak and pointing to a toad, said, I am weeping because God has made me a handsome creature, not repulsive like this reptile; and yet I have never confessed it, or thanked Him and praised Him.

[1] Cf. Luke 16:10, R.S.V.
[2] This is an application of the proverb that "Big things never come to one who despises little things"—one of the sayings that Luther afterwards chalked on the wall of his room near the stove. So *W.*, Vol. VII, p. 566, note 1
[3] *Die villeicht nit die helfft yhn gleich sind unnd doch wol mit got zufriden und loben yhnen*

The cardinal was struck with penitence at what the man said. He fell from his horse, and had to be led away. He cried, O, St. Augustine, you said truly that the ignorant rise up and capture heaven before us, and we with all our skill linger in our flesh and blood.[1] You will notice that the shepherd was neither rich nor handsome nor powerful, but he had nevertheless so probed into, and so deeply meditated on, God's blessings that he found much in himself that he could not pass over.

Mary acknowledged God's first work in her; it was that He had regarded her; and this was so important that all else depended on it and flowed from it. Whenever God turns His face towards us and regards us, it is due simply to His grace and salvation; and all the other gifts and works follow of necessity. Thus we read in Genesis 4 that God regarded Abel and his sacrifice, but did not regard Cain and his sacrifice.[2] Hence too arise the frequent prayers in the Psalter that God should turn His face to us and not hide it; that He should cause it to shine upon us; and so forth.[3] What Mary considered as most important is seen when she said, All generations shall call me blessed because He has regarded me.

Notice that Mary does not say that she will be well-spoken of, her goodness praised, her virginity or modesty belauded, or her conduct celebrated in song; but only that God regarded her, and that she would be called blessed. That is the way to give all the honour to God, from the purest motives. She pointed out that God had regarded her, and she said, *Ecce enim ex hoc*, "For, behold, from henceforth all generations will call me blessed, etc.", namely, from the time when God regarded me in spite of my unimportance, I shall be called blessed. Not she, but God's grace towards her was to be praised. Indeed she was of no account, and she held herself of no account. When God regarded her in spite of her insignificance, she boasted of the blessing by telling what God had done for her; she put all the emphasis on God's regard for her in her insignificance.

This shows the nature of true reverence, and how we

---

[1] Cf. Aug. *Confessions*. 8.8.19   [2] Gen. 4:5
[3] Cf. Ps. 31:16, 67:1, 80:3, 30:7, 22:4

revere and serve her. How ought we to address her? Consider
the words as they stand, and they will teach you to say,
"O thou blessed virgin, mother of God, how came you to
such lowliness and to be so despised? Yet God regarded you
in His great grace and generosity, and did great things for
you. You were unworthy of any of them; yet God has shown
a rich and overflowing grace, far above your merits. How
favoured you are; from now to all eternity, you are blessed in
having found such a God, etc." Do not imagine that she
would be reluctant to hear it said that she was unworthy of
such grace. There is no question but that she spoke sincerely
when she called herself unworthy, and insignificant; and that
God regarded her, not at all because of her merits, but purely
and simply of His grace.

She does not like listening to those vain babblers, who
preach and write a great deal about her merits, trying to
make much of her powers, but failing to see that they minim-
ize the Magnificat, accuse the mother of God of untruth, and
make little of the grace of God. The more the merit we
ascribe to her, the more is taken from God's grace, and the
more the Magnificat loses. The angel's greeting spoke only of
the grace of God, said that God was with her, and that she
was blessed above all other women. It follows that all who
ascribe much praise and honour to her, and maintain that
these are her due, are almost making an idol of her. Our
attitude to her is then exactly as if we worshipped her and
expected benefits from her. But this she repudiates, and
wants God to be praised in herself, and, through herself, lead
everyone to a sound trust in God's grace.

To revere her rightly, we must not see her just as herself,
but also in relation to God, recognizing that she is far beneath
God, making her quite lowly. We must (as she says) take
account of her lowliness, and then marvel at the overflowing
grace of God, who took notice of such a lowly, negligible
person, and blessed her amply by His grace. When you have
envisaged the facts in this way, you will be moved to love
and praise God for these acts of grace. You will be roused to
expect everything that is good in such a God, a God who
regards and does not condemn; who regards the lowly, the

despised, and those of no account. Nothing could seem better to Mary than that you should come to God through her, and learn of her to trust God, and fix your hope in Him, and this when you, too, are cast down and abased. Whenever that happens, whether in life or at the hour of death, she does not desire you to come to her, but through her to God.

Secondly, you must learn to fear all the haughty ways that people adopt, for you notice that God found no pride in Mary, nor would He have borne it. But our masters, who picture the virgin to us, despise her lowliness, and only see her exalted and imposing. They simply contrast us with the mother of God, but do not contrast her with God; they make us diffident and faint-hearted, veil the idea of comforting grace, like the altar-pieces during Lent.[1] Nothing remains to give us courage, for they exalt Mary till she has no peer. Yet she should, and she would gladly, be regarded as the most outstanding example of God's grace. She would win everyone to trust, love, and praise the divine grace, till every heart was brought by her to such a delight in God that all might well say, "O thou blessed virgin, and mother of God, how truly has God given us profound comfort through you. He graciously regarded you in your unworthiness and insignificance. From this fact we are at once encouraged to think that, as your example shows, He will not despise us poor, good-for-nothing people, but will regard us with grace."

Remember also that David, St. Peter, St. Paul, St. Mary Magdalene, and others like them, by the great grace that was given to them in their unworthiness and for the encouragement of all mankind, are instances meant to strengthen our confidence and faith in God. So, too, the blessed mother of God should rightly and properly be such an example to all the world. Nowadays, she cannot offer such an example on account of the excessive number of panegyrical sermons and the amount of merely empty talk. They never explain that

[1] In this season, curtains were hung over the pictures in church; and the altar-pieces, with paintings of the great saints, were closed. The backs of the wings were thus brought to sight, often with scenes from the life of Christ in subdued colours. The high altar was hidden from sight by a curtain which also cut off the choir. The curtain was known as the Lenten curtain. Cf. *W.*, Vol. VII, p. 569 note, and Vol. XIX, p. 112, note 1

this verse shows how the overflowing wealth of God came into harmony with her deep poverty, the divine honour with her insignificance, the divine dignity with her ignominy, the divine greatness with her littleness, the divine goodness with her lack of merit, the divine grace with her unworthiness; nor how her joy and love for God grew into complete trust; yet that is the reason why the lives and deeds of the saints have been recorded.[1] Yet some people seek help and comfort from her as if she were divine; and I fear that there is now more idolatry in the world than ever before. But I shall not discuss that point just now.

I have translated the Latin *omnes generationes* as "children's children", although literally it should be "all generations or races". The phrase is so obscure, however, that some have toyed with the question how it can be true that all generations call her blessed, when Jews, pagans, and many wicked Christians scoff at her, or scornfully refuse to call her blessed. In other words, they take the word *generation* to mean mankind as a whole; but it should be understood otherwise. If we take the natural order of birth, where one is born of another, father, son, son's son, such a series is known as a generation. This was the meaning in her mind, namely, that her praise would endure from one generation to another and there would never be a time when she was not praised. She expresses this fact when she says, "Lo, from henceforth, all generations", meaning, it begins now and will last through all generations for ever.

Similarly, the word *macaruisti* has a wider connotation than "call . . . blessed", it means "save", "give salvation to". This is something that is not done by saying certain words, or by genuflection; or by bowing your head, or doffing your hat, or painting pictures, or building churches; these the wicked can do. Rather it comes about when people use all their strength, and in complete sincerity. Their heart, (as already explained), by virtue of God's regard for Mary's lowliness, and by His grace, becomes filled with joy and

[1] The variant readings of this last sentence are no less difficult than the exact translation: *yhe und aller heyligen leben und that beschrieben sind.* Cf. *W.*, Vol. VII, 570, note I

delight in God. Then with all their heart and mind, they say, "O thou blessed virgin Mary, such a blessing is rightly thine for it is proper to thee."

(iv) *For He who is mighty has done great things for me, and holy is His name*[1]

Mary's song in this verse includes all the blessings which God had given and continued to give. In the preceding verse she sang of God's regard for her, and of His grace; and, as I have said, this was the greatest, the chief of all blessings. Now, her song is of the works which He does and the gifts which He makes; for of a truth God gives riches to some people and adorns them in high degree, like Lucifer while still in heaven. But Lucifer cast the gifts among the people and still does not value them. The outer gifts are only presents, of a temporary nature, but God's grace and regard are a heritage which endures eternally. Thus St. Paul says in Romans 6, Grace is eternal life.[2] When giving possessions, God gives His goods; but when it is grace or regard, He gives Himself; with the goods we grasp His hand, but with His grace and regard, we receive His heart, spirit, mind, and will. The blessed virgin therefore paid regard to the main thing, to what came first. She did not begin by saying, "Every child of God will bless me because He has so greatly endowed me", as the present verse says; rather first of all she said, "He regarded me in my insignificance", as was said in an earlier verse. When grace is active, gifts are given; but you cannot convert the proposition and say that gifts are a sign that grace is active. Hence the second verse is in order after the first. Similarly, we read in Genesis 25 that Abraham gave gifts to his secondary wives or concubines; but to Isaac, the legitimate son of his true wife Sarah, he gave the whole heritage.[3] In the same way, it is not God's will that His true children should build on His benefactions and gifts, great as they are, and whether spiritual or physical; but only His grace, yet without despising His gifts.

Mary mentions no benefactions in particular, but speaks of them collectively in a single word and says, He has done

---

[1] Luke 1:49   [2] Cf. Rom. 6:23   [3] Cf. Gen. 25:5f.

great things for me. All that He has done for me is great—
which teaches us that when our reverence issues from the
depth of our spirit, our words are but few. She felt it quite
impossible to put into words all her happy thoughts and
feelings. The few words used by the spirit are always com-
prehensive and profound; no one can grasp them, even though
to some extent we share the same spirit. To those who are
not spiritually minded, there is little to find in the words,
which seem quite without sap or savour; but such people talk
loudly about their own affairs. In Matthew 6, Christ declares
that when we pray we are not to use a multitude of words,
like the pagans who believe they will be heard if they speak
much.[1] The churches are well-attended; there are organs and
singing, declamations and lectures; but, I fear, very little
praising of God whose will it is to be praised in spirit and in
truth, as it says in John 4.[2]

Solomon says in Proverbs 27, He that praises his neighbour with a loud voice, rising early in the morning, is to be
regarded as a slanderer,[3] for he raises suspicion, and everyone
thinks he is trying to conceal some wrong. The warmer his
praises the worse it all sounds. On the other hand, anyone
who slanders his neighbour with a loud voice, rising early in
the morning (i.e. he is not lazy, but sets to work energetically)
is to be regarded in the same way as if he uttered praises; for
people think it is false, and that his motives are hatred and
envy, and this makes his own case worse and his neighbour's
better. Similarly, if we think to praise God with oratory,
declamation, and shouting, we are acting as if He were deaf
or ignorant and as if we were trying to rouse Him or instruct
Him. Such a foolish notion of God tends to a man's own
shame or undoing rather than to his credit. But he who
meditates deeply in his heart on what God has done, thinks of
it with such wonder and gratitude that he breaks out into
rapture, and groans rather than speaks. The words stream
forth like a flood (not thought out or in due order). The spirit
boils over and, at the same time, the words live and have
hands and feet; it is as if the whole body with all its life and
organs were trying to find utterance. That is the right way to

---

[1] Cf. Matt. 6:7   [2] Cf. John 4:24   [3] Cf. Prov. 27:14, A.V.

praise God in spirit and in truth. The words are aflame,
alight, and alive; like David in Psalm 118, Lord, Thy word is
all fire; and again, My lips shall utter Thy praises;[1] just like
hot water which begins to simmer and bubble, because it
cannot contain itself in the kettle any longer on account of
the great heat. So, too, the words uttered by this blessed
maiden in the course of this song, though few, are deep and
full. It is what St. Paul in Romans 12 calls fervent in spirit,[2]
or spiritual fervour and passion, and it teaches us to make it
ours.

The great thing was purely and simply that she had become
the mother of God. She had received so profound and great a
blessing that it passed all her comprehension, and issued in
much honour and happiness. She was raised above all the
rest of womankind, and was without an equal. She had a child
by the heavenly father, and such a child. She herself was
unable to give Him a name on account of His surpassing
greatness. She had to be content with fervour and exaltation.
It was so great a matter that it exceeded all telling or comprehension. Hence all our reverence is comprised in a single
phrase when we call her the mother of God; nothing better
could be said to her or about her, not if we had as many
tongues as there are leaves in a forest and blades of grass in
the fields; or stars in the sky and grains of sand in the sea.
It is in the heart that you comprehend what it means to be
the mother of God.

Mary freely acknowledged the grace of God, and claimed
no merit of her own; although she was free from sin, this gift
of grace was so surpassingly excellent that she was quite
unworthy of it. How could any mortal woman, indeed, be
worthy of becoming the mother of God? We ask this in spite
of certain writers who keep babbling about her fitness for
such a motherhood. But I believe her rather than them.
She declares that God had regarded her in spite of her insignificance, and had not rewarded her for her merits; rather
she said, "He has done great things for me, done by Him
alone, apart from my merits". In all her life she had never
had such a thought, still less prepared and made herself

[1] Cf. Ps. 119:140, 171   [2] Rom. 12:11

ready for becoming the mother of God. The message took her quite by surprise, as Luke says. A person of merit is not unprepared for his reward, but thinks of it and makes ready for it.

In the hymn, *regina celi letare*, we sing, "Whom thou wast worthy to bear" and in another passage, "Whom thou didst worthily bear, etc." But this is not a conclusive argument, because we use the same phraseology in singing of Christ's cross which, after all, was a piece of timber and unable to merit anything. Hence we are to understand the hymn to mean that she was to be the mother of God, and therefore that she was a woman, a virgin, of the tribe of Judah, that she also believed the angel's message, and so was suitable in every way, as the Scriptures had said of her. Just as the timber had no other value or worth than that of being suitable for the cross, and of being so ordained by God, so Mary's worthiness for this motherhood was simply that she was suitable for it and was ordained for it. It was purely a matter of grace and not a reward for merit; so that nothing could be detracted from God's grace and praise and honour by giving too much to her. It were better to make less of her than to detract from God's grace. In fact we cannot go too far in belittling her, for, like all God's creatures, she was created out of nothing. On the other hand, it is easy to detract too much from God's grace, which is dangerous in itself and unwelcome to Mary. There ought to be a rule, moreover, not to go too far in giving her such a high-sounding appellation as the queen of heaven. She may indeed be the queen of heaven, but that does not make her a secondary God, nor, as some think, induce her to give more help the more we pray to her as if she were a deity. She gives nothing. It is God alone who gives, as I shall now explain.

He who is mighty

In these words, Mary denies all might and power to any created being, and ascribes it to God alone. That is an exceedingly bold and far-reaching denial to be made by a very youthful and lowly maiden like her. She dares in a single phrase to make all the powerful powerless, all the eminent ineffectual, all the wise men fools, all the famous ashamed; she ascribes power, action, wisdom, fame, and all, to God alone. The phrase, He who is mighty, is as much as to say there is no one else who does anything, but, as St. Paul says in Ephesians 1, It is God alone who made everything, who works in everything; and the work of every creature is God's work.[1] Similarly, in the creed we say, I believe in God the Father almighty. He is almighty because nothing except God's power operates in all, through all, and over all. Samuel's mother sang, I Samuel 2, No man is able to do anything by his own power,[2] and St. Paul says in 2 Corinthians 3, Not that we are sufficient of ourselves to claim anything as coming from us; our sufficiency is from God.[3] This is indeed a lofty assertion; it includes much within itself, and sweeps away all arrogance, pride, presumption, fame, and false self-confidence; it exalts God alone. It explains why God alone is to be exalted, namely, because He does everything. That is easily said, but it is meant to be profoundly believed, and to be acted upon in daily life. Those who follow this faith in practice, will be contented, serene, straightforward, untroubled, knowing well that all depends, not on themselves, but on God.

When the holy mother of God used these words, she meant to say, None of these things, none of these great blessings depend on me, but all are brought about by Him who has done great things for me. The term, mighty, does not connote power which is inactive and at rest, like an earthly king whom we call mighty even when he is sitting still and doing nothing; but an operative force, a continual activity ceaselessly in being and at work. God is never at rest; He is ever at work, as Christ says in John 5, My Father is working still, and I am working,[4] and similarly St. Paul in Ephesians 3, He is mighty and able to do more than we ask[5]: in other words He is always able to do more than we ask; that is His nature, and that is how His might operates. For this reason, I said that Mary had no wish to be a secondary God. She herself does nothing; God does all. We should pray and beseech of

---

[1] Cf. Eph. 1:11   [2] Cf. 1 Sam. 2:9   [3] 2 Cor. 3:5, R.S.V.
[4] John 5:17, R.S.V.   [5] Cf. Eph. 3:20

her that, through her intercession, God may grant our petitions, and so fulfil our prayers. All the other saints should be addressed in the same way, for whatever is done is always done by God Himself.

Mary therefore goes on to say, *And Holy is His name.* Her meaning is, "Just as the work is not mine, so neither is the repute or the honour; because the repute and the honour belong solely to Him who does the work. It is unreasonable for one person to do the work, and another to have the repute and gain the honour. I am only the instrument with which He operates; I have made no contribution to what He has done. Nobody, therefore, ought to praise me or do me honour because I have become the mother of God; rather it is God and His work that are to be praised and honoured in me. It is enough if you rejoice with me and bless me, because God has used me to do His work." In this way, she ascribes everything to God, and claims to have done nothing, earned neither honour nor fame. Rather she continued to live in the same way as when she had none of this experience; nor did she seek more honour than before, did not elevate herself, put herself forward or cry out in rapture,[1] that she had become the mother of God. She did not demand to be revered, but went off to work in the house as before; milked the cows, did the cooking, the washing up, and the brushing. She acted as a serving maid or a housewife ought, in the little unconsidered duties, just as if the superlative blessings and graces had not been given her. The neighbours and other women paid no higher regard to her than formerly; nor did she wish it. She remained a poor village woman among others of low estate. What a pure unsullied heart she had, what a marvellous character, what great matters were hidden under such a humble form. How many met her, talked, ate, and drank with her, perhaps despised her and thought her an ordinary, poor, and inconsiderable[2] village woman; and might have been incensed against her had they known about her experience.

That is the meaning of the phrase, His name is holy, for "holy" means that which is set apart, and dedicated to God, that which none may touch or soil, but all must hold in

---

[1] Cf. *supra*, p. 222   [2] *Schlecht*

honour. In this context, "name" means good repute, fame, praise, and honour. Everyone should use restraint in mentioning the name of God, not violate it, or lay special claim to it. Exodus 30 describes how Moses made a precious ointment, but, at God's command and stern order, it was not to be used for anointing the bodies of ordinary men.[1] This means that no one should ascribe God's name to some such man. We should desecrate His name if we let ourselves be belauded or honoured; or ourselves delighted in, or boasted of, our works or blessings as the world does, God's name being continually desecrated and profaned. Since the works are God's alone, the "name" should remain His alone; and all who hallow His name and show forth its honour and fame, do truly honour Him. They themselves will be honoured in their turn. It is written in Exodus 30 that the precious ointment was so holy that it sanctified everybody that it touched. In other words, when God's name is hallowed by us, and we claim no works, or fame or anything for our own satisfaction, then God is truly honoured; He draws near and sanctifies us.

We must therefore be on our guard because, in this life, we cannot exist without God's blessings, and, therefore, not without name and honour. If anyone praises us and holds us in repute, we must follow the example of the mother of God, and be ready to quote this verse in response. Our attitude to praise or honour will be correct. Either openly or in our hearts, we shall say, "O Lord God, Thine is the work that is praised and lauded; let the name and the fame also be Thine. It is not I, but Thou, who hast done it, O Thou who art almighty, and doest all things, for holy is Thy name." The praise or the honour must not be refused as if it were wrongful; nor despised as if it were of no account; but because it is too exalted and precious a thing, a thing which should be offered up to heaven, to Him to whom it belongs. That is the teaching of this verse, and that is the answer to the question whether we ought not to honour each other. Indeed St. Paul says in Romans 12 that we ought to be eager to honour one another.[2] But no one ought to accept honour as his due, or let it rest upon himself; but hallow it and ascribe it to

---

[1] Exod. 30:22-33   [2] Rom. 12:10

God, to whom it belongs together with all the blessings and the works in which the honour is rooted. No one should live an unhonoured life; but if he lives honourably, then honour is due. But the honourable life is the gift and work of God, and therefore His name is alone holy, untouched by our own self-seeking. That is our petition when we repeat the Lord's Prayer, and say, Hallowed be Thy name.

(v) *And His mercy is on those who fear Him from generation to generation*[1]

We must accustom ourselves to the usage of Scripture which gives "generations" the meaning of the natural sequence of parents and children, the latter being born of the former, as already said.[2] The German word *Geschlechte* is not satisfactory, but is the best available in that language, tribes and friendly groups of the same blood also being called *Geschlechte*. In the present context, however, generation means the natural sequence of parent, child, and his children, in such a way that any member of the same series belongs to and makes one generation. We can therefore translate the original fairly well by saying, "His mercy endures from son to son among those that fear Him." This idiom is almost universal in the Bible, and derives originally from the words which God spoke on Mount Sinai in the first commandment given to Moses and all the people; He said, "I am thy God, strong and jealous, punishing the sins of the fathers on the children to the third and fourth generation of them that hate Me, and showing mercy for a thousand generations on those that love Me and keep my commandment."

Once Mary had sung outright of the benefits with which God had blessed her, she turned separately to the various works of God which He does for mankind in general; and, in singing to us about them, she also teaches us how to understand aright the work, the character, the nature, and the will of God. Many philosophers of great intelligence have discussed these questions, seeking eagerly to discover what God is like. They have written much about Him, and expressed different views among themselves; but all have been

[1] Luke 1:50. R.S.V.   [2] Cf. *supra*, p. 220

too blind to see clearly that the greatest thing in heaven and
on earth is to know God rightly as far as it is within human
power to do so. The mother of God teaches those who are
willing, and, in this passage almost repeats what she had
taught already,[1] and had experienced in herself. How can one
rightly learn to know God except by His own works? If we
understand His work aright, we cannot go astray as to His
nature, will, heart, or mind. Hence the art of recognizing His
works. To enable us to grasp it, Mary enumerated six divine
works in six different persons, one after the other in the next
four verses. She distinguishes two kinds of worlds, each with
three different kinds of divine operation, and three different
kinds of men: each being the counterpart of the other. She
shows what God does in each case, and pictures Him in a way
that cannot be improved.

The classification is well-conceived and logically arranged,
beside being based on several passages of Scripture; in
particular, Jeremiah 9, where the prophet says, Let not the
wise man glory in his wisdom. Let not the mighty man glory
in his might. Let not the rich man glory in his riches: but let
him that glorieth glory in this, that he understandeth and
knoweth that I am the Lord that exerciseth loving-kindness,
judgment, and righteousness in the earth: for in these things
I delight, saith the Lord[2]—a noble text, harmonizing with
the song of the mother of God. Here, too, we see that
Jeremiah divides the whole world into three parts: wisdom,
power, and wealth; and shatters them all when he says that
we are not to glory in these things, for God is not found
among them, and has no delight in them. In contrast with
these, he puts the other three: loving-kindness, judgment, and
righteousness. These are my works, saith God, and all that I
have created is in harmony with them. I am at thy hand,
and I make everything, not only in heaven, but also on
earth; and there am I to be found. He who knows me in
this way can take comfort; let him glory in it. If he is not
wise in his own conceit, but of a humble spirit, my loving-
kindness shall be upon him; if he is not proud, but humble,
my judgment shall be with him, and encourage him; if he is

[1] Cf. *supra*, pp, 213f.   [2] Jer. 9:23f., A.V.

not rich, but poor and needy, all the more shall my righteousness be near him.

In His wisdom, everything is included: especially spiritual
blessings and lofty benefits, in which we can find pleasure,
pride, and approbation. The next verse says that here are
wisdom, reason, common sense, skill, piety, virtue, the good
life; in brief, all the highest gifts of religion and the spirit,
except those that are identified with God Himself. He
exercises power over all in authority, over friends, rank, and
honour, over men and things temporal or spiritual, whether
of the church or of the laity (although the Bible knows
nothing of ecclesiastical authorities and powers, but only of
service and humility) with all their inherent rights, liberties,
privileges, etc. The idea of wealth includes health, rank,
pleasure, strength, and everything that comes as an outward, bodily advantage. Contrasted with them are another
three: the poor in spirit, the heavy-laden, those who lack the
necessities of life. But it is now time to consider the six
works and kinds in proper order, one after the other.

God's first work: loving-kindness

This verse says, His loving-kindness endureth from generation to generation, to those that fear Him. His mercy begins
with the greatest and most exalted, namely, the spiritual,
inward qualities which the proudest, haughtiest, most stiff-
necked people on earth reveal. No rich man, no powerful
lord, who is as high and mighty as a knowall who feels and
believes he is in the right, knows all there is to know, and is
wiser than other folk, especially when matters reach a crisis,
and he must either give way, or be in the wrong. Then he
becomes very insolent, and loses all fear of God. He may even
boast that he is not in error, that God is on his side and the
devil on the other. He presumes to claim God's judgment. If
he is also in a position of authority and power, he carries on
headlong, persecutes, judges, slanders, slays, chases, destroys,
all who would withstand him; and then he declares he has
done it all for the sake and the glory of God. He feels more
fully assured of much gratitude and merit in God's sight than
do most of the angels in heaven. O how hollow he is! The

Bible has a great deal to say about people of that sort. It
threatens them severely; but they feel it less than the anvil
feels the hammer-blows of the smith. People of this sort are
very common.

It is of them that Christ speaks in John 17 and says, The
time is coming when they who kill you and persecute you,
will think that they are doing God a notable service.[1] And the
Psalms say of the same type of man, He overpowers all his
opponents and declares, I shall meet no evil.[2] It is much as if
he were to say, I am in the right. I am doing well. God will
reward me highly for it. Such were the people of Moab in
Isaiah 16 and Jeremiah 48: We have heard of Moab that he
is more arrogant than most; his haughtiness, his pride, his
pushfulness, his boasting, and his wrath, are greater than his
power.[3] This shows that such people readily overreach themselves because of their pride. The Jews were of this character
when dealing with Christ and the apostles; so, too, were the
friends of St. Job when they reproved him severely, but
praised God highly and preached Him insistently. Such
people never listen, never let one speak; they feel it is impossible that they themselves are wrong and should give
way;—always headlong, even though the heavens fall.[4]
The Bible cannot condemn too strongly forlorn people of
this kind. Sometimes it calls them adders who stop their ears
lest they hear;[5] sometimes stubborn unicorns;[6] sometimes
roaring lions;[7] sometimes great, immovable rocks;[8] sometimes dragons;[9] and much else besides.

Equally well are they depicted in Job 40 and 41, where the
same kind of people are called Behemoth.[10] Behema means a
single animal, but behemoth means a number of such animals,
in other words, a race which has an animal mind, and does not
allow the spirit of God to rule in it. The Bible describes them
as having an eye like the red of dawn, for there is no measure
to their cunning, and their skin is so tough that they only
scoff at a stab or a sting. In other words, if preachers denounce
these people, they make light of it, for they feel that what is

---

[1] John 16:2   [2] Cf. Ps. 5:10f.   [3] Cf. Isa. 16:6; Jer. 48:29f.
[4] *Nur hindurch und solt die welt gar drob zu drummern gahn*
[5] Cf. Ps. 58:4   [6] Cf. Ps. 22:21   [7] Ps. 7:2   [8] Jer. 5:3
[9] Cf. Ps. 74:13   [10] Job 40:10ff., 41:10ff.

right in their eyes cannot be open to reproof. Further, the monsters' scales overlap, and leave no intervening space; for these people hold closely together, and the spirit of God cannot enter them. Their heart (says God) is as hard as the anvil of a smith,[1] and is the devil incarnate, handing over everything straightway to the devil. Such people in our time,[2] more than in all others, are the pope and his entourage, and have long been so; for they fulfil, and more than fulfil, what is here described: they refuse to listen or reform. It is no use arguing, advising, begging, threatening, or anything else; their answer is "We are in the right". That is the end of the matter, in spite of anyone else, or, indeed, the whole world.

But it may be asked, Is that satisfactory? Ought we not to hold fast to the truth? Ought we to abandon the truth? Are we not commanded to be ready to die for the right and the truth? Have not the holy martyrs suffered for the gospel's sake? Was not Christ Himself innocent? Here, as elsewhere, these people appear at first glance (and, as they plead, in God's eyes) to be in the right, to act fairly and wisely. My reply is, It is high time to open one's eyes: that is the crucial need. Everything depends on our being properly taught about what is right. Truth depends on it, and for the sake of truth we ought to suffer all things, and not deny it however small a matter it may be. Sometimes, it may well be that these people have right on their side; but their case is spoiled when the right is not done by them in the right way; they do not act with fear, nor as if they kept God before their eyes. They believe it is enough, and that it is right to decide and to proceed on their own authority, and finish with it. Thus they make right wrong even when it is fundamentally right. Much more dangerous or difficult is it when they believe themselves to be right, but do not know for certain the relation between their sense of right and those high matters which have to do with God and what He judges to be right. In the first place, however, we shall discuss the rough, human

[1] Cf. Job 40:15 to 41:34
[2] In this and the following paragraphs, there seems to be a clear reflection of Luther's experiences at Worms only a week or two earlier

idea of the right, and begin with a homely instance that can
be easily understood.

Is it not true that money, property, body, honour, wife,
child, friends, and the like, are good things created and given
by God Himself? Grant that they are God's gifts and not
your own property, and that He wishes to test whether you
are willing to sacrifice them and more just for His sake, rather
than cling to these gifts of His, good as they are. In such a
case, He ordains an enemy for you, who deprives you of a
part if not the whole, and does you harm; or, by death or
destruction, you suffer loss otherwise; do you believe that
you have now good grounds for ranting, raging, and using
force and violence to get them back again? or for being
impatient until you possess them once more, even granted
that they are good in themselves and God's creation, made
by Himself, and that they are called good everywhere in the
Bible? Will you now hold to the Word of God? Will you use
body and soul to defend these things or to get them back?
Or will you do without them willingly, and patiently let
them go? Would that not seem to be the finer response? If
you are really anxious to do the right, you must not act
headlong; what then? You must fear God, and say, "These
things are good and are given by Thee, as Thine own word
says in Scripture; but I do not know whether it is Thy will
that they should be mine. If I knew that I must not have
them, not for a moment would I receive them back again;
if I knew that Thou wouldest have them to be mine rather
than theirs, I would obey Thy will, and give body and soul
striving to get them back; but since I know and understand
nothing of present events, nor whether Thou willest that I
should have them or not; I leave it all in Thy hands, and will
wait to know what I ought to do, for I am ready either to
have them or to let them go."

Now that is straightforward, and shows fear of God; there
is the gentleness of spirit of which the mother of God sings
in the present verse. Here we have a basis for understanding
the grounds on which Abraham, David, and the people of
Israel in former days, strove well, and struggled hard:
they set forth in obedience to God's will, were in fear and

trembling, not about possible failure, but because God had laid His will upon them, as the history books record and depict, when they believed themselves to be faced with God's command. Notice that this does not deny the truth; the truth avers that it is a good thing, and made by God. And indeed, the same truth says and teaches that you must let a good thing of this kind take its course. You must always be ready to do without it if God so wills, and depend only on God. Truth does not compel you to recover things when it merely declares them to be good, nor does it compel you to deny that they are good; rather you ought to leave them alone, and yet acknowledge that they are good and not evil.

That is how we must deal with what is right and with the various blessings of reason and wisdom. What is right is a good thing, given by God, as no one doubts. The Word of God itself declares that the law or what is right[1] is good, and no one ought to say in this connection that any affairs of his which are good or right are wrong or evil, but rather die for them, abandoning everything that is not of God. Indeed it would be a denial of God's Word to deny that the right is good and not evil. On the other hand, would you shriek, shout, and raise Cain, if this right was taken from you and suppressed? There are people who cry to heaven, make much ado, destroy the countryside and its inhabitants, and fill the world with wars and bloodshed. How do you know whether it is God's will for you to retain these gifts and rights? Everything is His, and He may take them from you either to-day or to-morrow, whether outward things or inward things, by friends or foes, or as it pleases Him. He tests you to see whether, for His sake, you will forgo your rights, accept injustice and suffering, bear disgrace for His sake, and depend on Him alone. If, then, you fear God, let this be your thought: Lord, it is Thine, and I do not wish it mine; for I know that, whatever betides, Thou wilt provide, if only Thou art my God.

Now consider the verse: "And His loving-kindness is over them that fear Him", and who would do nothing aside from

---

[1] The German word *Recht* includes both the legal and the ethical sense of what is right, leaving many passages ambiguous

His will. Mark now that God's will is done in both respects:
you know that what is right, your reason, your knowledge,
your understanding, and your views are right and good in
the way God's word speaks of these things. Secondly, that
you would willingly go without these things for God's sake,
even though you be wrongfully ruined and brought to shame
in the eyes of the world. God's word teaches: "Two things are
right and good, namely to know and to obtain." For you, it is
sufficient to know that you are on the side of the good and
the right. If you cannot obtain, let God have the glory.
You are commanded to know, but God has reserved to
Himself the victory. If it is His will that you should also
obtain, He will see to it Himself, or grant it to you without
thought on your part. It will be put into your hands or
obtained by you in a way you had never thought of, nor
desired. If it be not His will, be content with His loving-
kindness. If you are robbed of the victory of the right, still
no one can deprive you of the knowledge thereof. Mark well,
we are not to dispense with God's benefactions, but to be
free from a wicked and perverse clinging to them. We must
be able to do without them, or to use them, with a serene
mind, in order that, in either case, we may depend on God
alone. That is something that ought to be understood by all
princes and men in authority, who are not satisfied with
knowing the right, but desire to obtain and conquer at
once, without any reverence for God, filling the world with
blood and cries of woe. They believe they are acting well
and doing right, because their cause is right or they think it
is. But that is the pride of arrogant Moab which esteemed
itself worthy of, and to have the right to possess, the noble
and lovely gifts and graces of God. If Moab could see himself aright, as in God's sight, he would find himself unworthy
to live on the earth, or to eat a crust of bread to keep himself
alive. What blindness! What blindness! Who is worthy of
one of the least things which God has created? And yet, on
the one hand, we would possess His highest creations, righteousness, wisdom, and honour; but, on the other hand, shed
blood in wrath, undergo and incur all sorts of misfortune.
Then off we go to pray, fast, hear mass, or found churches;

while all the time our temper is bloodthirsty, irate, and wrathful, till it would be no marvel if the stones were to leap up at us before our faces.

This immediately raises the question whether a lord ought not to defend his land and his people against wrong, or remain inactive and allow himself to be deprived of everything. What would be the practical consequences of this policy? I shall give my opinion as briefly as possible. An earthly authority ought to protect its subjects, as I have repeatedly said. Such authorities carry the sword in order to overawe those who do not abide by godly teachings; and to give other people peace and quietness. In this they must not act selfishly, but seek the common good and the glory of God. They would prefer to be inactive and let their sword remain in its sheath, if God had not ordained that the wicked must be punished. Yet that protection should not be given at the price of much waste, beginning with a spoon and ending with a bowl.[1] It would be foolish if one were to endanger a whole town for the sake of defending one man, or to rouse up a whole country for the sake of one village or castle. However, such an act may be specially commanded by God, as in earlier times. A thief may steal a citizen's goods, but if you proceed to order your army to punish the wrong, you make the whole country pay. In a case like this, which has done the greater harm, the thief or the ruler? David was often forbearing where he could not punish one man without hurting another. Those in authority should always act on that principle. A landowner must often put up with an annoyance for the sake of the common good, and not demand that, for his own sake, everyone else should suffer a greater loss. Circumstances vary; Christ would not let the tares be uprooted, lest the wheat be uprooted at the same time. If a man were to take offence at every slight, and never overlook anything, we should never have peace, and moreover we should endure much loss. It follows that the question of right or wrong is never a sufficient cause in itself and without

---

[1] A saying frequently used by Luther, and once with the explanatory note which may perhaps be rendered: If you can't end it, don't try to amend it. Cf. *W.*, Vol. VII, 583, n. 1

discrimination, for inflicting punishment or waging war. There is sufficient ground for appropriate punishment if it can be inflicted without hurting a third party. A ruler or an authority should always consider what purpose the whole matter serves, and not just one element in it. No head of the family will prosper if he throws away the whole pillow just because it has lost a feather.[1] But I do not intend to discuss war just now.

Similarly as regards religion: here matters like faith and the gospel are the highest blessings, and no one must leave them out of account. But the question of right, prosperity, honour, pleasure, and the like, must also be put into the scales, and then let God decide. This must be done not just to gain your point, but for you to understand the case thoroughly and be ready to suffer. It may be that the offender is a wrong-doer, a deceiver, a heretic, a wastrel, a sinner, and so on; and that all the world spurns, persecutes, pursues, burns him up, or otherwise chokes him off. Yet the above principle holds good, and God's mercy is at hand. Faith and truth cannot be taken away from you even if you lose your life. But when faith and truth are the issue, there are few who will cry out loud or act with vigour as is the case where temporal rights and advantages are concerned; for there are few who are ready to make an outright confession of their faith. And such men, if needs be, must be ready to endure suffering and reproach for the sake of those poor souls whose salvation is endangered because the gospel has been suppressed. The prayers and petitions of those who are suffering hurt to their souls are much more important in God's eyes than the prayers and petitions which the Moabites offered because of their temporal goods and rights, as I have already said[2]. For, where God's word does not win through and triumph, the pity is not for those who confessed their faith in vain, but for those who failed to be made strong by the word.

We see in the prophets, in Christ, and in the apostles, much suffering and much wrong, because the word of God was suppressed; but they were glad to suffer any wrong or

---

[1] Another of the proverbial sayings of which this whole passage is full
[2] Cf. *supra*, p. 231

hurt to themselves on account of the fact that their object was to win blessings for all other men. In a case like this, no one ought to use force to claim or to obtain the rights of the gospel by violence or unreasonable means; rather, we ought to humble ourselves before God, for perhaps it is that we are unworthy of being the agents through whom such great benefits should come. We must surrender everything to His tender mercy, with prayer and tears.

Mark, that is God's first work with us: He is merciful to any who gladly go without all their fancies, rights, wisdom, and other spiritual advantages, and willingly remain poor in spirit. These are they who truly fear God, who do not imagine they deserve anything, no matter how small; but gladly, for the sake of God and the world, remain poor and humble. What they possess, they regard purely as gifts of grace to the undeserving; they use them with praise, thanks, and the fear of God, as if they belonged to someone else; not for their own will, pleasure, praise, or honour, but only for the sake of Him whose they are and whom they seek. They exhibit the fact that God takes much more pleasure in showing them mercy, His noblest work, than in force, its opposite. Hence Mary says that such is the work of God without ceasing, from generation to generation among those that fear Him, and that His work endures into the third and fourth generation. The next verse sets neither term nor time, as we shall now see.

God's second work: He destroys spiritual pride:

(vi) *He has shown strength with His arm,*
He has scattered the proud in the imagination of their
hearts[1]

Let no one be confused by the difference of translation between "show strength" and "act forcefully". In any case we find the truest interpretation if we leave the tense out of consideration, and think simply of expressing God's nature and the work which He has always done, always does, and will always do. It would be much as if I were to translate:

[1] Luke 1:51

God is a Lord whose works are of such a character that He brings down the proud by His power, and is merciful to all who fear Him. God's arm is the Biblical term for His personal power, which He exercises without the intermediation of any created thing; and thus He can act so quietly and secretly that no one is aware before the event. This power or arm can only be understood or known through faith. It is on this account that Isaiah 53 complains that only few have faith in His arm; he says, Who has believed our preaching and who have knowledge of God's arm? It does everything, and the passage continues, It acts in secret, with no proper appearance of possessing such power.[1] Habakkuk says that horns are in God's hands to show His great strength; and he nevertheless declares that His strength is hidden there.[2] How is this to be understood?

In this way: when God works through the agency of created things, it is obvious where the strength and where the weakness lie; as the proverb has it: God helps the strongest.[3] It follows that it is God who defeats the others through the prince who wins the war. If a wolf devours someone's sheep, or the sheep is hurt otherwise, it all happens through some created thing. Therefore God makes or breaks one of His creatures through another of them; he who is then overcome is overcome, and he who then stands stands. But where God Himself takes action by His arm, the events are different. Destruction comes unexpectedly; and reconstitution unexpectedly, and with no man watching. God does this kind of work only between the two parts of the world: the godly and the wicked. He lets the godly man become powerless and oppressed until everyone thinks he is ruined and is finished. Yet in that very man, God is most powerfully present, although hidden and in secret. Those who suffer the oppression do not perceive His presence but have faith in it. God is there in full strength and with all His arm. Where human power ebbs away, God's power enters, provided faith

---

[1] Cf. Isa. 53:1   [2] Cf. Hab. 3:4

[3] Based ultimately on the Latin tag, *Fortes fortuna adiuvat*; cf. also Voltaire's *On dit que dieu est toujours pour les gros bataillons*; but Luther avoids the cynicism of both sayings, and sees the matter in a purely religious light

is present and expectant. When the oppression ceases, the nature of the strength that endures stress becomes evident. Notice that Christ lacked power in this way on the cross, and yet there did His greatest work, and overcame sin, death, the world, hell, the devil, and all wickedness. This too was the nature of the strength and the victory of the martyrs; and it is of this that Joel 2 speaks, Let the weak say, I am strong,[1] but it is in faith, and unawares until the end comes.

God also lets those of the other kind grow big and rise high. He withdraws His own power and lets them inflate themselves from their own resources; for when human strength enters in, God's power goes out. Then when they are fully inflated, and it is the universal opinion that these people are on top and have won, and they themselves are confident and think their success complete, God punctures the balloon, and that is the end of the story. Fools do not know that, in the very fact of their rise and power, they have been cast out by God, and His arm is not near them. Their affairs endure for a time, but afterwards disappear like a bubble, and become as if they had never been. Psalm 72 discusses this case because the writer had greatly marvelled that the wicked were very rich, assured, and powerful in this world. In the end, he says, I could not understand it until I penetrated into the secret of God, and saw what would be their ultimate end. I saw that only by deceiving themselves were they raised on high, and that they were brought low by what raised them up. How quickly were they cast down, and how soon were they desolate, and it was as if they had never been; like a dream which flies away when we awake.[2] Psalm 36 says, I have seen a godless man grow great and high, like a cedar on the mountain of Lebanon. I passed by soon thereafter, but he had already gone. I sought after him, but he could not be found.[3]

It is revealed only to faith that we can last but for a short time in this way; otherwise we should see clearly how God's mercy and all God's power are with those that fear Him, and that God's arm is against the proud in full earnest and force. Those of us who are faithless, grope for the mercy

---

[1] Cf. Joel 3:10   [2] Cf. Ps. 73:16ff.   [3] Cf. Ps. 37:35f.

and the arm of God; and when we do not feel them, we think ourselves forlorn, beaten by the enemy; we feel that God's grace and mercy have gone from us, and His arm is against us. All this means that we do not know His true works, and therefore, we know neither Him, nor His mercy, nor His arm, because it is His will to be known only by faith. Therefore the sense and meaning must be present; but the eye that offends us must be plucked out and thrown away.[1] Notice that the two works of God are mutually opposed; from which we may learn that it is God's way to be far from the wise and clever, and near to the simple and those who suffer wrong.[2] This in turn makes us love and praise God, comforts us in body and soul, and encourages all our powers.

Consider now the words, He scattereth the proud in the imagination of their hearts.[3] The scattering takes place, as I have said, when they are at the height of their cleverness and full of their own wisdom, and when God's wisdom is absent. How could He better bring them down than by emptying them of His own wisdom, and letting them become full of their own, temporal wisdom, which quickly fades? Mary speaks of "the proud in the imagination of their hearts", that is, those who are well-pleased with their own opinions, feelings, and understanding, all being given them, not by God, but by their own heart, which, they believe, is the most upright, the best, the wisest. On this basis, the proud are overbearing to the fearful, detract from their opinions, and their rights, put them to shame, and persecute them to the full: all because their own ways are right and must hold good. When they reach this stage, they boast, they exalt themselves like the Jews against the Christians; but do not see that meantime their own interest wastes away to disgrace, and Christ is raised to honour.

It has now become plain that this verse is speaking of things spiritually good, and telling how they reveal both sides of God's work; and its point is that we should gladly be poor in spirit and suffer wrong. We must let our opposite numbers have their way. They will not prosper for ever, because the pledge is too strong. They cannot escape God's

---

[1] Cf. Matt. 5:29   [2] Cf. Matt. 11:25   [3] Luke 1:51

Q<small>ML</small>

arm; they must be abased as much as they have exalted themselves: that is what we believe. Where there is no faith, God does not work in this way. He leaves them alone, and works openly through the things He has created, as I have already said.[1] But these are not the appropriate works by which we may know Him, for the powers of created things are intermingled with them. They are not purely and simply God's own works, for then, of necessity, no man works with Him, but He alone does the work. This takes place when we become weak, oppressed in our rights or our being, and suffer God to work in us: these are noble works.

Mary deals with the false hypocrites in a masterly fashion, and looks, not at their hands or their outward appearance, but into their hearts. She says, "The proud in the imagination of their hearts", meaning, in particular, those who are hostile to God's truth, as the Jews were, and still are, to Christ. For those who are knowledgeable and saintly in this way, are not arrogant in clothes and bearing; they are given to much prayer and fasting; they preach and study diligently, attend mass, walk with bent heads, wear poor clothes; they believe that there are no greater foes of arrogance, unrighteousness, and hypocrisy than themselves, and no greater friends of truth and God than they. How could they do hurt to the truth when they are such saintly, pious, and learned people? These ways of theirs give the right appearance, and deceive and sway the masses. Moreover, they are very much in earnest, offer petitions to the good Lord, and pity the poor Jesus, who did much wrong, and was proud, and not so godly as they themselves are. Matthew 11 speaks of them and says, Divine wisdom is justified by her children.[2] In other words, they are more righteous and wise than I, who am the divine wisdom; what I made is not right, and it will be remodelled by them.

Those are the most poisonous and dangerous men on earth. That pride is in the heart, profound, devilish. It cannot be remedied, because it will not listen. They think what is said does not fit them. They apply it to the poor sinner who needs such teaching; they themselves do not require it. John the

---

[1] Cf. *supra*, p. 239   [2] Cf. Matt. 11:19

Baptist, in Luke 3, calls them the brood of vipers,[1] and so also does Christ.[2] These are the righteous who do not fear God, and only serve to destroy belief in God with their pride; because no one persecutes the truth and the right more than they, although, as I have said, they do it for the sake of God and His righteousness. That is why they rank first on the side of the three foes of God; for the wealthy are the least dangerous foes; the powerful are worse; but these people of learning have no peers, and they bewilder others. The rich wipe out the truth among themselves, the powerful drive it away from others, but the learned wash it out of themselves and put something else in its place: the imagination of their hearts, and they do not want it to come back again into the light. Truth as such is much better than the people in whom it dwells; and the learned are much worse than the powerful and the wealthy. God is particularly hostile to them, as is only right.

The third work: to abase those on high:

(vii) *He has put down the mighty from their thrones*[3]

The present work and those that follow are easily understood from the first two. For God destroys the wise and crafty in the pride and self-esteem which are their stay, and on which basis they attack those who fear God. The latter must then suffer wrong: their feelings and rights are trampled down, usually for the sake of the word of God. But He in turn overthrows the mighty and the great in the midst of the power and authority on which they trust, and through which they exercise their pride against the humble and the godly; for these cannot but suffer loss, pain, death, and other evils from them. And, just as God comforts those who are made to suffer wrong for the sake of the right and the truth, and for what they have said, so He comforts those who are put to shame and made to suffer; and the comfort He gives to them is as profound as the terror He inspires in their foes. All of this must be recognized with the eye of faith and then awaited, for He does not destroy the mighty immediately

---

[1] Luke 3:7   [2] Matt. 23:33   [3] Luke 1:52

they deserve it. He gives time for their might to reach its highest pitch and its final end; if they do not then possess faith in God, they will be unable to maintain themselves; silently they collapse and break down. Then the oppressed rise, also silently, for God's power is within them, and they hold the field alone after the others have been brought low.

Notice, however, that Mary does not say that God breaks their throne, but that He expels the mighty. Nor does she say that He leaves the humble at the bottom, but raises them up. As long as the world lasts there must be authority, rule, power, and those who sit on thrones. But because they make evil use of these things, act against God, do wrong and violence to the godly; and because they take pleasure in so doing, advance themselves by it, and do not use their prerogatives in the fear of God, to His praise, and to guard what is right—He will not tolerate that condition very long. All experience and history show that He raises one rich man and abases another; advances one princedom and represses another; increases one people and destroys another, as He did with the Assyrians, Babylonians, Persians, Greeks, and Romans, who doubtless thought that they would sit for ever on their thrones. But God never destroys reason, wisdom, or righteousness; for, if the world is to endure, we shall need reason, wisdom, and uprightness. On the other hand, pride and the proud who serve their own interests as a consequence of their pride and find pleasure doing so; who do not fear God, who therefore persecute the godly and the divine righteousness, and who use the good gifts of God against God—these He destroys.

Now in matters where God is concerned, the crafty and the proud join sides with the powerful, and make them act contrary to the truth, as it says in Psalm 2, The kings of the earth have arisen, and the rulers of the earth have gathered against God and His anointed one, etc.[1] In other words, both the right and the truth are inevitably opposed by the crafty, the powerful, and the rich; that is, by the world and the greatest and highest forces of which it disposes. The Holy Spirit therefore comforts the people who hold to the right and

[1] Ps. 2:2

the truth, and, through the lips of the virgin, bids them neither turn aside nor be afraid. Those who are crafty, powerful, and rich, will not last very long. If the religious and the learned were to join forces with the powerful and the rulers and also the rich; if they did not oppose but rather supported the truth and the right, where would wrong abide? Who would tolerate any evil? Unfortunately, this does not happen; for the learned, the religious, the mighty, the great, the rich, and the worldly upper classes, inevitably strive against God and the right, and act as the devil's own. It is as Habakkuk says in chapter I, their food is tender and choice: meaning, Satan has a delicate palate, likes to eat of the best, the daintiest, the rarest—like beer and honey; hence the learned, the hypocritical holy men and women, the great lords, the rich, the devil's lickspittles! On the other hand, as St. Paul says in 1 Corinthians 1, God chooses what the world rejects: the poor, the humble, the simple, the lowly, the despised.[1] God ordains that the lowliest must suffer at the hands of worldly upper classes, in order to make it plain that our salvation is not due to any man, but only to God's power and works, as St. Paul says.[2] Hence the truth of the proverb, The greatest scholars are the biggest fools;[3] a prince in heaven is as rare as venison on earth;[4] on earth the rich, in heaven the poor;[5] for the learned cling to pride in their hearts, the mighty keep on oppressing, and the rich will not forgo their pleasures; and so it continues.

The fourth work: raising the lowly:

And He has exalted those of low degree[6]

The term "low degree" should not be understood to mean only the humble, but also those whom the world ignores and counts as nobodies. It is the equivalent of what Mary said earlier of herself: He has regarded the lowly estate of His

[1] Cf. 1 Cor. 1:28   [2] Cf. 1 Cor. 3:7
[3] *Die gelerten die vorkeretenn,* a saying frequently quoted by Luther
[4] *Ein fuerst wiltprett ym hymel,* a saying occasionally used by Luther
[5] Derived ultimately from the parable of Dives and Lazarus, Luke 16:19ff.
[6] Luke 1:52

handmaiden. The truly humble are those who really prefer
to be of low degree and counted as nothing, and do not seek to
be advanced. Similarly the term "exalted" does not mean that
God sets them on the throne or in the room of those whom He
has deposed. Similarly, when He has mercy on the fearful, He
does not set them on the seats of the learned, otherwise, the
proud. Rather, He gives them much more—He exalts them
in Himself and in the spirit above all thrones and powers
and all the critics[1] both on earth and in heaven, for they are
wiser than all the learned and the mighty. How this takes
place, I have explained already[2] in connection with the first
work, and I need not repeat it here. God's purpose is to
comfort the oppressed and terrify the tyrants. If our faith
were sufficient, we should see it happening.

The fifth and sixth works

(viii) *He has filled the hungry with good things,
and the rich He has sent empty away*[3]

As I have already said,[4] those of low degree are not to be
understood as outwardly negligible or despised; they prefer
and choose to be of that kind, especially when flung down for
the sake of the right or of God's word. Similarly, the hungry
are not just those who take little or no food; rather, they are
glad to suffer privation, especially if they are oppressed by
others, for the sake of God and the truth. This is to be of low
degree, of less account, and more in need than the devil and
the damned; more than evil-doers who suffer punishment, or
are starving and in distress; more than those who rebel at
their lowliness or need, and whose condition affords them no
help, but rather increases and multiplies their grievances. Of
such the mother of God is not speaking, but of those who are
one with God, and God one with them; of those who believe
in Him and trust Him.

Moreover, what harm was it to the holy patriarchs
Abraham, Isaac and Jacob, to be rich? What harm was the
throne to David? or power in Babylon to Daniel? or to all

[1] *kunst richter*　　　[2] Cf. *supra*, p. 230.
[3] Luke 1:53　　　[4] Cf. *supra*, p. 210

those who were and still are of high rank or great wealth—
as long as their hearts are not in these things and are not
self-seeking? In Proverbs 16, Solomon says, God weigheth
the spirits;[1] in other words, He judges, not according to the
outward appearance or form, whether they are rich, poor,
high, low; but according to the spirit which abides within.
Different kinds of people and ranks are necessary on earth in
our present life; but our hearts must neither cleave to, flee
to, nor depend on the exalted or the rich; nor flee from the
lowly and the poor. Hence Psalm 7 says, God trieth the
reins and the heart, and therefore He is a just judge.[2]
Men on the contrary judge by appearances, and hence often
go astray.

These works, like those already mentioned, are done by
God in secret, and no one is aware of them till they are
complete. A wealthy man is never aware how very empty and
pitiable is his condition; but when he is dying, or otherwise
brought low, he sees that every one of his possessions is as
nothing. As Psalm 75 says, They have fallen asleep (meaning,
died) and then have found that none of the men of wealth
have anything to call their own.[3] On the other hand, the
hungry are unaware how well they are nourished—until the
end comes. Then they discover how truly Christ said,
Luke 6, Blessed are you that hunger and thirst, for you shall
be satisfied;[4] and also how true and comforting are the words
of the mother of God: He has filled the empty with good
things. It is quite impossible that God will let anyone who
trusts in Him die of hunger: rather it must be that all the
angels will come and feed him. Elijah was fed by the ravens,
and with a handful of meal he did eat at the house of the
widow of Zarephath for many days.[5] God cannot abandon
those who trust Him, and therefore David says in Psalm 36,
I was young and now am old, but I have never seen the
righteous forsaken nor his seed begging bread. He that trusts
in God is rightly placed,[6] and again in Psalm 33, the rich
remained hungry and thirsty, but they that seek the Lord do
not lack anything that is good;[7] and St. Hannah, Samuel's

---

[1] Prov. 16:2 [2] Cf. Ps. 7:9, 11 [3] Cf. Ps. 76:5 [4] Cf. Luke 6:21, R.S.V.
[5] Cf. 1 Kings 17:6, 15 [6] Cf. Ps. 37:25 [7] Cf. Ps. 34:10

mother, says in I Samuel 2, Those who have eaten their full, have had to sell themselves to get bread; but the hungry have been well-fed.[1]

A fatal unbelief keeps blocking the way and preventing God from doing these works in us, and so we neither experience nor understand them. We desire to be satisfied and to have enough of everything before hunger and thirst come upon us. We worry about preparing for future hunger and thirst so that we shall never need God and His works. What sort of a faith is it with which to trust God, while you are devising and planning how to profit yourself? The effect of unbelief is that we see God's word and the truth and the right are overborne, and wrong is victorious. We keep quiet, make no protest, say nothing about it, offer no defence, let things take their course. Why? Because we fear that our turn will come and we shall be impoverished and starving, and always then be humble folk. This way of thinking means setting temporal possessions higher than God, and putting an idol in His place. But we are not listening properly and do not understand the encouragement of the divine message that God raises those of low degree, abases the proud, provides for the poor, deprives the rich. We therefore never come to understand His works, and without that understanding there is no salvation for us; we must be eternally damned. Psalm 27 says, They regard not the works of God, and understand not the operation of His hands. Therefore wilt thou destroy them and never again build them up.[2]

Moreover that is fitting, because they did not believe His message, but thought it the words of a lightly-spoken and faithless God. They never ventured to put any weight on His word, and launch out: so little do they make of His faithfulness. But we must always venture and dare when supported by His word; for Mary did not say, He has filled the sated and exalted the proud, but He filled the hungry and raised those of low degree. To know what hunger and thirst are, you must be hungry in a thirsty land, where there is neither store, nor stay, nor any man at hand, but only God; where no one else can meet your needs but God alone. Hence, you

---

[1] Cf. 1 Sam. 2:5   [2] Cf. Ps. 28:5, A.V.

must not only speak about humility but actually become humble and remain so. Then, when other men cannot help you, God alone will do His work in you. At least that must always be your desire, and you must not turn aside to avoid it. Here indeed is the reason why we are Christian at all, and have been given a gospel which neither the devil nor worldly men can tolerate; which makes us poor and lowly, so that in us, too, God may do His own works. Consider the point for yourself: ought He to feed you before you are hungry, or raise you before you are abased? If so, He must appear to be a hypocrite and quite unable to forgive. His works would be only worthy of scorn. Yet it is written in Psalm 110, His works are truth and earnestness.[1] If He were to intervene as soon as you became needy or humbled, or somewhat needy and cast down, then His works would be too mean for divine power and majesty; Psalm 110 says: The works of God are great and sought out for the needs of everyone.[2]

Let us now consider the other side: if He were to shatter the rich and great before they became rich and great, how would He set about it? Obviously, first of all they must become so exalted and so rich that they themselves and everyone else thinks (and it would be fundamentally true) that no man could ruin them, no one resist them. They become self-confident also, and say what Isaiah 47 says of them and of Babylon, Listen, you who live in luxury, who are very certain of your position, and who say in your hearts, "Here am I, and no one troubles me. I am certain I shall not be a widow or without children (meaning, without strength or support);" but these two losses will fall upon you in a single day, etc.[3] Then God can work His works in them. Similarly, God let Pharaoh lord it over the children of Israel and oppress them, as God Himself says in Exodus 9: For this cause have I raised thee up, to show in thee my power, and that thereby my name might be declared throughout the world.[4] The Bible is full of such instances, inculcating God's work and God's word, and rejecting man's works and words.

Mark well what profound encouragement it affords when, not man, but God gives to the hungry and completely satisfies

[1] Cf. Ps. 111:7   [2] Cf. Ps. 111:2   [3] Cf. Isa. 47:8f.   [4] Exod. 9:16, A.V.

them. Mary adds, "With good things", meaning a satisfaction which is perfect, useful, and happy; that it does every possible good for body and soul. This fact, in turn, is a sign that, before, they were entirely lacking in good things and were in complete need. As I said above, riches, in this context, should always be understood to include the different kinds of temporal goods for satisfying creature comfort; and the soul itself takes pleasure in it all. On the other hand, hunger, in this context, signifies, not merely lack of food, but of any temporal goods. Since a man can do with a certain lack of food, and almost all good things are there for the sake of supporting life; yet no man can live without any food, although he can perhaps manage without clothing, house, money, property, and friends or neighbours.[1] Hence, in Scripture, the term for hunger embraces temporal goods in the case of utter necessity and neediness and intolerable poverty; in such a way that the Bible calls those who are greedy for ecclesiastical and temporal advantages, slaves of their stomachs; and Paul says that their God is their belly.[2] How could anyone give stronger or greater encouragement willingly to bear hunger and poverty than is given by these most apposite words of the mother of God—that God will satisfy all the hungry? The man who is not encouraged by these words, and by this respect and praise given to poverty, is certainly as lacking in faith and trust as a pagan.

Moreover, who could give greater assurance in promising wealth, or put the rich in more dreadful fear than Mary does when she lets God Himself be the teacher? O how great and overwhelming is it for us either when God fulfils His will, or when He forsakes us. How utterly vain is the help or the counsel which anyone can give. It makes us afraid if we hear of our own father's denial or one's master's disfavour; yet when we are exalted or rich we are not in terror when we hear that God refuses us, and not only refuses, but threatens to ruin us, to bring us low, and to deprive us of all. On the other

[1] This present paragraph lacks clear expression of any single thought. Luther seems to be struggling to resolve a mental contradiction of the kind that he suffered during his first strenuous years as a monk, when he tried in full earnest to fulfil his vocation and his vows
[2] Phil. 3:19, cf. also Rom. 16:18

hand, what a joy when our father is kindly or the master gracious, and not only overlooks many a fault, but even spares us in both body and goods. In the present text we have a promise of this kind given by God, which is a great source of strength. Yet we can neither use it nor enjoy it, neither be thankful nor happy. O hollow unbelief, stubborn and hard as stone, for you are unaware that such great things exist.

I have now said enough about the six works of God.

(ix) *He has helped His servant Israel in remembrance of His mercy*[1]

After having told of God's work in herself and all mankind, Mary returns to the beginning: to the first clause. She concludes the Magnificat with by far the most important of all God's works, namely, the incarnation of the Son of God. She now freely acknowledges that she is a handmaid, a servant to all mankind, insofar as she fulfils the work of God in her own self, and confesses that it is for the good, not only of herself, but of all Israel.

It is true that she divides Israel into two parts, putting in front only that part which serves God; for those alone serve God who let Him be their God, and work His own works within, in the way I have already discussed.[2] It is a pity that the term *Divine Service* is now used with such a remote meaning that its sound does not recall these works, but rather church bells, church buildings, censers, candle flames, church gossip, the gold and silk and precious stones in the hats of the choir, vestments at mass, chalices, monstrances, organs, pictures, processions, churchgoing, and most of all, mumbling even when praying the rosary. To such a pass has Divine Service[3] fallen, that God has nothing to do with it, whereas it is all the service we ourselves know anything about. Daily we sing the Magnificat in church, with splendid ceremony, but less and less do we bring out its true tone and meaning. Our text remains like a rock, however, and if we do

---

[1] Luke 1:54   [2] Cf. *supra*, pp. 224f.
[3] The term *Gottesdienst* in German allows a certain play on the words which cannot be reproduced in English; *Gottesdienst* is the ordinary word for public worship, but its literal meaning is service of God

not learn or allow God's true work, there will soon be no divine service, no Israel, no grace, no mercy, no God; not even if we sang and rang ourselves to death in the churches and surrendered our worldly goods altogether. He has not commanded anything at all of this sort and, therefore, without any doubt, He takes not the least pleasure in it.

But to that kind of Israel which does serve God, the incarnation of Christ is a benefit. They are the people after His own heart. For their sake He became incarnate, and redeemed them from the power of the devil, of sin, of death, of hell; and led them into righteousness, eternal life, and bliss. That is how we should understand the song of Mary in this verse; so, too, St. Paul says in Titus 1 that Christ gave Himself for us that He might purify a people to be His heritage for Himself;[1] similarly, St. Peter in 1 Peter 2, You are a holy people, a people that God Himself has won, a royal priesthood.[2] That is the wealth of God's unfathomable mercy, and we come to possess it, not by any merit, but by pure grace. Hence Mary's words are, He has remembered His mercy; she does not say, He has remembered our merits and deserts. We were in need, but were also unworthy; owing to that fact, we praise and worship Him, and we suppress all our boasts and claims. He had no reason for acting except that He was merciful, and that He willed to make His mercy known. Why then does Mary go on to say, not that He was partial to us, but that He remembered His loving-kindness? The reason is that He had promised it as the next verse says. He had delayed so long, however, that He gave the impression, and allowed it to appear, that He had forgotten it (just as all His work looks as if He had forgotten us); when Christ came it was plain that God had not forgotten, but had always intended to fulfil His promises.

It is true, of course, that the name Israel really means the Jews and not us gentiles; yet because they repudiated Christ, He chose certain people, apart from them, worthily to bear the name of Israel and from then onwards to constitute a spiritual Israel. This is proved in Genesis 32, when the holy patriarch Jacob wrestled with an angel and was lamed in the

[1] Cf. Tit. 2:14   [2] Cf. 1 Pet. 2:9

thigh[1] to prove that thenceforward the Israelites were not to boast of their physical descent, like the Jews; for Jacob then did away with the name and blotted it out, in order that he might afterwards be called Israel, meaning "God's lord". It is indeed a high and holy name, and implies a great miracle, namely, that by God's grace, a man might become equal to God in strength with the result that God does that man's will. Thus we see that, through Christ, Christian people are united with God like a bride with her bridegroom; the bride has a right to and power over the bridegroom's body and all that he possesses. This is what takes place through faith, for then a man does God's will and, reciprocally, God does the man's will. Thus Israel is a man in divine form and with divine power; in God, with God, and through God, he is a lord who is able to do all things, and actually does them.

That is the meaning of the name Israel, for the Hebrew *saar* means a lord, a prince; *el* means God. Combine the two in accordance with the Hebrew idiom and the result is Israel.[2] Such an Israel wants to have God, because when Jacob had wrestled with the angel and won, the latter said, Your name shall be Israel, for you have prevailed with God; and you shall prevail with men also. Much else could be said, for Israel is a rare and exalted mystery.

(x) *As He spoke to our fathers,*
to Abraham and to his posterity for ever[3]

This verse vanquishes all claims of merit and prerogative, and exalts the pure grace and loving-kindness of God; for God did not choose Israel because of that people's deserts, but on account of His own promise. He made that promise out of pure grace, and by pure grace did He fulfil it. Hence St. Paul, in Galatians 3, says that God gave the promise to Abraham 400 years before He gave the law to Moses, lest

[1] Cf. Gen. 32:24ff.
[2] This etymology, which is incorporated in the A.V. margin, is now outmoded, as even the R.V. margin shows; unfortunately much of Luther's argument depending on the etymology as he understood it, is invalidated too
[3] Luke 1:55

any should boast or claim that, by the law or the works of the law, he had merited this promise and this act of grace.[1] The mother of God in the present verse praises and exalts the same promise above all else, and ascribes the work of the incarnation of God simply to the divine, gracious, unmerited promises which had been given to Abraham.

God's promise to Abraham is written more particularly in Genesis 12 and 22, and is quoted in many a passage. It runs: By myself have I sworn: in thy seed shall all the races or people of the earth be blessed.[2] St. Paul and all the prophets rate the words of God highly, as is right. For in these words, Abraham and all his posterity are chosen and redeemed; and we, too, cannot but be redeemed thereby, for the words include Christ, and promise Him as the saviour of the world. And the bosom of Abraham is the place where all born before Abraham are safe. Apart from this divine word, no one would have been saved, even if he had done every possible good work, as we shall see.

The first conclusion to be drawn from this God-given word is that apart from Christ the whole world, with all its accomplishments and knowledge, lies under sin and condemnation, and is execrated. The verse says, not some, but all nations shall be blessed in the seed of Abraham; therefore, apart from that seed, Abraham would not have been a blessing to all nations. What need would God have to promise a blessing in full earnest and with a solemn oath, if blessing and not a downright curse had already been there? The prophets have drawn weighty conclusions from this fact, namely, that all men are wicked, vain, liars, false, blind, and, in brief, ungodly; or, again, that in the Scriptures it is no great honour to be called a man, for man as such no longer counts in God's eyes for anything else than an open liar, and one who is pronounced faithless before the world. So completely has mankind suffered destruction through Adam's fall that he and his nature and his being are born under a curse.

The second conclusion is that the seed of Abraham in this case cannot mean that which is born in the way of nature: of

---

[1] Cf. Gal. 3:17   [2] Cf. Gen. 22:16, 18 and 12:3

a man and a woman; because this very birth has been
execrated and simply produces execrated fruit, as I have
explained. If then all the world is to be redeemed from the
curse by the seed of Abraham, and so become blessed
according to God's promise under oath, then the seed must be
previously blessed, and untouched and unsoiled by such a
curse. It must be naught but blessing, full of grace and truth.
Further, since God, who cannot lie, so spoke and swore that
oath, it must be Abraham's natural seed, or a child genuinely
born in the natural way of his flesh and blood. Moreover that
same seed must be truly natural man of the flesh and blood of
Abraham. Thus we have two contradictory statements; to
be the natural flesh and blood of Abraham, and yet not born
in the natural way of man and woman. That is why God said
"Thy seed" and not "Thy child"—in order that it might be
quite clear and certain that it was to be his natural flesh and
blood, such as his seed is. A child need not be one's own
child in the course of nature as we know. At the point where
the contradictories clash, we discover the means by which
God's sworn word stands inviolate.

God can fulfil what He promises, and has done so, although
no one imagined it before the event. This is because His
words and works do not require a basis of reason, but demand
a faith which is both unconstrained and pure. Now mark
how he harmonized these two elements: by the Holy Spirit
and without any act of man's, He made Abraham's seed into
a son born in the course of nature from one of his descendants,
namely, Mary, the undefiled virgin. In this case, natural
conception and birth, with their malediction, did not operate,
and could not have affected this seed; and yet Abraham's
natural seed was as truly present here as in all the rest of
Abraham's descendants. Indeed this is that very seed of
Abraham which blots out the malediction from all the world.
To him who believes in this seed, prays to it, confesses it,
and holds fast to it, all execrations are abolished, and every
blessing is given according to God's sworn word: In thy seed
shall all the nations of the world be blessed. To put it otherwise, everything which is to receive a blessing must be
blessed through this seed, and in no other way. Now this is

the seed of Abraham which is born, not from any of those sons of his to whom the Jews have always looked in expectation, but only from his daughter, Mary.

The sweet mother of this seed implied this truth when she said, He has helped Israel in accordance with His promise to Abraham himself and to all his seed. When she perceived that His promise to her had been fulfilled, she declared that it had been fulfilled, and that He was beginning to carry out His word, simply by remembering His mercy. Here too we see the foundation of the gospel, and why all its teaching and preaching leads to faith in Christ and to the bosom of Abraham. There is neither help nor hope, except by faith in the seed which has received the blessing. In fact the whole of the Bible depends on the oath which God swore; for the whole Bible is concerned with Christ. Further, it is plain that all the forefathers in the Old Testament, and all the holy prophets, possessed the same faith and the same gospel as we possess. Therefore St. Paul says in 1 Corinthians 10, For all of them maintained a firm faith in God's oath and Abraham's bosom.[1] They continued in this way, without believing in the seed promised in the future; we, however, believe in the seed which has been manifested and presented to us. The essence of the matter is the truth of a promise, and therefore also, it is a faith, a spirit, a Christ, a Lord, yesterday, to-day, and for ever, as St. Paul says in Hebrews 13.[2]

At a later date, the law was given to the Jews. It follows that the promise was not given just in order that, through the light of the law, they might better understand the curse which lay on them, and that they might yearn more warmly and earnestly after this promised seed of blessing, in which they had an advantage over all the gentiles in the world. But they transformed the advantage and made it a disadvantage; they tried to fulfil the law by their own powers, yet did not use it to understand the malediction on their own selves. Rather, they closed the door against themselves so that the seed had to pass them by; and this is still the case, though, please God, not for long. Amen. Here too is the cause of the contest which all the prophets waged with them, for the prophets well

---

[1] Cf. 1 Cor. 10:1ff.   [2] Cf. Eph. 4:5 and Heb. 13:8

understood the meaning of the law; and that, through it, we should come to comprehend human nature and its curse, and learn to call on Christ. The prophets therefore condemned all good works, the whole way of life of the Jews who did not follow this path. The Jews were then wrath and killed them, and thus rejected the service of God, good works, and the good life. This is what hypocrites and the graceless "religious" always do, and of which much could be said.

When Mary said, "to his seed for ever", the phrase means that the blessing abides in Abraham's blood (including the Jews) from yesterday, to-day, and till the last day. Although the great majority are stubborn, yet there are always a few who turn to Christ and believe in Him. God's promise is not false; and the promise was made to Abraham and his seed, not for one year, nor for a thousand years, but for all time, from one generation to another without ceasing. It follows that we should not be very unfriendly towards the Jews. Daily some of them become, or will become, Christians. Moreover, it is they and not we gentiles who possess the promise that evermore there shall be Christians who recognize in Abraham's seed the seed which has received the benediction. Our own condition depends on pure grace and is independent of any promise given by God. He knows the times and the seasons, the ways and the means. If we lived as Christians, and brought the Jews with kindness to Christ, that would surely be a true example for them. Who would be tempted to become Christian when he sees Christians dealing with other men in so unchristian a fashion? Not so, dear Christians. Speak to them the truth in kindliness; if they refuse it, leave them alone. There are too many Christians who do not respect Christ, nor listen to His word, and are worse than pagans and Jews; they go quietly off, and kneel before Him, and worship Him just as if He were an idol. But let us say no more of this just now, but pray God for a true understanding of the Magnificat, which is not only a light-bringing word, but also a life-giving fire in body and soul. May Christ grant this to us through the intercession, and for the sake, of Mary his beloved mother. Amen.

I now draw to a conclusion, your Highness, and I pray

that your Highness will forgive my presumption. I know well enough that your royal Highness's youthfulness daily receives plenty of good teaching and exhortation, yet I cannot be unmindful of my sincere and deep concern for your Highness. The hope of us all is that, in due time, God will grant, of His saving grace, to give the rule of Saxony into your Highness's hand. This will be a very precious thing if your counsellors are wise, but dangerous and regrettable if they are foolish. We must always hope and pray for the best, but nevertheless fear and prepare for the worst.

Your Highness should ponder the fact that, in the whole Bible, God has not let any praise be given to a pagan king or prince throughout the history of the world, but has always punished them the more severely. That is an awe-inspiring thought for all ruling lords. Moreover, in the people of Israel, who were actually His own people, He never found a king to praise or to leave unpunished. Above all, among the people of Judah, who were the crown of the entire human race, and whom God raised and loved above all others, there were only a few, not more than six, praiseworthy kings. The most attractive of them all was David, the best-loved; of his like there was none before him, contemporary with him, or after him, among temporal rulers. He reached decisions and acted, not according to his own wisdom, but entirely in the fear and wisdom of God, and only at His behest. Nevertheless, he stumbled on several occasions. Since Scripture could not censure his rule, but had to record the misfortune which fell on the people through David, it attributed the guilt, not to David, but to the people. It said that God was wrath with the people and had let the devil mislead David, the holy man, by causing him to number the people, seventy thousand dying of a plague as a consequence.

God had ordained all this in order to overawe those in authority, to keep them in fear, and to warn them of danger. Great wealth, great prestige, great power, great prosperity, together with the flatterers, whom no ruler can avoid having, are all round about a prince's heart; they urge him on to pride, to forgetting God, to caring little about the people and the common good; to sensuality, wantonness, presumption, idleness; in brief, to all kinds of evil and wrong-doing. No castle or city is ever so closely besieged or stormily attacked as a prince's heart. How is it possible for a prince to endure if he does not take these examples home, and if the fear of God is not his bulwark and defence? When a ruler or a person in authority does not love his people or ceases to care not only for his own well-being, but also that his people might prosper through him; then already his days are numbered, and his authority only serves the destruction of his soul. It will be of no use to him to found anniversaries, cloisters, altars, or similar endowments. God will require from him and from no other, a reckoning of his rank and office.

For these reasons, my gracious lord and prince, I commend to your royal Highness the Magnificat, particularly the fifth and sixth verses, which stand in the middle of it. I beg and pray your Highness, all your life long, to fear nothing so much on earth or in hell as that which the mother of God here calls the *mens cordis sui*, the imagination of one's heart. That imagingtion is the greatest, nearest, strongest, most harmful enemy of all men, especially those in authority. The things necessary to combat such imagination are reason, good views or thoughts, out of which all counsel or rule must issue; and your Highness cannot be saved from the dangers of that imagination unless you treat it at all times with caution, and follow it in the fear of God. I do not wish to counsel your Highness alone, but also all those who sit in council with you: let nothing be contemned and nothing trusted: what then?

This, that your Highness will not abandon prayer to monks' hoods or churches, as is the vain habit to-day; for this leads one to depend on other people's prayers, and to trust in them to the neglect of one's own. Rather, your Highness must assume an unrestrained, joyful attitude of mind. Set aside your bashfulness. Speak with God in your own heart in some private place. Give Him the key of your life, and implore Him to take control. Your prayer may be phrased like this: Lo, my God and Father, it is Thy work and Thy ordinance that I have been born to this rank and reign.

No one can deny it, and Thou, also, knowest it. Whether I
be worthy or unworthy, here am I, as Thou seest, and all
men know. Therefore, my Lord and Father, grant that I
may rule Thy people to Thy praise and their good. Let me not
follow my own counsel, but be Thou my counsellor. And
similar petitions.

With such a standpoint of your own, let happen what may,
just as God wills. How well-pleasing to God is this kind of
prayer and this attitude of mind, God Himself revealed to
Solomon, who also offered such a prayer. I have translated
this prayer at the end of this sermon[1] in order that your
Highness might have it as an example, that it might lead to
an encouraging confidence in God's grace, and that those
two things be continued that are hymned in the fifth verse.

Now I commend myself to your royal Highness, and may
God grant you a happy reign. Amen.

How king Solomon offered a princely prayer to God, as
an example to all princes and ruling lords; from the third
book of Kings, Chapter 3.[2]

"In Gibeon the Lord appeared to Solomon in a dream by
night and God said: ask what I shall give thee. And Solomon
said, Thou hast showed unto Thy servant David my father
great mercy according as he walked before Thee in truth,
and in righteousness, and in uprightness of heart with Thee;
and Thou hast kept for him this great kindness, that Thou
hast given him a son to sit on his throne, as it is this day.
And now, O Lord my God, Thou hast made Thy servant king
instead of David my father: and I am but a little child:
I know not how to go out or to come in. And Thy servant is
in the midst of Thy people which Thou hast chosen, a great
people that cannot be numbered nor counted for multitude.
Give therefore Thy servant an understanding heart (that
hears and obeys God) to judge Thy people, that I may
discern between good and bad: for who is able to judge this
Thy so great a people?

"And the speech pleased the Lord that Solomon asked this
thing. And God said unto him, Because thou hast asked

---

[1] I.e. the exposition of the Magnificat   1 Kings 3:5-14; cf. A.V.

this thing, and hast not asked for thyself long life; neither hast thou asked riches for thyself, nor hast asked the life of thine enemies; but hast asked for thyself understanding to discern judgment; behold, I have done according to thy words: lo, I have given thee a wise and understanding heart; so that there was none like thee before thee, neither after thee shall any arise like unto thee. And I have also given thee that which thou hast not asked, both riches and splendour: so that there shall not be any among the kings like unto thee all thy days. And if thou wilt walk in my ways, to keep my statutes and commandments, as thy father David did walk, then I will lengthen thy days."[1]

[1] Luther's version is very close to A.V., except for the added note in v. 9, and the word "splendour" in v. 13; Did Tyndale base his English version very faithfully on this translation, and was it lateer incorporated in A.V.?

7
SELECTED BIBLICAL PREFACES

THE PREFACE TO THE BOOK OF PSALMS

Introduction

LUTHER graduated Doctor of Holy Scripture at the University of Wittenberg on October 18, 1512, three weeks before his twenty-ninth birthday. He had undertaken the necessary studies at the urgent instance of John Staupitz, who held the chair of Holy Scripture, and who was the Superior of the Augustinian Order, a post which demanded more than all the time and strength he could give. He therefore immediately resigned his professorship and conferred it on the young doctor, whom he commended to Frederick the Wise as one whom he had been at pains to form into a "very special Doctor of Holy Scripture".[1]

Luther began work in his new appointment, so far as we know, with a course of lectures on the Psalms, and delivered them in Latin. The course lasted from 1513 to 1516.[2] His second course on the Psalms was begun in 1519 and continued to 1521, when it was broken off by the emperor's command that Luther should attend the council of Worms. The course therefore ended at Psalm 22, and Luther allowed it to remain incomplete; for Bugenhagen had published a complete commentary on the book of Psalms, to which Luther used to refer his students. Luther himself only resumed the work in 1532, and continued it for several years. But, throughout the whole of his life, the Psalms remained a favourite study. His first publication was an exposition of the seven penitential psalms,[3] and he constantly turned to the Psalms in his sermons, his popular writings, and his lectures.

No part of the Bible, apart from the Pauline corpus, influenced Luther more strongly than did the Psalms, and he seems to have had their thought and language constantly in his mind; he continually quoted them from memory, at first by translating from the Latin of the Vulgate, but afterwards using his own translation based on the Hebrew. He derived much of his personal idiom from this source, to say nothing of the fact that many of his hymns are spirited versions of the corresponding Psalms; and it was in the Psalms that he best shewed his marvellous gift as a translator.

He regarded the book of Psalms as a "little Bible" in itself, a "genuine school" in which one "learned to believe in God and have a good conscience towards Him". He felt that the variety and multiplicity of emotion expressed in the various Psalms enabled

[1] So Grisar, *Luther*, Vol. I, p. 40
[2] Cf. *W.*, Vol. III, pp. 1-652   [3] *W.*, Vol. I, 154/58-220

him to see deeply into the hearts of the writers, to hear them speaking with God, and to listen to prayers which were full of "sap, force, impetuosity, and fire"; and that we, too, could accept their sure confidence in God's mercy and faithfulness when we were passing through times of severe suffering or sharp temptation. Luther would have had all Christians know the entire Psalter by heart. He felt that it could never be exhausted, and he felt that no one could rightly claim that he fully understood even a single psalm.[1]

The Psalms lifted Luther into that fellowship of believers which, in his new conception, constituted the church universal;[2] and in this fellowship the Psalms helped him as much as or more than any other part of the Bible to clarify his own religious experiences, give them certainty, and make him feel that these experiences were essential elements in a profound and connected whole. It was this whole which dominated his deepest thought and, in spite of all the objections of his critics, past or present, preserved the essential objectivity of his thought.

The sense of this whole to which he referred his thought is seen in his understanding of Scripture, towards which he felt a highly characteristic mixture of authority and freedom,[3] a combination which his contemporaries, friend or foe, scarcely grasped, and which many future generations of Protestants perverted and then ossified. Luther's sense of the authority of Scripture had nothing to do with Literalism, but was owing to his recognition of the all-pervading presence of God in the book of books; his freedom was due to the quality of his religious endowment which enabled him, like Paul or Augustine, to handle the Bible as if it were something that he owned, or rather of which he understood the operation from within. It had given him life, and, over and over again, its life-giving power took prior place in determining the meaning of a passage. Abandoning the traditional, fourfold[4] understanding of Scripture, Luther, at least after 1519 and his contest with Eck at Leipzig, held that valid exegesis depended essentially on the plain meaning of the words. Yet this alone was not enough, for the prophetic content of the documents was far too important and urgent ever to let him regard philological arguments as sufficient. His outstanding quality, especially in his own era, is seen in the way in which he avoided allegorizing, while yet, as a born preacher and religious writer, making abundant use of picturesque analogies and parallels to press his points home.

Luther published a special separate edition of the Book of

[1] Cf. A. E. Berger, *Luthers Werke*, 1917, Vol. III, pp. 20f., to which work I owe much
[2] Cf. our Vol. I, pp. 87f.
[3] Cf. K. Holl, *Ges. Aufs.*, 1st ed. Vol. I, pp. 544ff.
[4] I.e. verbal, allegorical, moral, anagogical

Psalms in German in 1524, by which time he had translated three-quarters of the Old Testament. When the second edition of the booklet appeared in August 1528, it was given the present preface, which ranks among the best of his Biblical prefaces.

The original is reproduced in the *Weimar Bible*, Vol. IV, *ad loc. Ps.* and a critical edition is to be found in Arnold Berger's selection which is provided with useful notes and other aids.

Text and Notes

MANY of the fathers have loved and praised the Book of Psalms above all the other books of the Bible. Although the book itself is a sufficient monument to the writers, we ought to express our own praise and thanks for it. In years gone by, all our attention has been taken up by innumerable legends of saints, many Passionals,[1] books of edification, and moral stories, which have been in circulation while this book was put away on the top shelf, and so utterly neglected that scarcely a single psalm was properly understood. Yet the Book of Psalms continued to radiate such a sweet and lovely fragrance that every devout man was sustained and encouraged when he came upon its unfamiliar phrases, and so grew to love it. No books of moral tales and no legends of saints which have been written, or ever will be written, are to my mind as noble as the Book of Psalms; and if my purpose were to choose the best of all the edificatory books, legends of saints,[2] or moral stories, and to have them assembled and presented in the best possible way, my choice would inevitably fall on our present[3] Book.

In it we find, not what this or that saint did, but what the chief of all saints did, and what all saints still do. In it is shown their attitude to God, to their friends, to their foes; and their manner of life and behaviour in face of manifold

[1] Accounts of the lives and sufferings of the saints arranged according to the saints' days in the Church calendar
[2] In the *Betbüchlein* of 1522, Luther mentioned the desirability of a substitute for this kind of literature and in 1529 published his own Passional, which included, for the first time, woodcut illustrations suitable for the use of his adherents. Cf. *W.*, Vol. X, ii, pp. 331ff.
[3] Germ. *itzige*: perhaps our present German edition of the Book of Psalms

dangers and sufferings. Above all this, the book contains divine and helpful doctrines and commandments of every kind. It should be precious and dear to us if only because it most clearly promises the death and resurrection of Christ, and describes His kingdom, and the nature and standing of all Christian people. It could well be called a "little Bible" since it contains, set out in the briefest and most beautiful form, all that is to be found in the whole Bible, a book of good examples from among the whole of Christendom[1] and from among the saints, in order that those who could not read the whole Bible through[2] would have almost the whole of it in summary form, comprised in a single booklet.

The virtue of the Book of Psalms is unique, and is more finely exhibited than elsewhere when we compare it with the multitude of other books which continually babble about the saints and their doings, but seldom or never quote their words. Here the Book of Psalms is unique. It tastes good and sweet to those who read it, and it gives a faithful record of what the saints did and said: how they communed with God and prayed to Him in the old days, and how such men still commune with Him and pray to Him. In comparison with the Book of Psalms, the other books, those containing the legends of saints and other exemplary matter, depict holy men all with their tongues tied; whereas the Book of Psalms presents us with saints alive and in the round. It is like putting a dumb man side by side with one who can speak: the first is only half alive. Speech is the most powerful and exalted of human faculties. Man is distinguished from animals by the faculty of speech, much more than by shape or form or any other activity. A block of timber can be given a human shape by the art of the woodcarver; and an animal is a man's equal in seeing, hearing, smelling, singing, running, standing, eating, drinking, fasting, thirsting; or in bearing hunger, cold, and hardship.

The Book of Psalms has other excellencies: it preserves, not the trivial and ordinary things said by the saints, but their deepest and noblest utterances, those which they used when

[1] I.e. the pious in Old Testament times
[2] Luther's thought has now passed to the conditions of his own times

speaking in full earnest and all urgency to God. It not only tells what they say about their work and conduct, but also lays bare their hearts and the deepest treasures hidden in their souls: and this is done in a way which allows us to contemplate the causes and the sources of their words and works. In other words, it enables us to see into their hearts and understand the nature of their thoughts; how at heart they took their stand in varying circumstances of life, in danger, and in distress. Legends and moral tales cannot, and do not, do this, and so they make much of the miracles and works of the saints. But it is impossible for me to tell the state of a man's heart by only looking at or hearing about his many remarkable activities. And, just as I would rather hear a saint speak than see his actions, so I would rather look into his heart and the treasures of his soul than listen to his words. What the Book of Psalms gives us in richest measure in regard to the saints is the fullness of certainty as to what they felt in their hearts, and what was the sound of the words which they used in addressing God and their fellowmen.

The human heart is like a ship on a stormy sea driven about by winds blowing from all four corners of heaven. In one man, there is fear and anxiety about impending disaster; another groans and moans at all the surrounding evil. One man mingles hope and presumption out of the good fortune to which he is looking forward; and another is puffed up with a confidence and pleasure in his present possessions. Such storms, however, teach us to speak sincerely and frankly, and make a clean breast. For a man who is in the grip of fear or distress speaks of disaster in a quite different way from one who is filled with happiness; and a man who is filled with joy speaks and sings about happiness quite differently from one who is in the grip of fear. They say that when a sorrowing man laughs or a happy man weeps, his laughter and his weeping do not come from the heart. In other words, these men do not lay bare, or speak of things which lie in, the bottom of their hearts.

The Book of Psalms is full of heartfelt utterances made during storms of this kind. Where can one find nobler words to express joy than in the Psalms of praise or gratitude?

In them you can see into the hearts of all the saints as
if you were looking at a lovely pleasure-garden, or were
gazing into heaven. How fair and charming and delightful
are the flowers you will find there which grow out of all
kinds of beautiful thoughts of God and His grace. Or where
can one find more profound, more penitent, more sorrowful
words in which to express grief than in the Psalms of lamentation? In these, you see into the hearts of all the saints as if
you were looking at death or gazing into hell, so dark and
obscure is the scene rendered by the changing shadows of the
wrath of God. So, too, when the Psalms speak of fear or hope,
they depict fear and hope more vividly than any painter
could do, and with more eloquence than that possessed by
Cicero or the greatest of the orators. And, as I have said, the
best of all is that these words are used by the saints in
addressing God; that they speak with God in a tone that
doubles the force and earnestness of the words themselves.
For when a man speaks to another man on subjects such as
these, he does not speak from his deepest heart; his words
neither burn nor throb nor press so urgently as they do here.

It is therefore easy to understand why the Book of Psalms
is the favourite book of all the saints. For every man on
every occasion can find in it Psalms which fit his needs, which
he feels to be as appropriate as if they had been set there just
for his sake. In no other book can he find words to equal them,
nor better words. Nor does he wish it. And there follows
from this a further excellence that when some such a word
has come home and is felt to answer his need, he receives
assurance that he is in the company of the saints, and that all
that has happened to the saints is happening to him, because
all of them join in singing a little song with him, since he can
use their words to talk with God as they did. All this is
reserved to faith, for an ungodly man has no idea what the
words mean.

Finally, the book of Psalms contains an assurance and a
valid passport with which we can follow all the saints without danger. The moral stories and legends of the saints whose
words are never given, advocate works that no man can
imitate, works that are, in most cases, the beginnings of

sects and factions, that lead and even drag one away from the fellowship of the saints. The Book of Psalms, on the other hand, preserves you from factions and leads you into the fellowship of the saints; for, whether in joy, fear, hope, or sorrow, it teaches you to be equable in mind and calm in word, as were all the saints. The sum of all is that, if you wish to see the holy Christian church depicted in living colours, and given a living form, in a painting in miniature, then place the Book of Psalms in front of you; you will have a beautiful, bright, polished mirror which will show you what Christianity is. Nay, You will see your own self in it, for here is the true γνῶθι σέαυτον,[1] by which you can know yourself as well as the God Himself who created all things.

Let us therefore take care to thank God for these immeasurable benefits. Let us accept, use, and exercise them diligently and earnestly to the glory and honour of God, lest by our ingratitude we earn something worse. For of old, in the dark times, what a treasure it would have been held to be, if a man could have rightly understood one single Psalm, and could have read or heard it in simple German. To-day, however, blessed are the eyes that see what we see and the ears that hear what we hear.[2] But beware (for unfortunately we witness it) lest it happen to us as to the Jews in the wilderness, who said of the heavenly manna, Our soul turns from this poor food.[3] For we ought to understand what is also said, "that they suffered from plagues and died", lest it happen to us, too. To this end, may we be helped by the Father of all grace and mercy through Jesus Christ our Lord, to whom be praise and thanks, honour and glory, for the book of Psalms in the common German tongue, and for all his innumerable and unutterable mercies for ever. Amen.

---

[1] Greek: know thyself   [2] Cf. Luke 10:23   [3] Cf. Num. 11:6

LUTHER AND THE NEW TESTAMENT

Introduction

THE project of translating the Bible into German must have been often in Luther's mind, especially when any of the half-score earlier efforts came to his hand. But he was duly impressed with the magnitude of the task, and felt he could never give enough study to the niceties of Greek and Hebrew idiom, or ever appreciate fully the help afforded by the experts who were willing to assist him. He himself possessed the outstanding qualification which set him apart from the others: he had for long years been immersed in every book of the Bible, which, as a whole and in detail, had become imprinted on his mind if only from his long established custom of reading the whole of it through twice every year.

When the disturbances, due largely to Carlstadt's excessive zeal, broke out in Wittenberg in 1522 while Luther was secluded in Wartburg castle, Melanchthon, Amsdorf, and others felt incapable of dealing with the situation. Luther, in the guise of Ritter George, appeared on the scene on December 4, and stayed at Amsdorf's house till his return on the 9th. He used these few days to excellent purpose, and quieted the troubles for the time being; incidentally, Cranach took the opportunity of making the famous sketch of Luther as a knight in armour. But Melanchthon and others also took the opportunity of the presence of Luther to persuade him to begin translating the New Testament into German. This task was nothing like so formidable as that presented by the whole Bible, partly on account of the much briefer compass, partly on account of the restricted number of books of reference that were available at Wartburg castle. But the urgent need now felt to have the book in the hands of all friends of reform, not only for use against the Romanists, but also to prevent perversion and excesses within the reforming camp, was the strongest argument. Luther, there as a knight in armour, must have felt greatly impressed by their arguments that he should provide a new sword of the spirit, a weapon of righteousness striking to both right and left.

Now, Lietzmann has pointed out: "The time which Luther spent in Wartburg castle was, historically, the critical period; in it the Bible changed from being merely a weapon against the papacy to a kind of rampart guarding the truth inside the wide area so protected, and enabling the new evangel to master the currents and opinions within the evangelical movement itself. Now, for the first time, the written word of God was used against friends and sympathizers. In it Luther sought and found the definitive frontiers of the faith."[1]

He arrived back in Wartburg castle on December 12, and seems to have set to work as soon as he had completed his discussion of the postil, *Ein klein Unterricht*.[2] This little writing is closely related in substance to the present Preface to the New Testament, and in the concluding paragraph Luther cried, "Would to God . . . that every Christian man had the plain Scriptures and the pure word of God in his hand." At any rate, he wrote two letters on December 18, to John Lang and Wenceslas Linck,[3] in both of which he remarked that he had set about translating the New Testament.

All his work as professor of Holy Scripture, since 1512, had been devoted to the exposition of the Bible; and he had done both extensive and intensive work on the New Testament, notably his immensely detailed lectures on Romans,[4] Galatians,[5] and Hebrews,[6] to say nothing more about his many sermons and lectures on selected passages, and the immense labours he had already devoted to lectures on the Old Testament, all on the basis of such systematic research as was then possible. These labours, together with his own profound, personal, religious experience, afforded him a unique insight into obscure passages, and constituted his qualification for the undertaking. "Only a man who had lived in this atmosphere, with all his faculties alert, all the powers of his mind in use, and all his heart given to the Bible, could have produced such a work."[7]

Nevertheless, it was more than a general although profound competence that led others to urge him to the work. There was a spirit in him that arose largely out of the stand that he had taken at Worms and that was felt by all his adherents. This spirit issued in two main principles, namely, the conviction of the priesthood of all believers; and the need for the Bible in the vernacular in the hands of the laymen. Believers must be in a position to judge for themselves if their new status were to be a real one, and to do this they "must drink at the divine spring".

Thus Luther set his hand to the work which was to be the most enduring of all the monuments to his work as a reformer. He

---

[1] *Jahrbuch der Luthergesellschaft*, 1922, p. 40
[2] *A brief instruction*, cf. *W.*, Vol. X, ii, pp. 8f.
[3] *Br.*, Vol. II, pp. 413-16, Nos. 445, 446
[4] *W.*, LVI the whole vol.; and Vol. LVII, xi-lxxxiv, p. 1-232
[5] *W.*, Vol. II, pp. 436/43-618; cf. also Vol. LVII, iii-xxvii, pp. 5-108
[6] *W.* Vol. LXVII, ii-xli, pp. 5-238. These lectures are all given their own pages in this volume, and simply bound into one large tome, hence the repetition of the page numbers
[7] Cf. H. v. Schubert, qd. *Bi.*, Vol. VI, xxxiv

seems to have had at hand in Wartburg castle at least Jerome's commentaries, and Erasmus's work of 1505 on Laurentius Valla's *Notes on New Testament translation and collation*; and also a rough and clumsy German translation printed in Augsburg in 1475. His actual text was Gerbel's *Novum Testamentum Graece*, published in 1521[1] and secondly the Vulgate in two forms: (i) a popular edition of 1509 and (ii) one with many notes printed in Basle in 1498. Then, at least after returning to Wittenberg in March 1522, he would have Erasmus's edition with copious notes, although Erasmus's work became ever less acceptable to him: "He promotes linguistics but retards the gospel."[2] The principles on which he relied for the work were quite clear in his mind, and are set out with considerable force in his essay, *On Translating*.

The first edition of the new work appeared on September 21, 1522, though the actual translation had been accomplished in the almost incredibly short time of eleven weeks, between the middle of December and the early days of March, when he left Wartburg castle for Wittenberg. After he had preached the famous eight sermons to settle the unrest which centred on Carlstadt, he sat down with Melanchthon and Spalatin to revise the whole manuscript and to see it through the press. The first sheets appeared on May 10, one press working on the section: Gospels to Acts, and another on Romans to Revelation; although a third press took over the book of Revelation in July because it offered special difficulties owing to the 21 woodcuts with which it was adorned by Cranach. Within a month after publication on September 21, the first edition of 3,000 copies was sold out, although the price was the equivalent of something like three pounds[3] to-day. Of separate editions of the New Testament and of the whole Bible when at last he had completed it, more than a million copies were sold during Luther's lifetime. But it also fructified the work of translators in other languages, our own Authorized Version owing far more to Luther's work than the ordinary man has ever suspected.

When the New Testament appeared, it was seen that Luther had taken every care to make it as attractive and comprehensible as possible. It was provided throughout with numerous woodcuts, which were, as we have already said, especially numerous in the book of Revelation; then, too, there were simple, exegetical, marginal notes on points that Luther thought should be impressed on or explained to humble readers; in particular so that

[1] It seems probable that Gerbel sent him a copy fresh from the press as a special present, cf. *Bi.*, Vol. VI, xl

[2] Cf. T.R., Vol. V, No. 5,670, p. 310

[3] The price varied from $\frac{1}{2}$ to $1\frac{1}{2}$ gulders, cf. *Bi.*, Vol. VI, xliii

they might link up the passage with the doctrine of justification by faith;[1] and he provided certain Prefaces, with which alone we are concerned in the present work. Most of the Prefaces simply introduced the reader to the subject matter quite briefly and then left him to proceed with his study of the text itself. A few of them are of value on account of the critical judgment which they express as to the authorship, the subject matter, or the religious value of the document concerned; whilst two, those to the New Testament as a whole, and to the epistle to the Romans, are outstanding contributions to the understanding and study of the New Testament, and to the nature of evangelical religion in its profoundest depths.

In the Preface to the New Testament he stresses the fact that there is only one gospel, only one faith, and only one God, whose grace in redemption apart from any deserts on our part is the one theme from cover to cover; and that this is the gospel which was promised to the forefathers in the Old Testament, of which the New Testament and its message are the fulfilment.

The last paragraph of this general Preface appeared only in the first edition, and, as will be seen, contains those critical remarks which Luther felt he must make to keep his readers in touch with certain problems offered by the New Testament from the new standpoint. This paragraph alone contains the famous judgment about the straw in the epistle of James (the true form being milder than has become traditional, and tradition says nothing about it appearing only in the first edition); but it is much more important on account of the unfettered criticisms, quite in the spirit of the nineteenth century, which Luther permitted himself to pronounce on the books of the Bible. He was far from being a literalist—that was an aberration devised by the succeeding generation, to plague all Biblical scholarship to the present day, whether Lutheran or not. Indeed, he was bold to remark on the unevangelical character which some books betray, notably in his earliest Preface to the book of Revelation, which he seems to have disliked at that time as much as did Dionysius of Alexandria in the third century; and he discussed the epistle of James with a calm and balanced judgment which is unexpected after his rather startling words already referred to.

It would seem to have been Luther's first intention to write only one Preface, which was to serve the whole of the New Testament. He never wrote a separate one for each of the gospels, and only in 1533 did he provide one for the book of Acts (shortly before the publication of the complete Bible in German). When, in 1522, he came to the second part of the New Testament, i.e., Romans to Revelation, he planned separate Prefaces for all the

---

[1] E.g. on Gal. 3:19; Phil. 3:3, to take two examples quite at random

distinct writings; his correspondence shows[1] that he wrote the Preface to Romans last of all. It can be said that, in this Preface, he not only ended his work of translating the New Testament, but also that he reached a climax. This Preface was intended to be a continuation of the general Preface and to stress its leading ideas once again.

The Preface to Romans is far from being a formal literary introduction to a familiar document. In his lectures on Romans in 1515-16,[2] he displayed extraordinary spiritual sensitiveness, and demonstrated for the first time the dominating influence of St. Paul on the whole of the New Testament. He found in St. Paul the message which was nothing other than the gospel itself. Having grasped the central place of St. Paul's teaching, he used it as a criterion to measure the value of each and all the books in the New Testament, and indeed the whole Bible. He wrote the Preface to Romans with a lively and compelling sense that the truth, the whole truth, of the gospel had been made plain to him; and although it was, of course, only after long, profound, and profitable study and deliberation, yet he wrote this Preface in the last few days before his complete New Testament in German was to be given to his fellow-countrymen. Every page betrays, not only the profundity of his religious insight, his scholarship, and his sense of ultimate spiritual values, but also his pent-up and exalted emotion, an emotion which has scarcely failed to find a response in any of its readers, either in his own time and country, or subsequently and elsewhere. John Wesley's experience, though probably unparalleled in its far-reaching consequences, was only typical of its effect on the reader's heart. Writing in his Journal under the date May 24, 1738, in which Wesley describes the first stages of his conversion, he says, in paragraphs 14 and 15 "In the evening I went very unwillingly to a society in Aldersgate Street, where one was reading Luther's Preface to the Epistle to the Romans. About a quarter before nine, while he was describing the change which God works in the heart through faith in Christ, I felt my heart strangely warmed. I felt I did trust in Christ, Christ alone, for salvation: and an assurance was given me, that He had taken away my sins, even mine, and saved me from the law of sin and death.

(15) I began to pray with all my might for those who had in a more especial manner despitefully used me and persecuted me. I then testified openly to all there, what I now first felt in my heart. . . ."

Another of the most important Prefaces is that to the book of Acts which, however, was first published, as we have already

---

[1] Cf. *Br.*, Vol. II, Nos. 531, 536, 537   [2] *W.*, Vol. LXVII

noted, only in 1533. Luther read Acts with characteristic independence of judgment, and in the light of his own clue to all the New Testament writings. He regarded the book as Luke's commentary on the Pauline epistles, and as written to stress the main principle of the Christian doctrine of redemption. This view is not given first place by many modern writers, but it nevertheless retains great value as a scholarly alternative to, or the essential spiritual principle of, other competent opinions put forward from time to time. This Preface is said to be a section from a major work, *de loco iustificationis*, which he was planning in 1530, but which he never accomplished.[1]

In sum, the spiritual background of Luther's work in translating the New Testament for the German people is faithfully reproduced in:

1. The General Preface, where he makes the point that the essence of the New Testament is the gospel, the kerygma; and that there is only one gospel, namely, the message about Christ and His work as they come home to faith.

2. The Preface to Romans, which epistle "is the chief document in the New Testament, and is quintessential gospel."[2] He regarded the four gospels and the book of Acts as illustrations of this quintessence.

3. The Preface to the book of Acts (1533) which is presented as an elaboration of the doctrine of *sola fides iustificat*.

4. The Preface to the book of Revelation was completely replaced in 1530 by a form in which Luther gave a brief running commentary on the whole book. By this time, he had come to regard Revelation mainly as an allegory of the history of the church, its heretics and schismatics and renegades; and also as containing a polemic against the medieval abuses of the papacy.

While this view shows the first faint glimmer of Gunkel's understanding of its imagery and purpose, it is of little value to modern New Testament scholars, and can therefore be neglected in the present volume without great loss. The Preface of 1522 was innovation enough in its time, and preserves everything of abiding importance to most students to-day.

The Prefaces to the New Testament writings are translated from the Weimar Edition of Luther's Bible, Vols. VI and VII, where they immediately precede the various writings to which they refer.

---

[1] Cf. *W.*, Vol. XXX, ii, pp. 643, 652ff., and *Bi.*, Vol. VI, p. 414
[2] Cf. *infra*, p. 284

Text and Notes

PREFACE

(later editions added the words: to the New Testament)

IT would only be right and proper if this volume were published without any preface, or without any name on the title page, but simply with its own name to speak for itself. However, many unscholarly expositions and introductions have perverted the understanding of Christian people till they have not an inkling of the meaning of the gospel as distinct from the law, the New Testament as distinct from the Old Testament. This distressing state of affairs calls for some sort of guidance by way of preface, to free the ordinary man from his false though familiar notions, to lead him into the straight road, and to give him some instruction. He must be shown what to expect in this volume, lest he search it for commandments and laws, when he should be looking for gospel and promises.

In the first place, then, we must grasp the importance of getting rid of the vain idea that there are four gospels, and only four evangelists; and we must dismiss once for all the view that some of the New Testament writings should be classed as books of law or history or prophecy or wisdom, as the case may be. The purpose of this classification is to make the New Testament similar to the Old (though I myself fail to see the similarity). Rather we must be clear and definite in our minds, on the one hand, that the Old Testament is a volume containing God's laws and commandments. It also preserves the records of men who kept them, and of others who did not. On the other hand, the New Testament is a volume containing God's promised evangel, as well as records of those who believed or disbelieved it. We can therefore take it for certain that there is only one gospel, just as the New Testament is only one book. So too, there is only one faith and only one God: the God who makes promises.

Evangel is a Greek word meaning glad tidings, good news, welcome information, a shout, or something that makes one sing and talk and rejoice. When David defeated the giant, Goliath, there was a great shout, and an encouraging message was passed round among the Jews to say that their terrible enemy had been killed, and that they were free to enjoy liberty and peace; thereupon they sang and danced and made merry. Similarly, God's evangel, the New Testament, is a good piece of news, a war-cry. It was echoed throughout the world by the apostles. They proclaimed a true David who had done combat with, and gained the victory over, sin, death, and the devil. In so doing, He had taken all who were enchained by sin, threatened by death, and overpowered by the devil. Though they had merited no rewards, He redeemed them, justified them, gave them life and salvation, and so brought them peace and led them back home to God. For these reasons, they sing thanks and praises to God, and they will ever continue to be happy if they remain firm in faith.

This kind of war-cry, this heartening news, this evangelical, divine message, is called a new testament. It is also like a testament when a dying man decides how his property shall be divided among certain heirs, whom he names. In the same way, Christ, before His death, decided and commanded that this evangel was to be proclaimed to all the world after His death. He thereby gave all believers possession of all His goods: namely, His life, by which He had vanquished death; His righteousness, by which He had washed away sin; and His holiness, by which He had overcome eternal damnation. No poor fellow chained in sin, dead, and bound for hell can ever hear anything more comforting and encouraging than this precious and lovely message about Christ; the sinner cannot help exulting from the bottom of his heart and rejoicing over it when he accepts its truth.

Now God, in order to strengthen such faith, often promised this evangel, this testament of His, through the prophets in the Old Testament. Thus Paul says in Romans 1, I have been set apart for the gospel of God which He promised beforehand through the prophets in Holy Scriptures, concerning His son who was born to Him from the seed, etc.[1] And, in order that we might apply certain of these words to our own selves,[2] God's first promise was spoken when He said, to the serpent, I will cause enmity between you and the woman, between your seed and her seed. He shall trample on your head, and you will trample on his heel.[3] Christ is the seed of the woman, and He has trampled down the devil's head, meaning, sin, death, hell, and all its powers. Without this seed it is impossible for any man to escape sin, death, hell.

Moreover, in Genesis 22, His promise to Abraham was, In thy seed shall all the nations of the earth be blessed.[4] Christ is the seed of Abraham[5] according to St. Paul in Galatians 3, and has given a blessing to all the world through the gospel; for where Christ is not found, there remains the curse which was pronounced on Adam and his descendants, after his sin. The effect of this curse was that they too were guilty of sin, and that death and hell would be their lot. But, contrary to the curse, the gospel brought a blessing to all the world when it proclaimed, for all to hear, that whoever believed on the seed of Abraham should be blessed, i.e., delivered from sin, death, and hell. Thus made righteous, he would live in eternal bliss. This is what Christ Himself said in John 11, He who believes on me shall never die.[6]

He gave a similar promise to David, 2 Kings 17, when He said, I will raise up your seed after you to build a house for me, and I will establish his kingdom for ever. I will be his father, and he shall be my son.[7] That is the kingdom of Christ proclaimed by the gospel. It is an eternal kingdom of life, blessedness, and righteousness; all who believe enter it, and are loosed from the bonds of sin and death. Promises of this kind are made abundantly by the gospel in the other prophets, e.g., Micah 5, And you, Bethlehem, though small among the thousands of Judah, from you shall come one who shall be a leader of my people, Israel; and, again, Hosea 13, I will deliver them from the hand of death, from death will I rescue them.[8]

---

[1] Cf. Rom 1:1   [2] *Der etlich antzihen*   [3] Cf. Gen. 3:15
[4] Cf. Gen. 22:18   [5] Cf. Gal. 3:16   [6] Cf. John 11:26
[7] Cf. 2 Sam. 7:12ff.   [8] Cf. Mic. 5:1 and Hos. 13:14

This proves that there is only one gospel, just as there is only one Christ because the *euangelion*, the gospel, neither is, nor can be, anything other than the proclamation of Christ the son of God and of David, truly God and man. By His death and resurrection, He has conquered sin, death, and hell for us and all who believe in Him. The gospel may be proclaimed in few words or in many; one writer may describe it briefly and another at length. If at length, then many of the works and words of Christ will be set down, as in the case of the four evangelists. Those who write it briefly, like Peter or Paul, say nothing of Christ's works, but tell succinctly how He conquered sin, death, and hell by His own death and resurrection on behalf of those who believe in Him.

Therefore, beware lest you make Christ into a Moses, and the gospel into a book of law or doctrine, as has been done before now, including some of Jerome's prefaces. In fact, however, the gospel demands no works to make us holy and to redeem us. Indeed, it condemns such works, and demands only faith in Christ, because He has overcome sin, death, and hell for us. Thus it is not by our own works, but by His work, His passion and death, that He makes us righteous, and gives us life and salvation. This is in order that we might take to ourselves His death and victory as if they were our own.

Christ in the gospels, and Peter and Paul in their letters, set forth many doctrines and regulations, and expounded those regulations. That they should have done so must be regarded as another of the many beneficial works of Christ. To know His works and His life's story is not the same thing as to know the gospel, because it does not mean that you know that He conquered sin, death, and the devil. Similarly, it is not knowledge of the gospel if you just know doctrines and rules of this kind. But you will know the gospel when you hear the voice which tells you that Christ Himself is yours, together with His life, teaching, work, death, resurrection, and everything that He has, does, or can do.

A further point to note is that He does not constrain us, but gently draws us, as when He says, Blessed are the poor, etc.;[1] and, similarly, the apostles use the words, I exhort, I

---

[1] Matt. 5:3

beseech, I pray. On every count, it is evident that the *euangelion* does not form a book of laws, but a proclamation of the good things which Christ has offered us for our own, if only we believe. On the other hand, Moses, in his books, urges, drives, threatens, lashes out, and severely punishes; for he is a maker and administrator of law. That, moreover, is why laws are not prescribed for believers. It is as St. Paul says in I Timothy I, Understand this, that a man is given righteousness, life, and salvation by faith; and nought is required of him to give proof of this faith.[1]

If he have faith, the believer cannot be restrained. He betrays himself. He breaks out. He confesses and teaches this gospel to the people at the risk of life itself. His whole life and all his effort are directed towards the benefit of his neighbour, and this not just in order to help him to attain the same grace; but he employs his strength, uses his goods, and stakes his reputation, as he sees Christ did for him, and therefore follows His example. Christ never gave any other commandment than that of love, because He intended that commandment to be the test of His disciples and of true believers. For if (good) works and love do not blossom forth, it is not genuine faith, the gospel has not yet gained a foothold, and Christ is not yet rightly known. Watch that you apply yourself to the books of the New Testament so that you may learn to read them in this way.

The books which are the best and noblest in the New Testament.[2]

You are in a position now rightly to discriminate between all the books, and decide which are the best. The true kernel and marrow of all the books, those which should rightly be ranked first, are the gospel of John and St. Paul's epistles, especially that to the Romans, together with St. Peter's first epistle. Every Christian would do well to read them first and most often, and, by daily perusal, make them as familiar as his daily bread. You will not find in these books

[1] Cf. I Tim. 1:9
[2] This concluding section appeared only in the first edition, the "September Testament," of 1522; and it is very revealing of Luther's spirit and standpoint

much said about the works and miracles of Christ, but you will find a masterly account of how faith in Christ conquers sin, death, and hell; and gives life, righteousness, and salvation. This is the true essence of the gospel, as you have learned.

If I were ever compelled to make a choice, and had to dispense with either the works or the preaching of Christ, I would rather do without the works than the preaching; for the works are of no avail to me, whereas His words give life, as He himself declared.[1] John records but few of the works of Christ, but a great deal of His preaching, whereas the other three evangelists record many of His works, but few of His words. It follows that the gospel of John is unique in loveliness, and of a truth the principal gospel, far, far superior to the other three, and much to be preferred. And in the same way, the epistles of St. Paul and St. Peter are far in advance of the three gospels of Matthew, Mark, and Luke.

In sum: the gospel and the first epistle of St. John, St. Paul's epistles, especially those to the Romans, Galatians, and Ephesians; and St. Peter's first epistle, are the books which show Christ to you. They teach everything you need to know for your salvation, even if you were never to see or hear any other book or hear any other teaching. In comparison with these, the epistle of St. James is an epistle full of straw, because it contains nothing evangelical. But more about this in the other Prefaces.

[1] Cf. John 6:63; 8:51

PREFACE TO THE EPISTLE OF ST. PAUL TO THE ROMANS

THIS epistle is in truth the most important document in the New Testament, the gospel in its purest expression. Not only is it well worth a Christian's while to know it word for word by heart, but also to meditate on it day by day. It is the soul's daily bread, and can never be read too often, or studied too much. The more you probe into it the more precious it becomes, and the better its flavour. God helping me, I shall try my best to make this Preface serve as an introduction which will enable everyone to understand it in the best possible way. Hitherto, this epistle has been smothered with comments and all sorts of irrelevances; yet, in essence, it is a brilliant light, almost enough to illumine the whole Bible.

The first thing needed is to master the terminology. We must learn what St. Paul means by such words as law, sin, grace, faith, righteousness, flesh, spirit, and the like; otherwise we shall read and only waste our time. You must not understand the term "law" in its everyday sense as something which explains what acts are permitted or forbidden. This holds for ordinary laws, and you keep them by doing what they enjoin, although you may have no heart in it. But God judges according to your inmost convictions; His law must be fulfilled in your very heart, and cannot be obeyed if you merely perform certain acts. Its penalties do indeed apply to certain acts done apart from our inmost convictions, such as hypocrisy and lying. Psalm 117 declares that all men are liars, because no one keeps God's law from his heart;[1] nor can he do so; for to be averse to goodness and prone to evil are traits found in all men. If we do not choose goodness freely, we do not keep God's law from the heart. Then sin enters in, and divine wrath is incurred even though, to outward appearance, we are doing many virtuous works and living an honourable life.

In chapter 2, St. Paul therefore asserts that the Jews are

[1] Ps. 116:11

all sinners. He says that only those who keep the law are righteous in God's eyes, his point being that no one keeps the law by "works". Rather, Paul says to the Jews, "You teach us not to commit adultery, but you commit adultery yourselves. Further, in judging others; you condemn yourselves, since you do the very things which you condemn."[1] It is as if he were to say, To outward appearance, you observe the law scrupulously, condemning those who do not observe it, and being quick to teach one and all. You see the splinter in the other man's eye, but are unaware of the timber in your own. Granted that, in appearance and conduct, you observe the law, owing to your fear of punishment or hope of reward, yet you do nothing from free choice and out of love for the law, but unwillingly and under compulsion; were there no law, you would rather do something else. The logical conclusion is that, in the depths of your heart, you hate the law. What is the use of teaching others not to steal if you are a thief at heart yourself and, if you dared, would be one in fact? Of course, the outer conduct of this kind is not continued for long by humbugs of this kind. It follows that, if you teach others, but not your own selves, you do not know what you teach, and have not rightly understood the nature of the law. Nay, the law increases your guilt, as Paul says in chapter 5.[2] A man only hates the law the more, the more it demands what he cannot perform.

That is why, in chapter 7, Paul calls the law spiritual;[3] spiritual, because, if the law were corporeal, our works would meet its demands. Since it is spiritual, however, no one keeps it, unless everything you do springs from your inmost heart. Such a heart is given us only by God's spirit, and this spirit makes us equal to the demands of the law. Thus we gain a genuine desire for the law, and then everything is done with willing hearts, and not in fear, or under compulsion. Therefore, because that law is spiritual, when it is loved by hearts that are spiritual, and demands that sort of mind, if that spirit is not in our hearts, sin remains; a grudge abides together with hostility to the law, although the law itself is right and good and holy.

[1] Cf. Rom. 2:1, 22f.   [2] 5:20   [3] Cf. 7:14

Therefore, familiarize yourself with the idea that it is one thing to do what the law enjoins, and quite another to fulfil the law. All that a man does or ever can do of his own free will and strength, is to perform the works required by the law. Nevertheless, all such works are vain and useless as long as we dislike the law, and feel it a constraint. That is Paul's meaning in chapter 3 when he says, "Through the works of the law shall no man be justified before God".[1] It is obvious—is it not?—that the sophisticators wrangling in the schools are misleading when they teach us to prepare ourselves for grace by our works. How can anyone use works to prepare himself to be good when he never does a good work without a certain reluctance or unwillingness in his heart? How is it possible for God to take pleasure in works that spring from reluctant and hostile hearts?

To fulfil the law, we must meet its requirements gladly and lovingly; live virtuous and upright lives without the constraint of the law, and as if neither the law nor its penalties existed. But this joy, this unconstrained love, is put into our hearts by the Holy Spirit, as St. Paul says in chapter 5.[2] But the Holy Spirit is given only in, with, and through, faith in Jesus Christ, as Paul said in his opening paragraph. Similarly, faith itself comes only through the word of God, the gospel. This gospel proclaims Christ as the Son of God; that He was man; that He died and rose again for our sakes, as Paul says in chapters 3, 4, and 10.[3]

We reach the conclusion that faith alone justifies us and fulfils the law; and this because faith brings us the spirit gained by the merits of Christ. The spirit, in turn, gives us the happiness and freedom at which the law aims; and this shows that good works really proceed from faith. That is Paul's meaning in chapter 3 when, after having condemned the works of the law, he sounds as if he had meant to abrogate the law by faith; but says that, on the contrary, we confirm the law through faith, i.e. we fulfil it by faith.[4]

The word SIN in the Bible means something more than the external works done by our bodily action. It means all the circumstances that act together and excite or incite us to

[1] 3:27f.   [2] 5:5   [3] 3:24f., 4:24f., 10:9   [4] Rom. 3:31

do what is done; in particular, the impulses operating in the depths of our hearts. This, again, means that the single term, "doing", includes the case where a man gives way completely, and falls into sin. Even where nothing is done outwardly, a man may still fall into complete destruction of body and soul. In particular, the Bible penetrates into our hearts, and looks at the root and the very source of all sin, i.e., unbelief in the depth of our heart. Just as faith alone gives us the spirit and the desire for doing works that are plainly good, so unbelief is the sole cause of sin; it exalts the flesh, and gives the desire to do works that are plainly wrong, as happened in the case of Adam and Eve in the garden of Eden, Genesis 3.[1]

Christ therefore singled out unbelief and called it sin. In John 16, He says, The spirit will convict the world of sin because they do not believe in me.[2] Similarly, before good or evil works are performed, and before they appear as good or evil fruits, either faith or unbelief must be already in our hearts. Here are the roots, the sap, and the chief energy of all sin. This is what the Bible calls the head of the serpent and of the old dragon,[3] which Christ, the seed of the woman, must crush, as was promised to Adam.[4]

The words GRACE and GIFT differ inasmuch as the true meaning of grace is the kindness or favour which God bears towards us of His own choice, and through which He is willing to give us Christ, and to pour the Holy Spirit and His blessings upon us. Paul makes this clear in chapter 5 when he speaks of the grace and favour of Christ, and the like.[5] Nevertheless, both the gifts and the spirit must be received by us daily; although even then they will be incomplete; for the old desires and sins still linger in us, and strive against the spirit, as Paul says in Romans 7 and Galatians 5.[6] Again, Genesis 3 speaks of the enmity between the woman's children and the serpent's brood.[7] Yet grace is sufficient to enable us to be accounted entirely and completely righteous in God's sight, because His grace does not come in portions and pieces, separately, like so many gifts; rather, it takes us up

[1] Gen. 3:6   [2] John 16:8f.   [3] Rev. 20:2   [4] Gen. 3:15
[5] 5:15ff.   [6] Rom. 7:14-23; Gal. 5:17f.   [7] Gen. 3:15

completely into its embrace for the sake of Christ our mediator and intercessor, and in order that the gifts may take root in us.

This point of view will help you to understand chapter 7, where Paul depicts himself as still a sinner;[1] and yet, in chapter 8, declares that no charge is held against those who are "in Christ",[2] because of the spirit and the (still incomplete) gifts. Insofar as our flesh is not yet killed, we are still sinners. Nevertheless insofar as we believe in Christ, and begin to receive the spirit, God shows us favour and goodwill. He does this to the extent that He pays no regard to our remaining sins, and does not judge them; rather He deals with us according to the faith which we have in Christ until sin is killed.

FAITH is not something dreamed, a human illusion, although this is what many people understand by the term. Whenever they see that it is not followed either by an improvement in morals or by good works, while much is still being said about faith, they fall into the error of declaring that faith is not enough, that we must do "works" if we are to become upright and attain salvation. The reason is that, when they hear the gospel, they miss the point; in their hearts, and out of their own resources, they conjure up an idea which they call "belief", which they treat as genuine faith. All the same, it is but a human fabrication, an idea without a corresponding experience in the depths of the heart. It is therefore ineffective and not followed by a better kind of life.

Faith, however, is something that God effects in us. It changes us and we are reborn from God, John 1.[3] Faith puts the old Adam to death and makes us quite different men in heart, in mind, and in all our powers; and it is accompanied by the Holy Spirit. O, when it comes to faith, what a living, creative, active, powerful thing it is. It cannot do other than good at all times. It never waits to ask whether there is some good work to do, Rather, before the question is raised, it has done the deed, and keeps on doing it. A man not active in this way is a man without faith. He is groping about for

[1] 7:9ff.   [2] Rom. 8:1   [3] John 1:13

faith and searching for good works, but knows neither what faith is nor what good works are. Nevertheless, he keeps on talking nonsense about faith and good works.

Faith is a living and unshakeable confidence, a belief in the grace of God so assured that a man would die a thousand deaths for its sake. This kind of confidence in God's grace, this sort of knowledge of it, makes us joyful, high-spirited, and eager in our relations with God and with all mankind. That is what the Holy Spirit effects through faith. Hence, the man of faith, without being driven, willingly and gladly seeks to do good to everyone, serve everyone, suffer all kinds of hardships, for the sake of the love and glory of the God who has shown him such grace. It is impossible, indeed, to separate works from faith, just as it is impossible to separate heat and light from fire. Beware, therefore, of wrong conceptions of your own, and of those who talk nonsense while thinking they are pronouncing shrewd judgments on faith and works whereas they are showing themselves the greatest of fools. Offer up your prayers to God, and ask Him to create faith in you; otherwise, you will always lack faith, no matter how you try to deceive yourself, or what your efforts and ability.

RIGHTEOUSNESS means precisely the kind of faith we have in mind, and should properly be called "divine righteousness", the righteousness which holds good in God's sight, because it is God's gift, and shapes a man's nature to do his duty to all. By his faith, he is set free from sin, and he finds delight in God's commandments. In this way, he pays God the honour that is due to Him, and renders Him what he owes. He serves his fellows willingly according to his ability, so discharging his obligations to all men. Righteousness of this kind cannot be brought about in the ordinary course of nature, by our own free will, or by our own powers. No one can give faith to himself, nor free himself from unbelief; how, then, can anyone do away with even his smallest sins? It follows that what is done in the absence of faith on the one hand, or in consequence of unbelief on the other, is naught but falsity, self-deception, and sin, Romans 14,[1] no matter how well it is gilded over.

[1] 14:23

FLESH and SPIRIT must not be understood as if flesh had only to do with moral impurity, and spirit only with the state of our hearts. Rather, flesh, according to St. Paul, as also according to Christ in John 3,[1] means everything that is born from the flesh, i.e. the entire self, body and soul, including our reason and all our senses. This is because everything in us leans to the flesh. It is therefore appropriate to call a man "carnal" when, not having yet received grace, he gibbers and jabbers cheerfully about the high things of the spirit in the very way which Galatians 5 depicts as the works of the flesh, and calls hypocrisy and hatred works of the flesh.[2] Moreover, Romans 8 says that the law is weakened by the flesh.[3] This is not said simply of moral impurity, but of all sins. In particular, it is said of lack of faith, which is a kind of wickedness more spiritual in character than anything else.

On the other hand, the term spiritual is often applied to one who is busied with the most outward of works, as when Christ washed His disciples' feet, and when Peter went sailing his boat and fishing. Hence, the term "flesh" applies to a person who, in thought and in fact, lives and labours in the service of the body and the temporal life. The term "spirit" applies to a person who, in thought and fact, lives and labours in the service of the spirit and of the life to come. Unless you give these terms this connotation, you will never comprehend Paul's epistle to the Romans, nor any other book of Holy Scripture. Beware then of all teachers who use these terms differently, no matter who they may be, whether Jerome, Augustine, Ambrose, Origen, or their like; or even persons more eminent than they. But let us now turn to the epistle itself.

The first duty of a preacher of the gospel is to declare God's law and describe the nature of sin. Everything is sinful that does not proceed from the spirit, or is not experienced as the outcome of faith in Christ. The preacher's message must show men their own selves and their lamentable state, so as to make them humble and yearn for help. St. Paul follows this plan and, in chapter 1, begins by condemning certain gross sins and infidelities which are plain as the day. Such

---

[1] John 3:6f.   [2] Gal. 5:19ff.   [3] Rom. 8:3

were the sins of the pagans, and so remain, because they live apart from the grace of God. Paul therefore says that through the gospel the wrath of God is revealed, coming from heaven upon all mankind, on account of their godlessness and wickedness. For, although they know and daily recognize that there is a God, yet human nature, in itself and apart from grace, is so evil that it neither thanks nor worships Him. Rather, it blinds its own eyes, and falls continually into wickedness; with the result that, in addition to worshipping false gods, it commits disgraceful sins and all kinds of evil. It knows no shame and, if unpunished, commits other sins.

In chapter 2, Paul extends these punishments and applies them to persons who only appear to be godly, or commit secret sins. Such were the Jews, and such too are all hypocrites, for they live without joy and love. In their hearts they hate the divine law and, as is the way with all hypocrites, they habitually condemn others. They regard themselves as spotless, although they are full of envy, hatred, pride, and all kinds of impurity, Matthew 23.[1] These are precisely the people who despise God's goodness, and heap up the divine wrath by their hardness of heart.[2] St. Paul therefore, as a true preacher of the law, asserts that no one is without sin; rather, he declares the wrath of God against all who try to live by following their own nature or idle fancies. He does not regard people of this kind as any better than open sinners. He even says that they are obstinate and unrepentant.

In chapter 3, he treats of both kinds together, and says, of one as of the other, all are sinners in God's sight. Moreover, the Jews have been given God's word, although many have not believed in it. This attitude has not made either God's truth or faith of no effect. He cites in addition what Psalm 50[3] says, namely, that God remains true to His word.[4] Then Paul returns to the fact that all men are sinners, and proves his case from Scripture. He declares that no one will be justified by fulfilling the requirements of the law, because the law was given only to show the nature of sin. He then

[1] 23:28   [2] Rom. 2:4f.
[3] Psalm 51 in the edition of 1546, which follows the Hebrew and no longer the Vulgate enumeration
[4] Cf. Ps. 51:6

elaborates his teaching of the right way to become godly and
sanctified. He says that all men are sinners, and that none are
approved by God. Salvation can only come to them, un-
earned, by virtue of faith in Christ. Christ has earned it for
us through His blood. For our sakes, He has become God's
"mercy seat", and so God forgives all the sins that we have
committed in the past. In this way, God shows that His own
righteousness, which He confers through the medium of faith,
is our only help. He revealed this righteousness when the
gospel was preached; but the law and the prophets had
already testified to it. Faith, then, lends its support to the
law, although, at the same time, it repudiates works done
according to the law, and denies the esteem in which they are
held.

In chapter 4, having shown the nature of sin in the first
three chapters, and taught how faith leads to righteousness,
Paul begins to deal with certain objections and difficulties.
The first to be discussed is the common case of all those who,
hearing that faith justifies us apart from works, proceed to
ask, Is there any need to do good works? Paul thereupon
claims the support of Abraham and asks, What did Abraham
do in the matter of works? Were they all in vain? Were his
works valueless? He concludes that Abraham, apart from
any works, was justified simply by faith. Indeed, before he
did the "work" of circumcision, righteousness was attributed to him by Scripture simply on account of his faith,
Genesis 15.[1] Although the work of circumcision had not
contributed to his righteousness, yet God had commanded
it, and, as an act of obedience, it was a good work. Thus it is
also certain that no other good works contribute to making a
man righteous. Like Abraham's circumcision, they are only
outward signs proving that his righteousness is contained in
his faith. Consequently, we are to understand that good works
are purely and simply outward signs. They proceed from
faith, and, like good fruits, prove that the man himself is
already righteous at heart in God's sight.

In this way Paul adduces a cogent example from Scripture
in support of his doctrine of faith in chapter 3. He now calls

[1] 15:6

David as a further witness, and he says in Psalm 33[1] that we shall be justified apart from works, although, when justified, we shall not continue without works. Paul then gives this example a broader application, and extends it to all other observances of the law. He concludes that the Jews cannot be heirs of Abraham merely by virtue of their descent, and still less by observing the works of the law. Rather, if they be truly his heirs, they must inherit his faith, because, prior to the laws of Moses and prior to circumcision, Abraham was justified by faith and described as the father of all believers. Moreover, the law issues in wrath rather than in grace, for no one fulfils it willingly and with joy.[2] Hence the works of the law produce reluctance rather than grace. It follows that only faith can obtain the grace promised to Abraham; and examples like this are written in Scripture for our sakes, so that we, too, may have faith.

In chapter 5, Paul comes to the fruits or works to which faith gives rise. These are peace, joy, love to God and all mankind; in addition, assurance, courage, confidence, and hopefulness in spite of sorrow and suffering. Where faith is at home, it is joined by all things of this kind because of the overflowing goodwill which God shows to us in Christ. For our sakes, God let Him suffer death, not only before we could intercede in prayer to Him, but even while we were still enemies. We therefore maintain that faith justifies us apart from any works, although we must not draw the conclusion that we have no need to do any good works. Nay, rather, works of the right kind must not be neglected, works of which the mere ceremonialists know nothing. They trump up their own kind of works, but these breathe neither peace, nor joy, nor assurance, nor love, nor hope, nor courage, nor certainty, nor anything that partakes of genuine Christian conduct or faith.

Paul now makes an interesting digression, and discusses the origin of both sin and righteousness, of death and life. He shows how Adam and Christ represent two contrary types,

---

[1] Ps. 32:1f.

[2] This statement seems contrary to good Jewish tradition, cf. Ps. 1:2, 119:72, and *Pirque 'aboth*, ed. P. Fiebig, I, i, b; II, a; p. 13, etc.

and says, in effect, that Christ had to come as a second Adam
and to transmit His righteousness by virtue of a new, spiritual
birth in faith. This is the counterpoise to what Adam did
when he transmitted sin to us through our earlier, physical
birth. That is how Paul proves his assertion that no one can
deliver himself from sin, or attain righteousness, by means of
works, any more than he can prevent his own physical birth.
At the same time, Paul proves that the God-given law, which
would have helped, if anything could help in attaining righteousness, not only gave no help when it did come, but only
increased sin. Our evil nature becomes all the more hostile
to it, and prefers to pursue its own devices, in proportion to
the strictness of that law. Thus the law makes Christ more
necessary to us, and increases the need for grace to help our
nature.

In chapter 6, Paul discusses the special function of faith.
The question at issue is that of the battle of the spirit
struggling against the flesh, and finally killing outright the
sins and passions that remain alive after our justification.
He teaches that faith does not free us from sin to the extent
that we can relax into laziness and self-assurance, as if sin
no longer existed. Sin still exists; but, on account of the faith
that battles with it, is not held against us to our condemnation. Throughout our whole lives, we shall be kept
fully employed with our own selves, taming our body, killing
its passions, controlling its members till they obey, not the
passions, but the spirit. This self-discipline is needed in
order that we might conform to the death and resurrection
of Christ, and also that we might complete the meaning of
our baptism; for baptism, too, signifies the death of sin and
the new life of grace. The final goal is that we should be
entirely liberated from sin, rise again in the body with
Christ, and live for ever.

Paul declares that this is possible because we are not under
the law, but under grace.[1] He gives a clear explanation of
what it means to live "not under the law". This is not the
equivalent of saying that no laws bind us, and that we can
all follow our own devices; but rather, to be "under the law"

[1] Rom. 6:14

means to live apart from grace, and to be occupied with fulfilling the works of the law. In a case like this, it is certain that sin dominates us through the law, since none take a natural delight in the law; and our condition is then very sinful.[1] But grace makes us take pleasure in the law; then sin no longer enters in, and the law is no longer against us, but on our side.

To have the law on our side is the very nature of freedom from sin and the law, and Paul continues his discussion of this state of affairs to the end of the present chapter. He says that this freedom consists of taking pleasure simply in doing good, or in living uprightly, without being constrained to do so by the law. This freedom is therefore a spiritual freedom; it does not abolish the law; rather it supplies and furnishes what the law lacks, namely, willingness and love. Thus the law is silenced and put out of action; it makes no further demands. It is as if you were in debt to a lender, and unable to pay; there would be two ways of settling the matter and setting you free. In the first, the lender would refuse to accept anything from you, but simply rule off the account in his ledger. Or, on the other hand, some kind person might give you enough to settle up and pay the account; and this is how Christ has set us free from the law. Our freedom is not a crude, physical freedom by virtue of which we can refuse to do anything at all; rather, it does much, in fact everything; it is freedom from the demands and obligations of the law.

In chapter 7, Paul consolidates his argument with an analogy drawn from married life. If the husband dies, the wife is exempt from the marriage bond. By the death of one, the other is made free and set at liberty. The woman is not obliged, nor even merely permitted, to take another husband; rather, the point is that she is now quite at liberty for the first time to please herself about taking another husband. She could not do this earlier, not before she was free from her former husband. Similarly, our conscience is bound to the law in its former state of the old sinful self. But when this self

---

[1] The precise meaning of this passage is very obscure; perhaps one may paraphrase: if we hate what the law of Moses requires, our hearts are very wicked

is put to death by the spirit, our conscience is set at liberty, and each is released from the other. This does not mean that our conscience has become inactive, but that now, for the first time, it can really cling to Christ as a second husband, and bring forth the fruit of life.

Paul then proceeds to give a broader description of the nature of sin and the law, explaining that only by virtue of the law does sin really come alive and grow strong. The old self becomes all the more hostile to the law when it can no longer render what the law requires. The nature of the old self is sinful, and cannot help being so. To that self, therefore, the law means death and all the pains of death, and this, not because the law is evil, but because our evil nature is averse to goodness, the very goodness which is demanded by the law.[1] Similarly, it is impossible to ask a sick man to walk about and leap and do what a healthy man does.

St. Paul therefore asserts at this point that if the law is rightly understood, and if it is construed in the best way, it only reminds us of our sins, uses them to kill us, and makes us liable to everlasting wrath. All this our conscience learns perfectly by experience when it meets the law face to face. Hence, if we are to be upright and attain salvation, we shall require something different from, and better than, the law. Those people who fail to understand the law aright, are blind; in their presumptuous way, they think they can fulfil it with works. They are unaware how much the law demands; in particular, a heart that is free and eager and joyful. Hence they do not read Moses aright; the veil still covers and conceals his face.[2]

Paul now explains how flesh and spirit contend with each other in our hearts. He cites himself as an example, in order that we may learn properly how to put our indwelling sin to death. But he applies the name of law to both the spirit and the flesh, because, just as it is the nature of the divine law to make requirements and demands, so does the flesh strive and struggle and rage against the spirit, and insist on its

---

[1] *Das gutte das es gutts von yhm foddere*: the precise meaning is very obscure

[2] Cf. Exod. 34:33ff.; 2 Cor. 3:13ff.

own way. Conversely, the spirit strives and struggles against the flesh, and insists on its own way. This wrangling continues within us as long as we live; more in some, less in others, according as the flesh or the spirit is the stronger. But we must understand that our complete self consists of both elements: spirit and flesh; we fight with ourselves until we become wholly spiritual.

In chapter 8, Paul gives comfort to those engaged in this warfare, and says that the flesh shall not condemn them. He also shows the nature of flesh and spirit, and explains that the spirit comes from Christ, who gives us His Holy Spirit. This makes us spiritual, constrains the flesh, and assures us that, no matter how violently sin rages within us, we are the children of God as long as we obey the spirit and strive to put sin to death. But, because nothing else is so effective in taming the flesh as are our cross and the sufferings we must bear, he comforts us in our sufferings by assuring us of the support of the spirit, of love, and of all created things. In particular, not only does the spirit sigh within us, but also every creature shares our longings to be free from the flesh and from sin. Thus we see how these three chapters discuss the real work of faith, namely, to put the old Adam to death, and to control the flesh.

In chapters 9, 10 and 11, Paul deals with the eternal providence of God. It is by this providence that it was first decided who should, and who should not, have faith; who should conquer sin, and who should not be able to do so. This is a matter which is taken out of our hands, and is solely at God's disposal—that so we might become truly righteous. And this is our greatest need. We are so weak and wavering that, if it were left to us, surely not a single person would be saved, and the devil would certainly overpower us all. On the other hand, God is constant, and His providence will not fail, nor can anyone prevent its fulfilment. We therefore have hope in spite of sin.

At this stage, we must put a stop to those impious and arrogant persons who use their reasoning powers here first, and in their high and mighty way begin to probe into the deeps of the divine providence, inquiring to no purpose whether they are among the elect; they cannot help bringing disaster on themselves, either by failure or by running needless risks. But you must study this epistle yourself, chapter by chapter. Concentrate first of all on Christ and His gospel, in order to learn how to recognize your sins and to know His grace. Next, wrestle with the problem of sin as discussed in chapters 1, 2, 3, 4, 5, 6, 7, and 8. Then, when you have arrived at chapter 8, dominated by the cross and passion of Christ, you will learn the right way of understanding the divine providence in chapters 9, 10, and 11, and the assurance that it gives. If we do not feel the weight of the passion, the cross, and the death, we cannot cope with the problem of providence without either hurt to ourselves or secret anger with God. That is why the Adam in us has to be quite dead before we can bear this doctrine, and drink this strong wine, without harm. So beware! Avoid drinking wine when you are still a suckling infant. Every doctrine requires us to be of the appropriate ability at the right age, and of the due maturity.

In chapter 12, Paul speaks of the true way of serving God. He shows that all Christians are priests, and that the sacrifices they offer are not money or cattle, as prescribed by the law, but their own selves after their passions have been put to death. He then describes the outward conduct of Christians under the discipline of the spirit; how they must teach, preach, rule, serve, give, suffer, love, live, and act towards friend, foe, and fellow-man. These are the works which a Christian does, for, as I have said, faith is not an inert thing.

In chapter 13, he teaches us to respect and obey the secular authorities. This subject is introduced, not indeed because such conduct will make the people good in God's eyes, but because it ensures the public peace and the protection of those who are good citizens; whereas the wicked will not be able to do evil without fear, or with easy minds. Such authority must therefore be held in respect by good people, although they do not require its services. But Paul ends by showing that love includes everything else; and he clinches the whole with the example of Christ, who has done for us what we too must do in following Him.

In chapter 14, Paul teaches us how to deal with any who

have an unstable conscience and to spare them. He teaches us not to use our Christian liberty to hurt the weak, but to help them. Where this is not done, dissension arises and the gospel comes into contempt, although all depends on it. It is therefore better to humour the weak in faith a little, till they grow stronger, rather than that the gospel should be lost altogether. Love alone can do a work like this, and it is particularly needed just now when the question of eating meat, and other matters of free choice, are being discussed intemperately and brusquely, disturbing to no purpose those of unstable conscience before they know the truth.

In chapter 15, Paul cites the example of Christ, and teaches that we should bear with others who are weak, even including open sinners and those who have disgusting habits. We must not cast them off, but be patient with them until they reform. That is what Christ did in our own case, and continues to do day by day; for He bears with many shortcomings and evil habits, as well as all sorts of imperfections on our part; yet He never fails to help us.

Then, in conclusion, Paul prays for them, praises them, and commends them to God. He explains his own status and message, begs them earnestly to give gifts on behalf of the poor at Jerusalem, and avers that he speaks and acts entirely out of love. It may therefore be said that this epistle gives the richest possible account of what a Christian ought to know, namely, the meaning of law, gospel, sin, punishment, grace, faith, righteousness, Christ, God, good works, love, hope, and the cross. It tells what our attitude should be to our fellows, whether righteous or sinful, strong or weak, friend or foe; and to our own selves. Moreover, everything is cogently proved from Scripture, and illustrated by Paul's own case or that of the prophets; it leaves nothing to be desired. Therefore, it seems as if St. Paul had intended this epistle to set out, once for all, the whole of Christian doctrine in brief, and to be an introduction preparatory to the whole of the Old Testament. For there can be no doubt that if we had this epistle well and truly in our hearts, we should possess the light and power found in the Old Testament. Therefore, every Christian ought to study Romans regularly and continuously. May God grant His grace to this end. Amen.

The final chapter consists of greetings. It includes, too, a noble warning in regard to man-made doctrines which were being disseminated side by side with the gospel, and which were doing harm. It is exactly as if St. Paul had foreseen that, out of Rome and through the Romanists, would come the misleading and vexatious canons and decretals, together with all the crawling maggots of man-made laws and regulations, which by now have eaten into the entire world, and which have not only swallowed up this epistle and all Holy Scripture, but prevented the work of the spirit, and destroyed our faith; so that nothing else remains than their God, the belly. Paul here depicts them as its servants. God deliver us from them. Amen.[1]

[1] This concluding paragraph was transferred in the editions of 1539 and subsequently, to a position in the preceding paragraph, which was altered a little in the wording

PREFACE TO THE ACTS OF THE APOSTLES[1]

WE ought to read this book with a different understanding from that which has been usual hitherto. The old view is that St. Luke recorded the lives and deeds of the apostles simply as examples of good works or the good life. St. Augustine and many others regarded it as affording the best illustrations of this sort, because the apostles shared all their possessions with other Christians; and so on in the same way. This state of affairs, however, did not last long, and soon had to be abandoned. The true purpose of the book is that St. Luke here teaches all Christians in every age the main article of Christian doctrine, namely, that we all need to be justified, and this simply by faith in Christ, without any addition of the law or any help from our work.

That proposition expresses his primary purpose, and was the reason why he wrote this book. It explains why he emphasized so strongly that the apostles preached faith in Christ, declaring that both Jews and gentiles must needs be justified by it apart from any merit due to works. He also explains how the example and the experience of the apostles show that the gentiles, as well as the Jews, were justified simply by the gospel and apart from the observances of the law. He shows, in chapters 10 and 15, how Peter testified regarding this issue, and said that God made no distinction between Jew and gentile. Rather, He gave the Holy Spirit through the gospel to the gentiles, who lived without the law; and similarly to the Jews, not by the law or because of their works and deserts, but through the gospel. St. Luke sets both these teachings side by side in the book of Acts: the doctrine of salvation by faith, and examples of that faith.

The book might well therefore be regarded as a running commentary on the Pauline epistles. What St. Paul teaches by his words, and urges by quotations from Scripture, St. Luke exhibits here by giving instances. His account shows that all took place, and necessarily so, in harmony with St.

[1] *Bi.*, Vol. VI, pp. 414-16 (A.D. 1533)

Paul's teaching, namely, that it was not law or works that made men righteous, but only faith in Christ. You will find this book is a splendid mirror which reflects the truth, *sola fides iustificat*; faith alone makes men righteous. Here are various examples and instances of this principle, all of them trustworthy and encouraging witnesses; nor will any of them deceive you or play you false.

Look and see how St. Paul himself was converted; again how Cornelius, a gentile, was converted by what St. Peter said: and how an angel had already told him that Peter would preach to him, and that he would be saved thereby; again, about Sergius, the governor, and all the towns where St. Paul and Barnabas preached. Read of the first council of the apostles at Jerusalem in chapter 15.[1] Read all the sermons of St. Peter,[2] St. Stephen,[3] and St. Philip,[4] and you will find that their whole purport is that we truly receive grace and are justified simply by faith in Christ and apart from works or the law. By understanding the book of Acts in this way, we can silence our opponents in no uncertain fashion; and when they talk about the law and our need of works, we can make their foolish lack of understanding plain to all the world.

Luke therefore declares that these instances of faith almost confounded those pious-minded Jews who had already become believers and that the rest were at a loss and in confusion. Nor is this surprising, since the Jews had been nurtured in the law and were accustomed to it from the time of Abraham. They could not help feeling mortified when the gentiles, who had neither their law nor their God, were made their equals in receiving the gifts of God's grace. But it is ten times worse when our own fellow-countrymen, all of us being gentiles, revile and try to suppress these teachings, especially since it is obvious and undeniable, that the grace of God and the knowledge of Christ were brought to our ancestors apart from law or merit, nay, when they were plunged in dreadful idolatries and given to blasphemy. But our opponents will only profit as much from reviling and suppressing these teachings as did the Jews with their raging and ranting. God had previously threatened the Jews and

[1] 15:6-30   [2] 3:12ff., 4:8ff., 10:34ff.   [3] 7:2ff.   [4] 8:27ff.

had declared, through the lips of Moses, I will make you wrath with a people that is not mine, and provoke you to anger with a foolish nation.[1] Similarly, in Hosea 2, I will call my people those who are not my people (i.e. living without the law and its works),[2] and He kept His word to them. It is the same God who speaks the same threats against the revilers of the present day. He has already made a beginning, and He will assuredly keep His word concerning them. But they will believe it only when, like the Jews, they learn from experience. Amen.

[1] Cf. Deut. 32:21   [2] Hos. 2:23

PREFACE TO THE EPISTLE TO THE HEBREWS[1]

THE books that we have dealt with hitherto have been most certainly the chief books of the New Testament. The four following[2] were differently regarded in ancient times. In the first place, the epistle to the Hebrews was not written by St. Paul, nor by any other of the apostles. This fact is proved in chapter 2, where it says that this teaching comes to us and is ours through those who heard it from the Lord.[3] It is therefore clear that the writer speaks of the apostles, as a disciple to whom this teaching had come from the apostles, perhaps long after them. St. Paul, however, in Galatians 1 declares with great force that he had received his gospel neither from any man, nor through any man, but from God Himself.[4]

Another great difficulty occurs in chapters 6 and 10, where the epistle flatly denies and refuses to recognize a sinner's repentance for sin after baptism;[5] and, in chapter 12, it says that Esau sought repentance and did not find it.[6] This contradicts all the gospels and St. Paul's epistles. Although one might attempt to explain it away by a gloss, the words are so clear that I do not know whether it could be done. In my view, the epistle is conflated from many fragments, and does not deal in an orderly fashion with one subject at a time.

However that may be, it is a very learned epistle. It gives a masterly discussion of Christ's priesthood, based on the Scriptures, a splendidly rich interpretation of the Old Testament. Thus it is plainly the work of an able and scholarly man who had been a disciple of the apostles, from whom he had learned much, and who was very well versed in the Scriptures. Although he does not profess to lay down the foundation of the faith, as he says in chapter 6,[7] this

---

[1] The original text of the Preface of 1522 will be found in *Bi.*, Vol. VII, p. 344. This Preface remained practically unchanged through all the editions published in Luther's lifetime

[2] In Luther's order: Hebrews, James, Jude, Revelation

[3] Cf. Heb. 2:3   [4] Cf. Gal. 1:1   [5] Heb. 6:4-6; 10:26

[6] Heb. 12:17   [7] Heb. 6:1

being the duty of an apostle, nevertheless he builds splendidly on it: gold, silver, precious stones, as St. Paul says in 1 Corinthians 3.[1] Therefore we must not let ourselves be held back even though some wood, straw, or hay be intermingled; but accept this splendid teaching with all respect; but we are unable to put it on the level of the apostolic epistles themselves.

It is not known who wrote it, nor is it likely to be known for some time yet; nor does anything important depend on that fact. We should content ourselves with the doctrine which the writer regularly draws from or bases on the Scriptures. At the same time, he shows a truly splendid grasp of the Scriptures, and gives us a criterion for reading and expounding them.

[1] 1 Cor. 3:1ff.

PREFACE TO THE EPISTLES OF ST. JAMES AND JUDE[1]

I think highly of the epistle of James, and regard it as valuable although it was rejected in early days.[2] It does not expound human doctrines, but lays much emphasis on God's law. Yet, to give my own opinion without prejudice to that of anyone else, I do not hold it to be of apostolic authorship, for the following reasons:

Firstly, because, in direct opposition to St. Paul and all the rest of the Bible, it ascribes justification to works, and declares that Abraham was justified by his works when he offered up his son. St. Paul, on the contrary, in Romans 4, teaches that Abraham was justified without works, by his faith alone,[3] the proof being in Genesis 15, which was before he sacrificed his son.[4] Although it would be possible to "save" the epistle by a gloss giving a correct explanation of justification here ascribed to works, it is impossible to deny that it does refer Moses's word in Genesis 15 (which speaks not of Abraham's works but of his faith, just as Paul makes plain in Romans 4[5]) to Abraham's works.[6] This defect proves that the epistle is not of apostolic provenance.

Secondly, because, in the whole length of its teaching, not once does it give Christians any instruction or reminder of the passion, resurrection, or spirit of Christ. It mentions Christ

[1] Cf. *Bi.*, VII-384-86. This preface was but little altered even as late as the edition of 1546

It will be noticed that Luther adopts in some respects a milder tone than in the few words in the last paragraph of his general introduction to the New Testament, cf. *supra*, p. 283, or at least a form of words that leaves less room for scoffing or parody. But his critical attitude is as firm as ever. He has much to say, unexpectedly, in appreciation of James's moral teachings, but nothing about the value of its purely religious content. He is right in reminding his readers that both epistles had difficulty in finding acceptance, and were only received late into the canon, which fact he attributes, however, to doubts about the validity of the teaching. He expresses a view which is still held by competent scholars: that James lays more emphasis on works than on faith, but his opinion that Jude is a mere extract from 2 Peter has not held its place. In any case, it would seem that his remarks on James are little more than an echo of Erasmus

[2] Cf., e.g., Jer., *de vir. ill.* ii, and Eus. *H.E.*, II, 23, 25, and III, 25, 3 (Schwartz)

[3] Rom. 4:3   [4] Gen. 15:6   [5] Rom. 4:1-22   [6] James 2:21ff.

once and again, but teaches nothing about Him; it speaks only of a commonplace faith in God. It is the office of a true apostle to preach the passion and resurrection and work of Christ, and to lay down the true ground for this faith, as Christ himself says in John 15, You shall be my witnesses.[1] All genuinely sacred books are unanimous here, and all preach Christ emphatically. The true touchstone for testing every book is to discover whether it emphasizes the prominence of Christ or not. All Scripture sets forth Christ, Romans 3[2] and Paul will know nothing but Christ, 1 Corinthians 2.[3] What does not teach Christ is not apostolic, not even if taught by Peter or Paul. On the other hand, what does preach Christ is apostolic, even if Judas, Annas, Pilate, or Herod does it.

The epistle of James, however, only drives you to the law and its works. He mixes one thing with another to such an extent that I suspect some good and pious man assembled a few things said by disciples of the apostles, and then put them down in black and white; or perhaps the epistle was written by someone else who made notes of a sermon of his. He calls the law a law of freedom,[4] although St. Paul calls it a law of slavery, wrath, death, and sin.[5]

Yet he quotes St. Peter's saying that "Love covers a multitude of sins", and again "Humble yourselves under the hand of God";[6] further, St. Paul's word in Galatians 5, The spirit lusteth against hate.[7] But St. James was killed by Herod in Jerusalem[8] before St. Peter's death, which shows the writer to have been far later than St. Peter or St. Paul.

In sum: he wished to guard against those who depended on faith without going on to works, but he had neither the spirit nor the thought nor the eloquence equal to the task. He does violence to Scripture, and so contradicts Paul and all Scripture. He tries to accomplish by emphasizing law what

---

[1] John 15:27   [2] Cf. Rom. 3:24ff.   [3] 1 Cor. 2:2
[4] 1:25; 2:12. Luther's exegesis seems fundamentally at fault here for once in a way; νόμος ἐλευθερίας means nothing more than "personal freedom"
[5] Cf. Gal. 3:23f. Rom. 4:15, 7:10ff.
[6] Cf. James 5:20; 4:10 and 1 Pet. 4:8; 5:6
[7] Cf. Gal. 5:17
[8] Luther's identification of the writer with James the brother of the Lord is not generally accepted to-day by competent scholars

the apostles bring about by attracting men to love. I therefore refuse him a place among the writers of the true canon of my Bible; but I would not prevent anyone placing him or raising him where he likes, for the epistle contains many excellent passages. One man does not count as a man even in the eyes of the world;[1] how then shall this single and isolated writer count against Paul and all the rest of the Bible?

The Epistle of St. Jude

No one can deny that this epistle is an excerpt from, or copy of, the second epistle of St. Peter,[2] for all he says is nearly the same over again. Moreover, he speaks of the apostles as would a disciple of a much later date.[3] He quotes words and events which are found nowhere in Scripture,[4] and which moved the fathers to reject this epistle from the canon. Moreover, the apostle Jude did not go into Greek-speaking lands, but into Persia; and it is said that he could not write Greek. Hence, although I value the book, yet it is not essential to reckon it among the canonical books that lay the foundation of faith.

[1] A proverb: A man alone is no man
[2] This view is not universally accepted by critics to-day
[3] Cf. Jude 17   [4] Jude 9, 14

PREFACE TO THE REVELATION OF ST. JOHN[1]

I would leave everyone free to form his own opinions about the book of Revelation, and would prefer not to bind anyone to my opinion or verdict; here I am setting down what I myself feel. I miss so many things in this book that I cannot hold it to be either apostolic or prophetic. First and foremost, it is not the way of the apostles to recount visions, but to prophesy in clear and simple words; this is done by St. Peter and St. Paul, and by Christ in the gospels. One of apostolic rank ought to speak of Christ and of what He did without using symbols and images; and there is no prophet in the Old Testament, not to mention the New Testament, who uses nothing but images and symbols. The result is that Revelation makes much the same impression on me as the fourth book of Esdras, and I cannot imagine that it owes its existence to the Holy Spirit.

In addition, the writer seems to me to be overstating his case when he commends his own book so emphatically, and more than is done in the case of other Biblical writings (to which much more importance is attached). He even commands, and issues threats, that if anything be taken away from it, God will deal in the same way with that man, etc. Again, he pronounces a blessing on those who fulfil what he has written;[2] yet no man knows its meaning, to say nothing of how to fulfil it; and this is no better than being without it. There are many better books for us to fulfil.

So, too, many of the early fathers rejected this book, although St. Jerome commends it eloquently and says it is above all praise. He admits however, that there are as many mysteries in it as there are words. But he is quite unable to prove these statements, and in many passages he is too free with his praise.

[1] Cf. *Bi.*, Vol. VII, p. 404. This Preface was omitted from editions after 1527, and was replaced by another in 1530 with much greater length and historical allegorization of detail. The latter was an important innovation, but otherwise the standpoint remained the same. The first preface, of 1522, gives all of consequence to most students to-day

[2] Cf. Rev. 22:18f.

Finally, let everyone judge the book as his own spirit leads him to do. My own type of mind does not fit in well with this book, and I regard as a sufficient reason for not thinking highly of it, that Christ is neither taught nor recognized in it. It is the first duty of an apostle to teach Christ, for Christ says in Acts 1, Ye shall be my witnesses.[1] I myself, therefore, abide by the books which give a clear and outright presentation of Christ.

[1] Acts 1:8

8

THE LORD'S SUPPER AND ORDER OF SERVICE IN GERMAN, 1526

Introduction

As soon as the movement of reform was felt far and wide in Germany, and the feeling had grown that reform was practical, efforts of many kinds were made to bring public worship into line with the new needs.

Luther having come safely through the ordeal at Worms, and various extremists having made different ventures both in their preaching and in pastoral service, Wolfgang Wissenburger in Basle and John Schwebel in Pforzheim ventured to draw up an Order of Public Worship for the service of the Lord's Supper in German instead of Latin. The following Easter, Thomas Müntzer of Allstedt introduced a German version of the service and in the next year published Orders of Service for Matins and Vespers, and for the Lord's Supper in a rich and solemn form. There are records of some half-dozen others of reforming sympathies, who drew up their own liturgies in various parts of the country, frequently complete with passages of Scripture, music for the intonations, and detailed directions for the conduct of the ceremonies.

All this was a welcome expression of the extent to which reform was taking practical expression; in their most solemn acts of worship together, the people were learning not only how to use their new freedom, but also how to rejoice in it. At this point, however, an inherent feature of the age-old religion began to make itself felt. The more widely reformed Services were adopted, and the more numerous the forms into which they were cast, the more their diversity became evident, and with that their lack of unity. The oneness of the church in space and time and ceremonial had received great stress for centuries, and even the reformers were careful to point out their own oneness with the apostles, the early fathers, and the inherent tradition of the faith. But as the new Orders of Service spread from the churches where each was first used into the immediately surrounding churches and even further afield, they came, as it were, into contact with each other, and the sense of variety in worship, so distressing still to many minds, became a deep concern. *Coenam dominicam aliter vos aliter Nurmbergeneses, aliter nos, aliter Norlingenses vicini nostri celebrant. Quod nimirum inconstantiae ac incertitudinis argumentum haud pauci existimant* was the complaint of the reforming ministers in Strassburg.[1]

Luther, when consulted about the problem and asked to suggest a solution, felt he could make no promise to set to work himself. "I feel unequal to a task which requires musical skill and at the

[1] Cf. *W.*, Vol. XIX, p. 45

same time must express a certain spirit"; but he went on to say that perhaps the time would come for it. Meanwhile he did not see much harm in the diversity as long as the variety of forms expressed a unity of spirit.[1]

About this time, the autumn of 1524, however, Carlstadt began to declare that at least the opening words *must* be in German; and ministers in Strassburg were using a form of service which they insisted should be entirely in German. The use of German was quite agreeable to Luther so long as it was not made compulsory —that, he declared, was to insist on too much; it was bringing in laws and regulations by the back door. "I should be glad if there were an Order of Service that fully harmonized with our German character. . . . But the extremists are insisting that it must needs be of a certain kind . . . requiring works of us as if commanded by God, when, in fact, He has given no such commands."[2] The natural result was that there was a widespread desire that Luther and his colleagues in Wittenberg would get together and prepare an Order of Service that all could freely adopt, and, if adopted by all, would then give the uniformity so much desired.

Luther delayed. Meantime, other leaders, in Nuremberg, Zürich, Sonnenwalde, and elsewhere, drew up liturgies which were steadily less tentative in character, some of which were submitted to Luther for his approval, and which he returned with a number of comments.

Eventually, in the autumn of 1525, Luther set himself to the task, and sent a first draft to the Elector. The time had now come to discuss the musical settings with two Wittenberg musicians; and, on October 29, the new draft was used at the Lord's Supper in the parish church. But it was not until the following summer that the new liturgy was printed and circulated. Special attention was drawn to the preface and to its remarks that the new Order was not to be regarded as an immutable requirement. The present form was only drawn up because not every minister was in a position to do the work suitably himself. It was published with the musical notes for the intonations, and full directions to the officiating clergy. These included suggestions for the abolition of most Saints' Days, and for the retention of certain feast and fast days, and their celebration for the present in their Latin form. Luther mentions in particular, Christmas, Easter, Whitsuntide, St. Michael, and the Purification, the observance of which was later to be abolished by many reformers, including John Knox in Scotland. Of the fasts to be retained and observed in Latin services, Luther mentions Palm Sunday and Holy Week, but goes on at

---

[1] Cf. *W.*, Vol. XIX, p. 45

[2] *Ibid.*, p. 46; cf. also "I find no people more distasteful than those who would do away with free and unobjectionable forms of Service, thus making a necessity out of liberty", *ibid.* note 1

once to say that the fasting must not be regarded as compulsory. He would also abolish the custom of veiling the altar pictures, crucifixes, and similar ornaments during Holy Week, and concentrate everything on the word and the sacrament, yet without using any constraint on participating in the services or the rites.

The Preface, besides its immediate application to introducing the new Order, includes much weighty teaching about the nature of Christian liberty, in a manner complementary to that of his tract *The Freedom of a Christian*.[1] And he has much of urgent importance to say about the teaching of the Christian facts to children and to the ignorant. These and other points make the Preface of abiding value, and an important contribution to Christian literature and to the understanding of the essential nature of the evangelical faith.

I have appended to the preface the concluding paragraph of the liturgy itself, for in it Luther comes back to what he had written by way of introduction to his text.

The present text follows the original as given in the Weimar Edition of Luther's Works, Vol. XIX, pp. 72-78.

[1] Cf. our Vol. I, p. 349ff.

THE LORD'S SUPPER AND ORDER OF DIVINE SERVICE

PREFACE BY MARTIN LUTHER

Text and Notes

MY first request, made in the kindliest way, and for God's dear sake, is that none of those who consider this Order for Divine Worship, or those who make use of it, should regard it in the least as an obligatory rule or binding on anyone's conscience. Rather, exercising Christian liberty according to their own good pleasure, all should use it how, where, and when it is found helpful, or as long as circumstances require it. We[1] should not like the impression to get abroad that we wished to constrain anyone to its use, or impose any regulations.[2] Since German forms of the Eucharist[3] and Divine Service are being imposed on all hands, many complaints and much offence arise on account of the numerous variations in the forms of Service. It would seem that any person at all draws up his own Order, some with quite innocent intentions, some even gaily and as if not to be outdone in producing something new; they display their ingenuity in their differences from other people. Even though all this is done in accordance with the principle of Christian freedom, yet that liberty is rarely used except to satisfy one's own private taste or for one's own advantage, and not for the glory of God and the benefit of our neighbours.

While the use of Christian liberty is a matter for each individual conscience, and no one has a right to forbid or

---

[1] The Wittenberg group of leaders

[2] Shortly after this liturgy was introduced at Reutlingen, the minister, Matthew Alber, wished to make certain changes, and Luther wrote: "Make what changes you please. I myself am making changes . . . and there is no need for you to adopt mine." *Br.*, Vol. IV, §7

[3] Germ., *Messe*, which is used equally for the R.C. mass and the reformed rites. Since the term Mass is used almost entirely in England and the U.S.A. for the Roman Catholic liturgy, it becomes necessary to translate by Eucharist, Lord's Supper, and the like, according to the requirements of the context

limit it, yet care must be taken to make it always the servant of love and of one's neighbour. But if some people should take offence and go astray because of our variety of usages, surely we ought to sacrifice our freedom, and, as far as possible, by what we do or leave undone, see to it that people are helped and not hurt by our ways. Nothing that can be called a matter of conscience in God's sight is involved in these liturgies, which are outward things, while yet it is granted that they contain something of value to our neighbour; for, as St. Paul teaches, we should strive lovingly to be of one mind,[1] and, as far as possible, adopt similar manners and customs.[2] We may notice, moreover, that God has given all Christians one baptism, one sacrament; and to none has He given one particular form.

Nevertheless, I must not be understood to desire that those who already possess a good liturgy, or who by God's grace are able to draw up one better than this, should abandon theirs and replace it by ours. It is not my view that the whole of Germany should adopt exactly our Wittenberg liturgy. In fact, up to the present time, religious foundations, cloisters, and parish churches, have never been alike in every particular. On the other hand, it would be a splendid thing if the liturgy were uniform throughout any single domain, and if the surrounding towns and villages followed the same usages as the city; but whether the neighbouring domains adopted the same usages or added to them, should be entirely at their choice. In a word, we are not publishing the present Order of Service for the sake of persons already Christian. They, of course, need nothing of this sort for they already worship God in spirit.[3] Liturgies are not things for which we live; they exist for the sake of making those of us Christian

---

[1] 1 Cor. 1:10; Rom. 15:5; Phil. 2:2; 3:15; Col. 1:10
[2] I.e. in Public Worship
[3] Luther's point is that people who indeed worship in spirit and in truth, can use equally well any suitable liturgy; or, when alone, act independently and worship as the spirit directs them. This is one exercise of the office of the priesthood of all believers (Cf. *W*., Vol. VI, pp. 370, 532). While true worship consists of expressions of faith, and is therefore independent of any outward acts, yet Luther insists that there is great gain in worshipping together (*W*., Vol. VI, pp. 372), and that the administration of the elements in the sacrament is a help just because they are material vehicles (*W*., Vol. VI, pp. 378)

who are not yet Christian. Liturgies are needed for the sake of those who have yet to become Christian,[1] or need to be strengthened. Similarly, a Christian as Christian has no need of baptism, of preaching, or the sacrament, for he is already in full possession of them; but he needs them as a sinner. Our greatest concern has regard to simple people and young folk, for they ought to be exercised and educated, day by day, in the Bible and the word of God. They must be made familiar with Scripture, expert, at ease, and knowledgeable in defending their faith; and, in the course of time, able to teach others and help in extending the kingdom of Christ. For the sake of such people, we must read, sing, preach, write, compose hymns. If it would help and were desirable to this end, I would have all the bells ringing, all the organs playing, and everything resounding that could resound.[2] The papist services are to be condemned in that they transform everything into rules, works, and merits. In so doing, they suppress faith. They do not direct their services to the young and simple with the purpose of exercising them in the Bible and the word of God; they cling to rites and ceremonies, holding that they are valuable in themselves, and essential for salvation: that is devilish; the early fathers know nothing of these rules and requirements.

There are three different kinds of Divine Service and Administrations of the Lord's Supper. The first is in Latin, and this I have already published under the title *Formula Missae*.[3] This I have no wish to abolish or change; we hold ourselves still free to use it in the form to which we are accustomed, in whatever place or time suits us, or if some cause moves us to do so. I have not the slightest wish to abolish the use of Latin in public worship,[4] for I am solely

---

[1] "The Christian life consists, not of merely being alive, but of being creative; not of the victory, but of the battle; not of our uprightness, but of being made right; not in having comprehended, but in striving to comprehend; not in purity, but in being purified", *Lectures on Galatians*, qd. Borcherdt and Merz, Vol. 3, p. 411

[2] Organs and the like had been forbidden by Zwingli's followers and by some other extremists, a ban which still persists among some sectaries

[3] *W.*, Vol. XII, pp. 197ff., first published in 1523. Here Luther was more conservative than later, and preserved the use of Latin throughout

[4] Luther still seems to have had the same view in March 1528; cf. *W.*, Vol. XIX, p. 74, note 2

concerned about our young people. If I could, and if Greek and Hebrew were as common among us as Latin, and if we had as many splendid tunes and hymns as we have in the Latin services, I would make a rota of the Sundays and use all four languages in turn: German, Latin, Greek, and Hebrew, for celebrating the Lord's Supper, and for the hymns and lessons.

I entirely disagree with those people who cling to one language, and think nought of all the others. I would like to train our youth and others in such a way that we should avoid the lot of the Waldenses in Bohemia.[1] In their case, faith was so fettered to their one language that they could not speak clearly and make themselves understood except to someone who had already learned that tongue.[2] That was not the way of the Holy Spirit in the earliest days. He did not wait till all the world came to Jerusalem and learned Hebrew, but endowed the office of preaching with the gift of tongues so that the apostles could preach wherever they went. I should prefer to follow their example. Moreover, it is only reasonable to train young people in several languages, for who knows how God will use them in the course of time? It is for this purpose, too, that our schools exist.

Secondly, the Lord's Supper and Divine Service in German, which is our present topic, should be drawn up for the sake of the ordinary laity. But we must arrange for these two Orders to be used publicly in our churches for all the people to share, since many will be present who do not yet believe and are not yet Christian. Rather the majority stand and stare, merely because it is something new; and then it is much as if we were holding Divine Service in some

[1] Luther refers to the Bohemian Brethren, who belonged to the Hussite movement in general, but adopted extreme positions

[2] Luther, at an earlier date, had already expressed the opinion that the Waldenses were wrong in considering a translation of the Bible into their own language as sufficient. In particular, they decided in 1524 to prescribe the vernacular to the exclusion of any other language for public worship. Cf. *W.*, Vol. XIX, p. 74, n. It should perhaps also be pointed out that Luther was very insistent that ministers should know Latin, Greek, and Hebrew; and that those "who knew the Bible only in their mother-tongue made many foolish blunders. My own experience is that reading the Scriptures in their original languages gives untold help in coming to a clear understanding of their meaning," *W.*, Vol. XI, 455

convenient place or resort among Turks or pagans. Obviously, it is not really a congregation with a proper constitution and rules, one in which the Christian people could be governed in accordance with the gospel. Public Worship is, rather, a public means of attraction to faith and Christianity.

A truly evangelical liturgy should have a third characteristic: worship must not be used in a public place in the midst of all and sundry; rather those who seriously wish to be Christian and confess the evangel by lip and life, must show that they are one by using a common name, and gather apart in some house for prayer, reading, baptism, receiving the sacrament, and discharging other Christian offices. By adopting such a method, those who do not remain truly Christian can be recognized, punished, corrected, excluded, or excommunicated, in accordance with Christ's command, Matthew 18.[1] Granted such a congregation, a common benevolent fund could be established among all Christians, to which there would be voluntary contributions, and which could be distributed among the poor, after the example of St. Paul in 2 Corinthians 9.[2] In such meetings there would be no need for frequent singing or long hymns. So too, a brief and excellent form of baptism and the sacrament could be observed, with everything directed to the word, to prayer, and to Christian love. Sound, but succinct instructions would be needed dealing with faith, the Ten Commandments, and the Lord's Prayer.[3] It is plain that if the people and the

[1] Matt. 18:17. It is plain that Luther was not satisfied with the ordinary parish church and its congregation, even when they had adopted the reform. He envisaged, rather, a "gathered community" consisting of the more earnest-minded people who felt a definite, personal commitment to the faith. Yet when a trial was made in Hesse on these Congregationalist lines, he was shocked, and condemned the attempt. He was much impressed with the danger of disunity and disorder to which it might lead, as is evident in the next paragraph or so, *infra* p. 321. Yet it is hard to see the reason in view of his own doctrine of the priesthood of all believers, with freedom in modes and forms of worship; and, on the other hand, his discontent with the state of his own churches in Saxony, as was plain to his eyes when he visited them. Cf. *W.*, Vol. XIX, p. 75, note 1

[2] 2 Cor. 9:1

[3] The need for such instruction in a concrete form was becoming increasingly apparent, and various efforts were made to meet the need. Eventually, however, in 1529 Luther himself put his hand to the work, and produced what proved the most valuable and one of the most beautiful of all his writings, his *Encheiridion*, or *Shorter Catechism*

individual persons were at hand who were eager to be Christian in earnest, the Orders of Service and the appropriate directions would be quickly drawn up.

At the moment, however, I am neither able nor willing to make rules for, or even inaugurate, such a group or congregation. The appropriate people and individual persons are not available, nor do I think many are pressing for it. Should it happen, however, that I must act, and that I am so constrained that I cannot with good conscience refuse to act, I will gladly do what I can to the best of my ability. Meanwhile, I shall leave the matter where it stands with the two Orders, and I will publicly help to promote this form of public worship among the people, to exercise young folk in the faith, calling and attracting others to it, besides my preaching. And I shall continue to do so until Christians yearn for the word, see their way clearly, and so discipline their own selves that no disorder arises. Then I should want to bring it into effect. We Germans are a wild, crude, turbulent, folk,[1] and we ought not lightly to set new things on foot among the people unless under extreme pressure.[2]

Let us proceed, in God's name. The most urgent need during Divine Service in German is for a plain, straightforward, and sound catechism. The term catechism means instruction, instruction by which pagans who want to become Christian may learn to understand what are the Christian facts which they will need to believe, perform, permit, and know. The name, catechumens, is therefore used for those young learners who have been accepted as pupils to undergo this instruction and learn what to believe, before being

---

[1] The peasants' revolt was a recent and dreadful experience. The dangers of disorder, and the need for emphasis on the due observance of law and order, were still very pressing. On the other hand, the existence of special groups of people conducting their own forms of worship would tend to disunity unless it were combined with a very high level of Christian character and a profound sense of responsibility to society. Yet Luther always remained faithful to the idea of Christian freedom; it dominated his thought in shaping the new evangelical church which was to be at once a state church and yet that of the people themselves: a church genuinely consisting of those who were united in the fellowship of faith and love. Cf. G. Gilbert, *Ecclesiola in Ecclesia*, qd. Borcherdt and Merz, *op. cit.*, p. 412

[2] A remark which is at variance with the view that Luther's reforming work was due to personal restlessness. Cf. also *W.*, Vol. XII, 485f.

baptized. It is impossible for me to give this teaching in simpler or better form than has been customary from the beginning of Christianity till now, namely, in the three subjects of the Ten Commandments, the Creed, and the Lord's Prayer.[1] Almost all that a Christian needs to know is to be found simply and briefly under these three headings. When none of those special kinds of meetings are available where preachers can give this instruction from the pulpit, either at certain seasons, or day by day, as necessity would seem to demand, then the instruction must be imparted by reading in the house at home, morning and evening, to the children and the members of the household. Nor will it be satisfactory if the catechumens learn and are able to repeat the words by heart, as hitherto; rather questions must be asked about each separate item, and the answers given must show how the meaning of each separate item has been understood. It is not possible, on any single occasion, to ask questions about the whole subject-matter, and therefore one part must be chosen for one day and another for another. If the parents or the teachers of the young people will not take the necessary care of them, or see that others take it, there will never be any religious instruction again. A special group would have to be arranged, as I have said.

Here is an example of the way in which young people should be catechized:

What prayer do you offer?

Answer: The Lord's Prayer.

What do you mean when you say, Our Father which art in heaven?

Answer: That God is not our earthly father, but our heavenly father, who will richly bless us in heaven.

What is the meaning of, Hallowed be Thy name?

Answer: That we ought to honour and glorify His name and not let it be blasphemed.

How is it blasphemed and desecrated?

Answer: When we, who should be His children, live wickedly, or learn and believe what is wrong. . . .

Continue in the same style, asking what is meant by the

[1] Cf. our Vol. 1, pp. 67ff.

kingdom of God, how it comes, what is meant by God's will, our daily bread, etc. . . .

In the same way, as regards the creed: What do you believe? *Answer:* I believe in God the Father . . . and so on, to the end.[1] Afterwards, if you have time, go from question to question, taken singly or two combined, e.g. What does it mean to believe in God the Father Almighty? *Answer:* It means to trust Him with all my heart and, both now and for ever, to be fully assured of His grace and favour and help. What does it mean to believe in Jesus Christ His Son? *Answer:* It means to believe in our hearts that, if Christ had not died for us, we should all have been lost for evermore . . . etc.

Similarly, too, in the case of the Ten Commandments, we must ask what the first, the second, the third, the fourth mean. For the purpose of putting these questions, you may make use of my *Betbüchlein*,[2] where I have dealt briefly with the three subjects; or you can follow your own plan. This must continue till the whole of Christian truth is held safely in our hearts as if in two purses, those, namely, of faith and love. The purse of faith has two pockets. In one pocket is the faith or conviction that we are sinners, totally ruined and condemned by Adam's sin, Romans 5, Psalm 50.[3] In the other pocket is the faith that we have all been redeemed through Jesus Christ from our ruined, sinful, and damnable condition, Romans 5, John 3.[4] The purse of love also has two pockets: in one is the faith that we must serve by doing good to everyone, as Christ did for us, Romans 13;[5] in the other is the faith that we must gladly endure suffering, and be patient.

[1] This brief phrase implies that the Creed should be taken, first as a whole, and then dealt with in detail, as the context shows
[2] *Little Prayer Book,* first published in 1522; cf. *W.,* Vol. X, ii, 331/75-482. This writing, which was greatly expanded in later editions, offers a training in devotion rather than a book of prayers as the name seems to imply; for it contains no prayers for the different situations in life, nor even a confession. Its main pillars are the Decalogue, the Creed, and the Lord's Prayer, largely based on the *Short Exposition* which he had published in 1520, and for which cf. our Vol. I, pp. 67ff. Even the later editions are not substitutes for the familiar Roman Catholic missal and other books of devotion, but were based directly on the Bible and its critical passages. Cf. also *T.R.,* Vol. V, §§ 6,013, 6,751
[3] Rom. 5:12; Ps. 51:7   [4] Rom. 5:18f.; John 3:16f.   [5] Rom. 13:8-10

WML*

When a child begins to grasp these truths, we must teach him the habit of asking about the texts of the sermons, bringing the questions home from church, and putting them to his parents when the family is gathered round the table for a meal (as was formerly the custom to practise conversing in Latin). Then the texts will be put into the purses and the pockets just as one puts pence, shillings and pounds into one's pockets. For example, the purse of faith is that for gold; we put into it this text, Romans 5, By one man's sin all men became sinners and were condemned,[1] and Psalm 50: Lo, in sin was I conceived, and my mother bore me in transgression.[2] Those are two golden sovereigns[3] in the purse. In the other purse goes the guinea piece[4] in the form of this text, Romans 5, Christ died for our sins and rose for our justification.[5] Again, John 3, Behold, the lamb of God who beareth the sins of the world.[6] Those are two goodly golden pieces in your purse. The purse of love is the purse for silver. Into the first pocket goes the text about doing good in Galatians 4, Serve one another in love;[7] Matthew 25, What you do to one of the least of my brothers, you have done to my own self.[8] Into the other pocket goes this text, Matthew 5, Blessed are you that are persecuted for my sake;[9] Hebrews 12, Whom the Lord loves He chastises, and scourges every son whom He accepts.[10] Those are two silver coins[11] for your purse. Let no one despise childish talk like this and think himself above it. When Christ wished to draw men to Himself, He had to become man. If we wish to attract children, we must become children with them. It is God's will that child's play like this should be done well; and if we were to comply, we should soon see the conversion of large numbers of Christian people with minds enriched by Scripture and the knowledge of God. They themselves would come to place more value on these purses as *locos communes*,[12] and

[1] Cf. Rom. 5:12, 18   [2] Cf. Ps. 51:7   [3] *Reynische gulden*
[4] *Ungerischen gulden*   [5] Cf. Rom. 4:25   [6] Cf. John 1:29
[7] Cf. Gal. 5:13   [8] Cf. Matt. 25:40   [9] Cf. Matt. 5:11   [10] Cf. Heb. 12:6
[11] Germ. *schreckenberger*, because, from 1492, silver was mined at Schreckenberg in the Erzgebirge of Saxony, whence the popular name for any silver coin
[12] The principles of the Christian faith. Melanchthon published the first systematic exposition of evangelical doctrine in 1521 under the title of *Loci Communes*

treasure therein the whole of the Bible. Unless this happens it will all be as before:[1] merely a going to and a returning from Service, with the people thinking that all you need is to listen during Divine Service, but no one thinking it necessary to learn anything and to remember it. Multitudes of people listen to sermons year in year out, and yet learn nothing. It is my daily experience that they listen to sermons three or four years on end, and learn nothing; they could not repeat a single sentence of the creed. Everything is accessible in books, but it cannot be said yet that everything has been taken to heart.[2]

*

Finally,[3] and in sum, this and every other Order of Service should be used on the understanding that if it lead to abuse, it must be abolished at once and another prepared; just as king Hezekiah broke up and did away with the brazen serpent[4] (which God Himself had commanded to be made,)[5] because the children of Israel abused it. Liturgies must always promote faith and nurture love; they must never be a hindrance to faith. If they no longer serve these purposes, they are already dead and done for, and of no further value. It would be just as if a sound coinage were counterfeited; and, because of the abuse, abolished; or even like new shoes which grow old and pinch; we wear them no more, but throw them away and buy others.

An Order of Service is an external thing; and, no matter how excellent, it may be abused. Then it is no longer an Order but a Disorder. Our point is that no liturgy has an independent value in itself, though this is how the papist liturgies have been regarded hitherto; rather, its proper use constitutes the life, value, force, and virtue of any liturgy whatsoever. Otherwise it is of no avail. May the spirit and grace of God be with us all. Amen.

MARTIN LUTHER.

---

[1] I.e. no progress made and nothing learned
[2] With this remark Luther ends rather than finishes the Preface; he immediately begins with detailed suggestion for the conduct of the Services. He concludes with the following paragraph of general import
[3] *W.*, Vol. XIX, p. 113   [4] 2 Kings 18:4   [5] Num. 21:8f.

Index of Scriptural References and Allusions

Index of Subjects

AACHEN, 129
Absolution, 92ff.
Acts, book of, 275ff., 301ff.
Affliction. *See* Suffering
Aldersgate Street, Wesley at, 276
Altar-pieces, 219, 315
Animals, 188, 216, 231, 239, 268
Antichrist, 84f., 86f., 88, 96. *See* Pope
Antilogiarum Mart. Lutheri Babylonia. See Faber, John
Antiquitates. See Josephus
Anxiety, 57
Apostles, 281, 301, 304f., 307f., 309
Appeal to the Ruling Classes. See Luther
Arians, Arianism, 153, 168
Assyrians, 244
Augsburg, 162, 274
Austria, 173
Authorities, *See* Secular power
Authority, limits to, 146

BABYLONIANS, 244
Baden, 163, 166, 169, 178
Baptism, 42, 94, 294, 317f., 320
Barefoot, Order, 197
Basle, 16, 110, 140, 159, 274, 313
Begards, 153
Belgium, 153, n.1
Betbüchlein. See Luther
Bible, 25, 75, 129, 148, 167, n.1, 181, n.3, 199, 231, 265ff., 270, 272ff., 284, 287, 308, 318, 323, n.2, 325. *See* Scripture, Holy; Word of God
Bishops, 118, 119, n.1, 120
  fealty to pope, 79
Blessing, 42, 45ff., 55ff., 61, 69, 205, 216; 221, 227f., 255f., 280. *See* Good
Bohemian Brethren, 319, n.1
Brandenburg, 87, n.3, 91, 102, 132, 162, 167
Brief Instruction. See Luther
Brussels, 130
Bull, papal, 73, 87, 91, 93ff., 145
Bundshuh, 161, n.1
Burning of the books, 74f., 77, 87, 101, 129, 180
Butter-eating, 111, 119, 121
By Faith Alone. See Kooiman

CANON LAW, 75, 77ff., 85, 88, 101, 119, n.1, 125
Cardinals and shepherd, story, 216f.
Carthusians, 197
Catechism, 320, n.3, 321
  example of, 322f.
Children, instruction of, 315, 321ff.
Christian, Christians, blessings, 48, 51
  boasting of Christ's merits, 69
  catechism, 321
  confidence, 69
  and death, 42, 53
  earthly obedience, 78
  force, use of, 83
  harassed by false teaching, 146
  liberty, 299, 315ff., 321, n.1
  at Lord's Supper, 104f.
  need of liturgy, 317f., 320
  poor and despised, 208
  priesthood of all, 298
  regulations, 79
  relation to Jews, 256
  sharing possessions, 301
  should know *Romans* by heart, 284
  should learn *Psalms,* 266
  sin, dread of, 25f.
  virtue, 165
  which books of Bible to read, 282
Christmas, 314
Church, Charles V's loyalty to, 130
  faith of, 65
  Holy Catholic, 66, 165, 168
  invisible, 64
  judgment of, 153
  obedience to, 102, 104
  oneness of, 313, 321, n.1
  prefigured by Tabernacle, 117ff.
  Roman, 74, 159. *See* Pope
  services, 251f.
  universal, 266, 271
Clergy, 117, 119. *See* Priest
Cologne, 73f., 77, 130
Commandments. *See* Ten Commandments
Communion, communicant, 66, 94f., 101ff. *See* Eucharist, Sacraments, Lord's Supper
Confession, confessional, 91ff.
Confessions. See Augustine
Conscience, 36, 92ff., 107f., 118 120, 146, 295f., 299, 317